FOND DU LAC PUBLIC LIBRARY

WITHDRAWN

D1466226

Midwest Living

BEST RECIPES
COLLECTION

Meredith® Consumer Marketing
Des Moines, Iowa

MIDWEST LIVING.
BEST RECIPES COLLECTION

Meredith® Corporation Consumer Marketing
Vice President, Consumer Marketing: Janet Donnelly
Consumer Product Marketing Director: Steve Swanson
Consumer Marketing Product Manager: Wendy Merical
Business Director: Ron Clingman
Senior Production Manager: George Susral

Waterbury Publications, Inc.
Editorial Director: Lisa Kingsley
Associate Editors: Tricia Bergman, Mary Williams
Creative Director: Ken Carlson
Associate Design Directors: Doug Samuelson, Bruce Yang
Production Assistant: Mindy Samuelson
Contributing Copy Editors: Terri Fredrickson,
Gretchen Kauffman
Contributing Indexer: Elizabeth T. Parson

Midwest Living® Magazine
Editor in Chief: Greg Philby
Creative Director: Geri Wolfe Boesen
Executive Editor: Trevor Meers
Senior Food Editor: Diana McMillen

Meredith National Media Group
President: Tom Harty
Vice President, Manufacturing: Bruce Heston

Meredith Corporation
President and Chief Executive Officer: Stephen M. Lacy
In Memoriam: E.T. Meredith III (1933–2003)

Pictured on the front cover:
Apple-Pear Praline Pie
(recipe on page 180)
Photographer: Kritsada Panichgul

Copyright © 2012 by Meredith Corporation.
Des Moines, Iowa.

First Edition.

Printed in the United States of America.

ISBN: 978-0-696-30142-1

All of us at Meredith® Consumer Marketing
are dedicated to providing you with
information and ideas to enhance your
home. We welcome your comments and
suggestions. Write to us at: Meredith
Consumer Marketing, 1716 Locust St.,
Des Moines, IA 50309-3023.

Orange-Honey
Sweet Rolls, page 53

Contents

**White-Chocolate Cheesecake
with Triple-Raspberry Sauce,
page 167**

The Taste of Happiness

Not every meal comes peppered with fanfare. And that's OK. But then along comes a food so sensational that one bite of it changes your culinary reality. You know the feeling. The helpless melting into your chair over a lush red velvet cake. The warm, contemplative bliss from a sweetly steaming latte eggnog. The fascinating budding on your tongue of the layered flavors of an herb-crusted tenderloin with red currant sauce. These are the foods we remember and the ones we want to experience again and again. These are the types we've harvested for this collection.

There's no magic recipe for making this happen, but we do know the main ingredients.

Our *Midwest Living* senior food editor, Diana McMillen (at right), culls the Midwest for outstanding recipes from cafes, inns, top restaurants and even from our readers. She and Test Kitchen Project Manager Colleen Weeden (at left) taste and test each one to ensure ultimate flavor and best preparation, working and reworking them as needed.

Then comes the alchemy. Sometimes on a spring day bursting with unleashable joy, a fresh rhubarb crunch is the perfect expression. Or a harried day when all you want is the solace of a sinfully all-out chocolate dessert. There is the cold autumnal drizzle in which the nostalgic scent of a simmering comfort food curls you in like a mother's arms. There are many more: holidays, weekend brunches, seeing an old friend, picnics, and yes, even the ordinary weekday.

When you pair a great food with your mood and moment, magic happens indeed. The recipes await. Happy tasting.

GREG PHILBY
EDITOR IN CHIEF

Goat Cheese & Fresh
Mushroom Crostini, page 14

APPETIZERS, BEVERAGES & SNACKS

Mini Italian Beef
Sandwiches with
Pepperoncini Slaw

Mini Italian Beef Sandwiches with Pepperoncini Slaw

Start to finish: About 20 minutes

- 1 17-ounce package refrigerated cooked beef roast au jus
- 2 cups frozen peppers (yellow, green, and red) and onion stir-fry vegetables
- 1 teaspoon dried Italian seasoning, crushed
- 1/8 to 1/4 teaspoon crushed red pepper
- 2 cups shredded cabbage with carrot (coleslaw mix)
- 1/2 cup pepperoncini salad peppers, stemmed and chopped, plus 2 tablespoons drained liquid
- 16 2- to 3-inch rolls, split
  Pepperoncini salad peppers (optional)

1. Place beef mixture in a medium saucepan, breaking up any large pieces. Add stir-fry vegetables, 1/2 teaspoon of the Italian seasoning and crushed red pepper to taste. Heat through just to boiling.

2. Meanwhile, in a medium bowl combine coleslaw mix, chopped pepperoncini and liquid and remaining 1/2 teaspoon Italian seasoning.

3. To serve, use a slotted spoon to divide meat mixture among roll bottoms. Top each with coleslaw mixture; add roll tops. Serve with additional pepperoncini peppers, if you like. **Makes 16 sandwiches.**

Nutrition facts per serving: 109 cal., 3 g fat, 16 mg chol., 322 mg sodium, 13 g carbo., 1 g fiber, 8 g pro.

Crispy Cheesy Potato Bites

Prep: 15 minutes Bake: 15 minutes Oven: 450°

- 1 30-ounce package frozen seasoned crisp potato rounds (Ore Ida Crispy Crowns) or 1, 32-ounce package fried potato nuggets (Ore Ida Tater Tots)
- 2/3 cup finely shredded Parmesan cheese or crumbled Cotija cheese
  Balsamic Ketchup or Chipotle Ketchup (recipes follow)

1. Line two 15x10x1-inch baking pans* with parchment paper or nonstick foil. Bake potatoes in the prepared pans according to package directions. Sprinkle with cheese and bake 4 to 5 minutes more or until cheese is golden brown.

2. Serve hot with toothpicks and desired ketchup for dipping. **Makes 14 servings.**

Balsamic Ketchup: Stir 1 tablespoon balsamic vinegar and 1 tablespoon snipped fresh basil into 3/4 cup ketchup.

Chipotle Ketchup: Stir 1 finely chopped canned chipotle pepper in adobo sauce and 1 tablespoon fresh lime juice into 3/4 cup ketchup. (See Tip, page 71.)

*Tip: If you don't have two pans, bake half the potatoes at a time. Bake second half while serving the first batch.

Nutrition facts per serving without ketchup: 175 cal., 11 g fat, 3 mg chol., 499 mg sodium, 17 g carbo., 2 g fiber, 3 g pro.

Sugared Bacon-Wrapped Smokies

Prep: 35 minutes Bake: 30 minutes Oven: 350°

- Nonstick cooking spray
- 1 16-ounce package small cooked smoked sausage links
- 15 slices bacon, each cut crosswise into thirds
- 3/4 cup packed brown sugar

1. Line a 15x10x1-inch baking pan with foil; lightly coat with cooking spray. Set aside.

2. Wrap each sausage link with a bacon piece, overlapping the bacon piece at the end. Press the end of the bacon piece to seal or secure with a wood toothpick.

3. Place brown sugar in a large resealable bag. Add several bacon-wrapped sausages at a time and seal. Shake bag gently to coat sausages with brown sugar; place in prepared pan. Repeat with remaining bacon-wrapped sausages.

4. Bake in a 350° oven about 30 minutes, or until the bacon is browned. Serve immediately. **Makes about 45 smokies.**

Make-Ahead Tip: Prepare recipe as directed above through Step 3. Cover and chill the sausages for up to 24 hours. To serve, uncover and bake as directed in Step 4.

Nutrition facts per smokie: 102 cal., 8 g fat, 15 mg chol., 210 mg sodium, 4 g carbo., 0 g fiber, 3 g pro.

Sugared Bacon-Wrapped Smokies

Mini Burger Party Platter

Prep: 45 minutes Broil: 8 minutes

¼ cup finely chopped green onions or
    onion
2 tablespoons fine dry bread crumbs
2 tablespoons water
1 teaspoon Worcestershire sauce or
    steak sauce
¾ teaspoon Montreal steak seasoning or
    Cajun seasoning
1 pound lean ground beef
2 1-ounce Swiss or cheddar cheese slices,
    cut into fourths
8 dinner rolls or cocktail-size hamburger
    buns, split
    Shredded red-tipped leaf lettuce
1 plum tomato, thinly sliced
    Balsamic Mayo, Chipotle Mayo, Garlic-
    Cumin Mayo, Herbed Goat Cheese
    and/or Citrus Ketchup (recipes follow)
    Spice-Dusted Waffle Fries (recipe
    follows)

1. In a large bowl, combine chopped onions, bread crumbs, the water, Worcestershire sauce and steak seasoning. Add beef; mix well.

2. Shape meat mixture into a 10x5-inch rectangle. Cut into 8 square-shape patties. Place patties on the unheated rack of a broiler pan. Broil 4 to 5 inches from heat for 8 to 10 minutes or until done (160°), turning once. Top with cheese; broil 30 seconds or until cheese slices are melted.

3. Top each dinner roll bottom with lettuce, tomato slice, mini burger, desired topping and roll top. If needed, secure buns with cocktail party picks. Serve with hot waffle fries. **Makes 8 appetizer mini burgers.**

Spice-Dusted Waffle Fries: Place 3 cups frozen waffle-cut French fried potatoes in a single layer on a baking sheet. Sprinkle with 1 teaspoon Montreal steak seasoning. Bake in a 450° oven for 15 to 20 minutes or until crisp. Makes about 2½ cups.

Nutrition facts per serving with Balsamic Mayo and fries: 402 cal., 24 g fat, 48 mg chol., 689 mg sodium, 35 g carbo., 3 g fiber, 16 g pro.

Balsamic Mayo: Combine ½ cup mayonnaise, 2 tablespoons balsamic vinegar and ⅛ teaspoon freshly ground black pepper. Cover and chill. Makes ½ cup.

Chipotle Mayo: Combine ½ cup mayonnaise and half to 1 chipotle pepper in adobo sauce, finely chopped. Cover and chill. Makes ½ cup. (See Tip, page 71.)

Garlic-Cumin Mayo: Combine ½ cup mayonnaise, 1 tablespoon lime juice, ¼ to ½ teaspoon garlic powder and ¼ teaspoon ground cumin. Cover and chill. Makes ½ cup.

Herbed Goat Cheese: Combine ½ cup soft goat cheese, crumbled (4 ounces); 2 tablespoons sour cream; and 1 tablespoon snipped fresh oregano, basil or thyme. Cover and chill. Makes ½ cup.

Citrus Ketchup: Combine ½ cup ketchup, ¼ teaspoon finely shredded lemon peel, 1 teaspoon lemon juice, ¼ teaspoon finely shredded orange peel and 1 teaspoon orange juice. Cover and chill. Makes ½ cup.

Jamaican Jerk Chicken Wings
(caption)

Jamaican Jerk Chicken Wings with Mango Salsa

Prep: 25 minutes Marinate: 4 to 24 hours
Grill: 20 minutes

12 chicken wings (about 2 pounds)
¼ to ½ cup Jamaican jerk seasoning
¼ cup cider vinegar
¼ cup orange juice
2 tablespoons lime juice
2 tablespoons olive oil
2 tablespoons soy sauce
    Mango Salsa (recipe follows)

1. Cut off and discard tips of chicken wings. Spread remaining wing portions open. With a sharp knife, cut each wing at its joint into two sections. Place chicken wing pieces into a resealable plastic bag set in a shallow dish.

2. For marinade: In a small bowl, stir together jerk seasoning, vinegar, orange juice, lime juice, olive oil and soy sauce. Pour over chicken wings; seal bag. Marinate in refrigerator for 4 to 24 hours, turning bag occasionally. Drain and discard marinade.

3. For a charcoal grill, grill chicken wing pieces on the rack of an uncovered grill directly over medium coals about 20 minutes or until chicken is tender and no longer pink, turning once halfway through grilling. (For a gas grill, preheat grill. Reduce heat to medium. Place chicken wing pieces on grill rack over heat. Cover; grill as above. For broiler, place chicken wings on the unheated rack of a broiler pan. Broil 5 to 6 inches from the heat about 8 minutes or until light brown. Turn wings. Broil for 8 to 10 minutes more or until chicken is tender and no longer pink.) Serve with Mango Salsa.
Makes 24 appetizers (serves 12).

Mango Salsa: Combine 2 cups chopped, peeled mangoes (two medium); ½ cup finely chopped red sweet pepper; 1 fresh jalapeño, seeded and finely chopped; 4½ teaspoons snipped fresh basil; 1½ teaspoons red wine vinegar; and ½ teaspoon sugar.

Nutrition facts per serving (with ¼ cup salsa): 95 cal., 4 g fat, 19 mg chol., 129 mg sodium, 9 g carbo., 1 g fiber, 5 g pro.

Chile-Lime Grilled Tiger Shrimp with Avocado Cocktail Sauce

Chile-Lime Grilled Tiger Shrimp with Avocado Cocktail Sauce

Prep: 20 minutes Marinate: 15 minutes
Grill: 7 minutes

Cocktail Sauce (recipe follows)
24 fresh or frozen jumbo shrimp in shells (about 1 ½ pounds)
 3 tablespoons lime juice
 3 tablespoons Asian chile sauce (such as Sriracha) or hot Thai chile sauce
 1 clove garlic, minced
 ½ teaspoon kosher or sea salt
 ⅛ teaspoon freshly ground black pepper
Lime wedges

1. Thaw shrimp, if frozen. Peel and devein shrimp, removing tails. Rinse shrimp; pat dry with paper towels. Place shrimp in a resealable plastic bag set in a shallow dish.

2. For marinade: In a small bowl, combine lime juice, Asian chile sauce and garlic. Pour marinade over shrimp; seal bag. Marinate in refrigerator for 15 minutes to 1 hour, turning bag occasionally (the shrimp will get spicier the longer it marinates). Remove shrimp; discard marinade.

3. Thread shrimp onto four or five metal skewers. Sprinkle shrimp with salt and pepper.

4. For a charcoal grill, grill shrimp skewers on the grill rack of an uncovered grill directly over medium coals for 7 to 9 minutes or until shrimp are opaque, turning once halfway through grilling. (For a gas grill, preheat grill. Reduce heat to medium. Place shrimp on grill rack over heat. Cover; grill as above.)

5. To serve, divide Cocktail Sauce evenly among eight chilled margarita, martini or wine glasses. Remove shrimp from skewers. Place three shrimp in each glass. Garnish each glass with a lime wedge.
Makes 8 servings.

Cocktail Sauce: In a medium bowl, combine four avocados, halved, seeded, peeled and chopped; one 14½-ounce can diced tomatoes, undrained; 3 tablespoons snipped fresh cilantro; 2 tablespoons lime juice; 1 tablespoon prepared horseradish; 1 tablespoon Worcestershire sauce for chicken; ¼ teaspoon salt; and ¼ teaspoon ground black pepper. Cover and chill for 2 to 6 hours. Makes about 4 cups.

Nutrition facts per serving: 238 cal., 15 g fat, 97 mg chol., 494 mg sodium, 13 g carbo., 6 g fiber, 15 g pro.

Bacon-Wrapped Shrimp

Prep: 20 minutes Grill: 8 minutes

 1 pound fresh large shrimp in shells (about 16 shrimp)
 8 slices bacon, halved crosswise
Barbecue sauce, heated (optional)

1. Peel and devein shrimp, leaving tails intact. Rinse shrimp; pat dry. Wrap each shrimp in a piece of bacon, securing bacon by skewering shrimp with wooden toothpick (neck to tail in a half-moon).

2. For a charcoal grill, grill shrimp on the lightly greased rack of an uncovered grill directly over medium heat for 8 to 10 minutes or until bacon is crisp and shrimp turn opaque, turning once. (For a gas grill, preheat grill. Reduce heat to medium. Add shrimp to grill rack. Cover; grill as above.)

3. If you like, serve with your favorite barbecue sauce. **Makes 16 appetizers.**

Nutrition facts per appetizer: 44 cal., 2 g fat, 37 mg chol., 119 mg sodium, 0 g carbo., 0 g fiber, 6 g pro.

Bacon-Wrapped Shrimp

Asian-Inspired Deviled Eggs

Prep: 20 minutes Chill: 24 hours

- 6 Hard-Cooked Eggs (recipe follows)
- ¼ cup purchased crème fraîche, mayonnaise, dairy sour cream and/or plain yogurt
- 1 teaspoon rice vinegar or white vinegar
- 2 tablespoons finely chopped celery or green onion
- ½ teaspoon grated fresh ginger or ⅛ teaspoon ground ginger
- ½ teaspoon Thai chile paste (optional)
  Coarsely ground pink or mixed peppercorns, or coarsely ground black pepper (optional)
  Snipped fresh mint or cilantro, or sliced green onion (optional)

1. Halve Hard-Cooked Eggs lengthwise and remove yolks.* Set whites aside.

2. Place yolks in a small bowl; mash with a fork. Add crème fraîche and vinegar; mix well.

Asian-Inspired Deviled Eggs

Stir in celery, ginger and, if you like, chile paste.

3. Stuff egg white halves with yolk mixture. Cover and chill until serving time (up to 24 hours). Garnish each top with ground peppercorns and mint, if you like. **Makes 12 servings.**

Hard-Cooked Eggs: Place six eggs in a single layer in a large saucepan (do not stack eggs). Add enough cold water to cover the eggs by 1 inch. Bring to a rapid boil over high heat (water will have large rapidly breaking bubbles). Remove from heat, cover and let stand for 15 minutes; drain. Run cold water over the eggs or place them in ice water until cool enough to handle; drain. To peel a hard-cooked egg, gently tap it on the countertop. Roll the egg between the palms of your hands. Peel off eggshell, starting at the large end. Makes 6 hard-cooked eggs.

*****Note:** Another way to present eggs is to cut tops off of hard-cooked eggs about one-third from the top; gently scoop out yolks with a small spoon. Cut a thin slice off of the rounded bottoms so eggs will sit flat. (Set aside tops for another use.)

Nutrition facts per serving: 62 cal., 5 g fat, 113 mg chol., 39 mg sodium, 0 g carbo., 0 g fiber, 3 g pro.

Shrimp-Stuffed Deviled Eggs: Prepare as above, except omit celery, ginger, chile paste and the garnishes. Stir 1 teaspoon spicy brown mustard or Dijon-style mustard, ½ teaspoon dried dillweed and ⅛ teaspoon bottled hot pepper sauce into yolk mixture. Fold in ¼ cup frozen peeled cooked salad shrimp, thawed, well-drained and chopped. Garnish each top with an additional salad shrimp and a small flat-leaf (Italian) parsley leaf or snipped fresh dill, if you like.

Italian Deviled Eggs: Prepare as above, except omit celery, ginger, chile paste and the garnishes. Stir 1 tablespoon grated Parmesan cheese, 1 tablespoon chopped toasted pine nuts and ¼ teaspoon dried basil, crushed, into the yolk mixture. Garnish each top with a thin red and/or white radish slice, small basil leaf or roasted red sweet pepper strip, if you like.

Goat Cheese & Fresh Mushroom Crostini

Prep: 30 minutes Bake: 15 minutes
Cook: 8 minutes Oven: 425°/375°

- 30 ¼-inch-thick slices baguette-style French bread (about 8 ounces)
- 2 tablespoons olive oil
- 2 tablespoons butter
- 4 shallots, coarsely chopped (about 1½ cups) or 1½ cups coarsely chopped onion
- 8 ounces fresh cremini mushrooms, coarsely chopped (about 1½ cups)
- 1 tablespoon packed brown sugar
- 3 tablespoons balsamic vinegar
- 1 tablespoon snipped fresh thyme
- ¼ teaspoon salt
- ¼ teaspoon freshly ground black pepper
- 6 ounces soft goat cheese
- 2 tablespoons snipped fresh Italian (flat-leaf) parsley (optional)

1. Arrange baguette slices on a large baking sheet. Lightly brush one side of each slice with some of the olive oil. Bake in a 425° oven for 5 minutes. Turn slices over and bake 2 to 4 minutes more or until lightly brown. Set aside. Reduce oven temperature to 375°.

2. Meanwhile, in a medium saucepan, melt butter over medium-high heat. Add the shallots. Cook for 3 minutes. Add the mushrooms and brown sugar. Cook and stir for 1 minute. Add the balsamic vinegar, thyme, salt and black pepper. Bring to boiling; reduce heat. Cook, uncovered, for 4 minutes or until most of the liquid is evaporated, stirring frequently.

3. Spread some of the goat cheese on each toasted bread slice. Bake about 8 minutes or until cheese is warmed through. Remove from oven. Top each with some of the mushroom-shallot mixture. Drizzle any remaining cooking liquid over crostini. If you like, sprinkle each with parsley. Serve immediately. **Makes 30 crostini.**

Nutrition facts per crostini: 63 cal., 3 g fat, 5 mg chol., 94 mg sodium, 6 g carbo., 0 g fiber, 2 g pro.

Goat Cheese & Fresh Mushroom Crostini

Ripe Olive Cheese Ball

Ripe Olive Cheese Ball

Prep: 15 minutes Stand: 45 minutes Chill: 4 hours

  2 8-ounce packages cream cheese
½ cup butter
½ cup crumbled blue cheese (2 ounces)
  1 4¼-ounce can sliced pitted ripe olives, drained
  2 tablespoons chopped green onion or snipped fresh chives
⅔ cup coarsely chopped almonds, toasted
    Snipped fresh parsley (optional)
    Assorted crackers and/or apple or pear slices

1. In a large mixing bowl, let cream cheese, butter and blue cheese stand 30 minutes to reach room temperature. With an electric mixer, beat mixture on low speed until smooth. Stir in olives and green onion. Cover and chill for at least 4 hours or up to 24 hours.

2. Shape mixture into two balls; cover and chill until serving time. (Or place in a freezer container and freeze up to 3 months. Let thaw in refrigerator overnight before serving.) To serve, roll in almonds. Let stand for 15 minutes. If you like, garnish with snipped parsley. Serve with assorted crackers and/or apple or pear slices. **Makes 2 balls (3½ cups).**

Nutrition facts per 1-tablespoon serving: 55 cal., 6 g fat, 14 mg chol., 69 mg sodium, 1 g carbo., 0 g fiber, 1 g pro.

Goat Cheese & Spinach Tart

Prep: 30 minutes Chill: 30 minutes
Bake: 35 minutes Stand: 15 minutes
Oven: 325°

    Rich Tart Pastry (recipe follows)
  1 10-ounce package frozen chopped spinach, thawed
  1 cup thinly sliced green onion
  3 tablespoons olive oil
  1 teaspoon dried oregano, crushed
½ teaspoon salt
¼ teaspoon ground nutmeg
¼ teaspoon ground black pepper
  3 eggs
  6 ounces goat cheese, crumbled
¾ cup milk

1. Prepare Rich Tart Pastry; set aside.

2. Meanwhile, drain spinach in a colander, pressing with the back of a spoon to press out excess liquid; set aside. In a large skillet, cook onion in hot oil over medium heat for 5 minutes or until soft. Add drained spinach, oregano, salt, nutmeg and pepper. Cook and stir until the spinach is heated through and any liquid has evaporated. Set aside to cool slightly.

3. In a medium mixing bowl, whisk eggs. Add goat cheese and milk, whisking until well combined. Stir in the cooled spinach mixture. Pour egg mixture into hot baked pastry shell. Bake in a 325° oven for 35 to 40 minutes or until a knife inserted near center comes out clean. Let stand for 15 minutes before serving.
Makes 8 to 10 servings.

Rich Tart Pastry: In a medium bowl, stir together 1 cup all-purpose flour and ½ teaspoon salt. Using a pastry blender, cut in ⅓ cup butter until pieces are pea size. Sprinkle 1 tablespoon ice water over part of the flour mixture; gently toss with a fork. Push moistened dough to the side of the bowl. Repeat moistening flour mixture, using 1 tablespoon water at a time, until all of the flour mixture is moistened, using 3 to 4 tablespoons water total. Form dough into a ball. Flatten the ball to a 1-inch-thick disk. Wrap dough with plastic wrap and refrigerate for 30 to 60 minutes.

On a floured surface, roll dough from center to edges into a circle about 12 inches in diameter. To transfer pastry, wrap it around the rolling pin. Unroll pastry into an 11-inch tart pan with a removable bottom. Ease pastry into pan without stretching it. Press pastry into fluted sides of tart pan and trim edges. Do not prick pastry. Line pastry with a double thickness of foil. Bake in a 450° oven for 8 minutes. Remove foil. Bake 4 to 5 minutes more or until lightly browned. Cool slightly on a wire rack.

Tip: To make in a 9-inch pie plate, line a 9-inch pie plate with pastry. Bake pastry as directed above. Cool slightly on a wire rack. Spoon filling in partially baked piecrust. Bake in a 325° oven for 45 minutes or until a knife inserted near the center comes out clean.

Nutrition facts per serving: 274 cal., 20 g fat, 111 mg chol., 510 mg sodium, 14 g carbo., 2 g fiber, 10 g pro.

Goat Cheese & Spinach Tart

Fiesta Dip

For an appetizer in minutes, Wendy Porterfield of the Washington House Inn in Cedarburg, Wisconsin, bakes her cheesy dip for 10 minutes, stirs, then spoons it into prebaked phyllo shells. Then she bakes the shells 5 to 10 minutes more. "The phyllo cup version makes a great appetizer for a more formal party, where the dip version is great for a crowd," she says.

Prep: 25 minutes Bake: 15 minutes Oven: 350°

- 1 cup mayonnaise
- 1 cup finely chopped Vidalia onion, Walla Walla onion or other sweet onion
- ¾ cup shredded Mexican-blend cheese (3 ounces)
- ⅓ cup shredded Monterey Jack cheese with jalapeño peppers (1½ ounces)
- ½ cup salsa
- 2 teaspoons liquid fajita marinade or Worcestershire sauce
- Baked Tortilla Chips (recipe follows) or tortilla chips
- Lime wedges

Fiesta Dip

1. In a bowl, combine mayonnaise, onions, cheeses, salsa and fajita marinade; mix well.

2. Transfer mixture to an ungreased 9-inch pie plate or 1-quart casserole. Bake, uncovered, in a 350° oven for 15 to 20 minutes or until bubbly around edges. Serve warm with Baked Tortilla Chips. Garnish with lime wedges. **Makes about 2½ cups.**

Baked Tortilla Chips: Cut five 6-inch flour tortillas into wedges. Place in single layers on ungreased baking sheets. Bake in a 350° oven for 10 to 15 minutes or until lightly browned and crisp.

Nutrition facts per ¼-cup serving: 276 cal., 24 g fat, 20 mg chol., 317 mg sodium, 10 g carbo., 0 g fiber, 5 g pro.

Heavenly Morel Tarts

Prep: 45 minutes Chill: 1 hour
Bake: 25 minutes Oven: 350°

- 1 8-ounce package cream cheese, softened
- ½ cup butter or margarine, softened
- 1½ cups all-purpose flour
- 6 ounces fresh morel mushrooms* or button mushrooms
- ½ teaspoon salt
- ½ cup chopped onion
- 3 tablespoons butter or margarine
- ¼ cup dairy sour cream
- 2 tablespoons all-purpose flour
- ¼ teaspoon salt
- ⅛ teaspoon dried marjoram, crushed
- ⅛ teaspoon dried rosemary, crushed
- 1 egg, lightly beaten

1. For pastry: In a large mixing bowl, beat together cream cheese and ½ cup butter with an electric mixer on medium to high speed until smooth. Add 1½ cups flour and beat on low speed until combined. Cover and chill at least 1 hour or until dough is easy to handle.

2. Clean mushrooms. Place morel mushrooms, if using, in a large bowl. Cover with cold water; add salt. Soak for 10 to 15 minutes. Drain, rinse and repeat two more times. Drain thoroughly; pat dry with paper towels. Chop mushrooms.

3. For filling: In a large skillet, cook onion in 3 tablespoons butter over medium heat until tender. Add mushrooms. Cook and stir for 3 to 5 minutes or until liquid is nearly evaporated. Remove from heat.

4. In a small bowl, stir together sour cream, 2 tablespoons flour, ¼ teaspoon salt, the marjoram and rosemary until combined. Stir sour cream mixture into mushroom mixture.

5. On a floured surface, slightly flatten the pastry dough. Roll dough from center to edges to ⅛-inch thickness. Cut dough into twenty-four 3-inch circles, rerolling dough as necessary. Using small cutters, make cutouts in the centers of half of the rounds or cut a slit in half of the rounds to let the steam escape during baking.**

6. Place 12 of the circles, without cutouts, on an ungreased baking sheet. Place about 1 tablespoon of the filling in the center of each. Moisten edges of filled pastry with a little water. Add the remaining 12 circles with cutouts or slits. Crimp edges together with a fork. Brush tops with beaten egg.

7. Bake in a 350° oven 25 minutes or until pastry is golden brown. Serve warm. **Makes 12 appetizer servings.**

Make-Ahead Tip: Cool the baked pastries, then wrap and freeze up to 1 month. To serve, place frozen pastries on an ungreased baking sheet. Bake, uncovered, in a 350° oven for 20 minutes or until heated through.

*Test Kitchen Tip: If fresh morels aren't available, substitute 1½ ounces dried morel or porcini mushrooms. In a small bowl, cover the dried mushrooms with hot water. Let stand for 20 minutes. Rinse under warm running water; squeeze out excess moisture. Slice the mushrooms.

**Note: Use small cutters to make cutouts from pastry scraps. Place on each brushed tart before baking. Brush again with egg.

Nutrition facts per serving: 237 cal., 19 g fat, 68 mg chol., 188 mg sodium, 14 g carbo., 1 g fiber, 4 g pro.

Heavenly Morel Tarts

Corn, Tomato &
Chipotle Chile Salsa

Corn, Tomato & Chipotle Chile Salsa

Prep: 30 minutes Stand: 20 minutes Chill: 1 hour

4 medium fresh ears of corn, husked, or 2 cups frozen whole kernel corn
2 teaspoons olive oil or cooking oil
2 cloves garlic, minced
2 cups grape or cherry tomatoes, quartered; 3 medium tomatoes, peeled and coarsely chopped; or one 14.5-ounce can diced tomatoes, drained
½ cup chopped green and/or red sweet pepper
½ cup finely chopped celery, red onion and/or green onion
¼ cup snipped fresh cilantro
¼ cup lime juice
1 to 2 teaspoons chopped canned chipotle chile peppers in adobo sauce (see Tip, page 71)
¾ teaspoon salt
Blue tortilla chips or scoop-shape tortilla chips

1. If using the fresh ears of corn, scrub corn with a stiff vegetable brush to remove silks. Rinse under cold running water. Place one ear of corn at a time in a shallow pan. Holding the ear at an angle, use a sharp knife to cut down across the tips of the kernels. Using the dull side of the knife, scrape the ear to release the milky juices into the pan. You should have about 2 cups of corn with its juices.

2. In a large nonstick skillet, heat oil over medium-high heat. Add fresh or frozen corn and garlic. Cook and stir for 3 to 4 minutes or until lightly browned. Remove from heat and cool slightly.

3. Stir tomatoes, sweet pepper, celery, cilantro, lime juice, chipotle chile peppers in adobo sauce and salt into corn mixture. Transfer to a large bowl. Cover and chill a least 1 hour or up to 24 hours before serving. Let salsa stand at room temperature 20 minutes before serving. Serve with tortilla chips. **Makes 4 cups (16 servings).**

Nutrition facts per ¼-cup serving (with chips): 112 cal., 5 g fat, 0 mg chol., 217 mg sodium, 17 g carbo., 2 g fiber, 3 g pro.

Chunky Fresh Tomato Salsa

Start to finish: 30 minutes

2 serrano chile peppers or 1 jalapeño chile pepper, stemmed and halved (see Tip, page 71)
1 clove garlic, peeled
2 large fresh tomatoes (about 1 pound)
⅓ cup loosely packed fresh cilantro leaves
1 green onion, thinly sliced
1 tablespoon lime juice or vinegar
Salt

1. In a food processor, combine chile pieces and garlic. Cover; process with on/off turns until finely chopped, stopping and scraping down sides as needed. Cut one of the tomatoes into quarters. Add tomato quarters and cilantro to food processor. Pulse four to six times or until a coarse puree. Transfer tomato mixture to a medium bowl.

2. Cut remaining tomato into ¼-inch pieces. Add tomato, green onion and lime juice to the bowl. Season to taste with salt, usually ¼ to ½ teaspoon. (Note: This salsa is best if eaten within an hour or two, but it will keep for a few hours in the refrigerator.) **Makes about 2 cups.**

*Note: For a milder salsa, seed the peppers.

Nutrition facts per ¼ cup: 13 cal., 0 g fat, 0 mg chol., 77 mg sodium, 3 g carbo., 1 g fiber, 2 g pro.

Chunky Fresh Tomato Salsa

Fresh Tomato Salsa

Start to finish: 30 minutes

6 roma tomatoes, coarsely chopped
1 small red onion, coarsely chopped
1 large fresh poblano chile pepper,
    seeded and coarsely chopped*
1 to 2 large fresh jalapeño chile peppers,
    seeded and coarsely chopped (see Tip,
    page 71)
2 tablespoons lime juice
1 tablespoon canola oil or cooking oil
1 teaspoon cumin seeds, toasted* and
    ground, or ½ teaspoon ground cumin
1 teaspoon coriander seeds, toasted**
    and ground, or ½ teaspoon ground
    coriander

½ teaspoon kosher salt or salt
¼ teaspoon ground black pepper

1. In a food processor, combine all ingredients. Cover; process with on/off turns until finely chopped. Cover and chill up to 3 days. **Makes 3 cups.**

Nutrition facts per serving: 30 cal., 1 g fat, 0 mg chol., 85 mg sodium, 5 g carbo., 1 g fiber, 2 g pro.

*Note: To toast seeds: In a dry small skillet, heat the cumin and coriander seeds over low to medium-low heat for 5 to 7 minutes or until fragrant, stirring often or shaking skillet to prevent seeds from burning. Remove from heat; allow to cool before grinding with a spice grinder or a mortar and pestle.

Mama Carolla's Bruschetta

This classic Italian appetizer comes from Mama Carolla's Old Italian Restaurant, housed in a 1920s stucco villa in Indianapolis, not far from the historic Monon Trail.

Prep: 30 minutes Grill: 3 minutes

4 medium roma tomatoes
1 tablespoon extra virgin olive oil
2 tablespoons thinly sliced green onion
1 tablespoon snipped fresh basil or
    1 teaspoon dried basil, crushed
1 tablespoon snipped fresh Italian
    (flat-leaf) parsley
1 tablespoon red wine vinegar
1 clove garlic, minced
    Salt and freshly ground black pepper
8 1-inch slices baguette-style French
    bread
2 tablespoons garlic-flavor olive oil or
    olive oil
2 ounces smoked mozzarella cheese,
    shredded (½ cup)
    Fresh basil (optional)

1. Wash tomatoes. To peel, dip tomatoes in boiling water for 1 to 2 minutes or until skins start to split. Dip in cold water; skin, core, seed and chop tomatoes.

2. For tomato topping: In a medium bowl, combine 1 tablespoon olive oil, sliced green onion, basil, parsley, vinegar and garlic. Add the tomatoes; toss to coat. Season to taste with salt and freshly ground black pepper. Set aside.

3. For toast: Lightly brush some of the 2 tablespoons garlic-flavor olive oil on both sides of each bread slice. For a charcoal grill, place bread slices on the rack of an uncovered grill directly over medium coals. Grill for 3 to 4 minutes or until grill marks appear, turning once. (For a gas grill, preheat grill. Reduce heat to medium. Place bread slices on grill rack. Cover and grill as above.) Or place on an ungreased baking sheet. Bake in a 400° oven for 4 minutes. Turn slices over and bake for 3 to 4 minutes more or until crisp and light brown.

4. To serve, use a slotted spoon to spoon about 2 tablespoons of the tomato topping onto each toast slice; sprinkle with mozzarella cheese. Garnish with fresh basil, if you like. Serve within 30 minutes.
Makes 8 servings.

Nutrition facts per serving: 125 cal., 7 g fat, 6 mg chol., 225 mg sodium, 12 g carbo., 1 g fiber, 6 g pro.

Warm Bruschetta Wedges: Prepare tomato topping as above, except substitute one 8-inch Italian bread shell (Boboli) for the baguette-style French bread. Place bread shell on a lightly greased large baking sheet. Brush garlic-flavor olive oil over bread shell. Use a slotted spoon to spoon tomato topping over bread shell; sprinkle with mozzarella cheese. Bake in a 400° oven for 10 to 15 minutes or until warm and cheese softens slightly. Cut into eight wedges. If you like, garnish with fresh basil. Serve hot.

Mama Carolla's Bruschetta

Fresh Tomato Salsa

Kicking Cajun Popcorn Mix

Prep: 10 minutes Bake: 15 minutes Oven: 250°

  1 3.5-ounce bag butter-flavor microwave
    popcorn
  ½ teaspoon Cajun seasoning
  1 tablespoon bottled green hot pepper
    sauce (optional)
  2 cups hot-and-spicy bite-size cheese
    crackers and/or jalapeño-flavor
    pretzel nuggets
  1 1.75-ounce package spicy seasoned
    peanuts (⅓ cup)

1. Pop popcorn according to package
directions. Open bag carefully; add Cajun
seasoning. Hold top of bag tightly and shake
vigorously until popcorn is evenly coated.

2. In a large shallow roasting pan, spread
popcorn; remove all unpopped kernels.
If you like, drizzle with green hot pepper
sauce; stir gently to coat. Stir in crackers and
peanuts.

3. Bake in a 250° oven for 15 minutes,
stirring once halfway through baking time.
Cool completely. Store tightly covered at
room temperature for up to 2 days.
Makes about twelve 1-cup servings.

Nutrition facts per serving: 105 cal., 7 g fat, 0 mg chol.,
201 mg sodium, 12 g carbo., 3 g fiber, 2 g pro.

Curried Snack Mix

Curried Snack Mix

Prep: 10 minutes Bake: 20 minutes Oven: 300°

  3 plain rice cakes, broken into bite-size
    pieces
  1 3-ounce can chow mein noodles
  2 cups bite-size square corn cereal or
    oyster crackers
  1 cup salted roasted soy nuts
  ⅓ cup butter
  2 teaspoons soy sauce
  1 to 1½ teaspoons curry powder

1. In a 13x9x2-inch baking pan, stir together
rice cake pieces, chow mein noodles, corn
cereal and soy nuts.

2. In a small saucepan, heat butter, soy
sauce and curry powder over low heat until
butter melts. Drizzle butter mixture over rice
cake mixture, tossing to coat.

3. Bake in a 300° oven for 20 minutes, stirring
once or twice. Cool before serving. Store in an
airtight container for up to 5 days.
Makes about 6 cups (twelve ½-cup servings).

Nutrition facts per serving: 144 cal., 8 g fat, 14 mg chol.,
236 mg sodium, 13 g carbo., 2 g fiber, 5 g pro.

Watermelon Lemonade

*Prep: 30 minutes Cool: 20 minutes
Chill: 4 hours*

  5 large lemons
  3 cups water
  1 cup sugar
  8 cups seeded and cubed watermelon
    (about 5 pounds with rind)
    Kiwi Cubes and/or Watermelon Cubes
    (recipes follow) or ice cubes
    Lemon twists (optional)

1. Using vegetable peeler, remove peel from
lemons in strips; juice the lemons for about
1½ cups juice.

2. For lemon syrup: In a medium saucepan,
heat and stir the lemon strips, the water
and sugar over medium heat until the sugar
dissolves. Remove from heat; cool for

20 minutes at room temperature. Stir in
lemon juice. Pour lemon syrup into a 1-gallon
jar or pitcher.

3. In a food processor or blender, puree half
of the watermelon until very smooth. Strain
through a coarse sieve set over a large bowl,
pressing through any pulp. Pour watermelon
juice into the same jar or pitcher as lemon
syrup. Repeat with remaining watermelon
(for about 10 cups total mixture). Cover;
chill for 4 to 8 hours. Strain Watermelon
Lemonade through a colander; discard
lemon strips. (If you like, cover and chill up to
24 hours more.)

4. To serve, fill eight 12-ounce glasses with
Kiwi Cubes and/or Watermelon Cubes or
ice cubes. Pour Watermelon Lemonade over
the ice. If you like, garnish each glass with a
lemon twist. **Makes 8 (10-ounce) servings.**

Kiwi Cubes: Peel four kiwifruits and cut into
eight pieces each. Fill compartments of two
ice cube trays with cut fruit. Add cold water;
freeze until firm.

Watermelon Cubes: Cut 1-inch cubes from
watermelon flesh. Place cubes in a single
layer in a 15x10x1-inch baking pan. Freeze
1 to 2 hours or until firm. If storing longer
than 4 hours, transfer to a plastic freezer bag
or container; freeze until needed.

Nutrition facts per serving: 155 cal., 0 g fat, 0 mg chol.,
5 mg sodium, 41 g carbo., 1 g fiber, 1 g pro.

Watermelon Martinis: Prepare Watermelon
Lemonade. Using 2 cups of the Watermelon
Lemonade, fill compartments of two ice
cube trays or 8x8x2-inch baking pan. Freeze
for at least 4 hours or until firm. If using
the baking pan, scrape frozen mixture or
break into small pieces. In a blender or food
processor, combine frozen Watermelon
Lemonade, 1¼ cups vodka or gin, and
⅓ cup melon liqueur. Cover; blend or
process until smooth. Pour the mixture into
chilled martini glasses. Garnish with a lemon
twist. **Makes 8 servings.**

Vanilla Vodka Cream Tini

Start To Finish: 15 minutes

Orange wedge
Vanilla Sugar (recipe follows) or
  granulated sugar
2 cups ice cubes
1 cup vanilla vodka*
½ cup Irish cream liqueur, whole milk,
  whipping cream, half-and-half or
  light cream
1 tablespoon Cointreau, Grand Marnier,
  orange liqueur or orange juice
Thin orange slices (optional)
White chocolate and/or dark chocolate
  shavings or curls (optional)

1. Rub the rims of four to six chilled martini glasses with a wedge of orange. Spread Vanilla Sugar onto a platter. Invert glasses into the sugar to coat rims. Set aside.

2. In a cocktail shaker or container with a tight-fitting lid, combine half of the ice cubes, half of the vanilla vodka, half of the Irish cream liqueur and half of the Cointreau. Cover and shake vigorously. Strain into two or three martini glasses; discard ice cubes. Repeat with remaining ice cubes, vodka, liqueur and Cointreau. Strain into remaining glasses.

3. Garnish drinks with orange slices and chocolate shavings, if you like.
Makes 4 to 6 drinks.

*Tip: If you do not have vanilla vodka, substitute 1 cup regular vodka and 1 teaspoon vanilla.

Vanilla Sugar: Fill a clean and sterilized 1-quart jar with 4 cups sugar. Using a sharp paring knife, slit one 4- to 6-inch vanilla bean lengthwise. Insert both halves into sugar, making sure all of the bean is covered with sugar. Secure lid and store in a cool, dry place for 2 weeks before using. (Will keep indefinitely.) Makes 4 cups.

Nutrition facts per serving: 232 cal., 4 g fat, 10 mg chol., 26 mg sodium, 8 g carbo., 0 g fiber, 1 g pro.

Green Tea Martini

Start To Finish: 5 minutes

1 cup ice cubes
¼ cup vodka (2 ounces)
2 tablespoons chilled double-strength
  green tea* or lemon herbal tea
  (1 ounce)
1 tablespoon Grand Marnier, Cointreau
  or orange-flavor liqueur (½ ounce)
Lemon wedge
Sugar (optional)
Thin strip lemon peel

1. In a cocktail shaker, combine ice cubes, vodka, tea and Grand Marnier. Shake for 1 minute; let stand for 1 minute.

2. Meanwhile, rub lemon wedge on the inside and rim of one or two chilled martini glasses. If you like, dip rim of glass or glasses in sugar to coat. Strain tea mixture into prepared glass or glasses. Garnish with a thin strip of lemon peel. **Makes 1 to 2 servings.**

*Double-strength green tea: Bring ½ cup water to boiling. Pour over tea bag in small bowl. Steep for 3 minutes. Remove tea bag.

Nutrition facts per serving: 177 cal., 0 g fat, 0 mg chol., 3 mg sodium, 7 g carbo., 0 g fiber, 0 g pro.

Green Tea Soda

Prep: 20 minutes Cool: 1 hour Chill: 4 to 24 hours

8 bags green, gingko or ginseng tea
½ cup honey
4 cups boiling water
1 cup orange or tangerine juice
½ cup lemon or lime juice
4 cups assorted fresh fruit, such as lemon
  slices, orange slices, white or regular
  nectarine wedges, blueberries,
  blackberries, raspberries and/or pitted
  dark sweet cherries
½ of a 1-liter bottle plain or flavored
  sparkling water, such as raspberry,
  strawberry or peach, chilled (2 cups)

1. In a heatproof medium glass bowl or a heatproof 2-quart pitcher, add tea bags and honey to the boiling water, stirring until honey dissolves. Cover; steep for 10 minutes at room temperature. Carefully remove tea bags, gently squeezing to remove liquid. Let cool 1 hour.

2. Add orange juice and lemon juice to brewed tea. Cover; chill tea mixture 4 to 24 hours.

3. To serve, fill eight to ten 12-ounce glasses with ice cubes. Divide tea among glasses; add fruit and fill with sparkling water.
Makes 8 to 10 servings.

Nutrition facts per serving: 119 cal., 0 g fat, 0 mg chol., 3 mg sodium, 31 g carbo., 2 g fiber, 1 g pro.

Vanilla Vodka Cream Tini

Green Tea Martini

Vanilla Cafe Latte

Vanilla Cafe Latte

Start To Finish: 5 minutes

¼ cup hot brewed espresso or hot
　　brewed strong coffee
2 teaspoons vanilla-flavor syrup (used to
　　flavor coffee) or 1 teaspoon sugar and
　　¼ teaspoon vanilla
2 to 3 tablespoons steamed milk
2 tablespoons frothed milk*
　　Ground cinnamon or grated chocolate

1. Into a 5- to 6-ounce cup, "pull" espresso
or pour in the coffee. Stir in vanilla-flavor
syrup. Add steamed milk and top with
frothed milk. Sprinkle with ground cinnamon
or grated chocolate. **Makes 1 serving.**

*Tip: To make frothed milk, use the steam
wand on your espresso machine to steam
and froth the milk. Or place hot milk in a
blender. Cover and blend until froth forms on
top of the milk. Or place the hot milk into a
deep bowl and use an immersion blender to
blend the milk until froth forms on top.

Nutrition facts per serving: 48 cal., 1 g fat, 4 mg chol.,
37 mg sodium, 8 g carbo., 0 g fiber, 2 g pro.

Mint Lemonade

Prep: 10 minutes Cool: 20 minutes
Chill: 4 hours

2 cups sugar
2 cups water
1½ cups lightly packed fresh mint leaves
6 lemons
3 limes
　　Chilled water
　　Lemon and lime slices and/or thin
　　wedges
　　Small mint sprigs (optional)

1. For mint syrup: In a medium saucepan,
heat and stir sugar and the 2 cups water
over medium heat until the sugar dissolves.
Remove from heat. Stir in 1½ cups mint
leaves; cool for 20 minutes at room
temperature. Strain mixture, discarding
mint leaves.

2. Finely grate 1 tablespoon of peel from
lemons and limes. Squeeze juice from
lemons and limes (to equal 2 to 2½ cups
total). In a 2-quart jar or pitcher, combine
cooled mint syrup, citrus peel and citrus juice.
Cover; chill for at least 4 hours to 24 hours.

3. Just before serving, stir mixture. To serve,
mix equal parts of citrus mixture and chilled
water (about ½ cup of each). Add slices or
wedges of lemon and lime. Pour into ice-
filled glasses. If you like, garnish each glass
with additional mint. **Makes 5 or 6 servings.**

Nutrition facts per serving: 359 cal., 1 g fat, 0 mg chol.,
12 mg sodium, 102 g carbo., 8 g fiber, 3 g pro.

Fizzy Frisky Whiskey: Prepare Mint
Lemonade. Just before serving, stir. For each
serving, pour equal parts fruit syrup mixture
concentrate from Step 2 and lemon-lime
carbonated beverage (about ¼ cup each)
into an ice-filled glass. Add 2 tablespoons
whiskey or bourbon; stir. Garnish with
orange twist and a maraschino cherry.

Winter Orange-Pomegranate Iced Tea

Prep: 10 minutes Stand: 5 minutes
Chill: 4 hours

3 cups water
1 navel orange, cut into ¼-inch slices
3 inches stick cinnamon, broken
6 whole cloves
4 orange-flavor or black tea bags
　　(decaffeinated, if you like)
1 cup orange juice
1 cup pomegranate juice
2 to 3 tablespoons sugar
12 orange wedges or chunks
6 lime wedges or chunks
6 6-inch wooden skewers
　　Ice cubes

1. In a medium saucepan, combine the
water, orange slices, cinnamon and cloves.
Bring just to boiling; remove from heat. Add
tea bags. Let stand, covered, for 5 minutes.
Remove tea bags; discard. Strain tea mixture
through a fine-mesh strainer; discard orange
slices and spices.

2. In a glass pitcher, combine strained tea
mixture, orange juice, pomegranate juice and
sugar, stirring to dissolve sugar. Cover and
chill for at least 4 hours or up to 24 hours.

3. To serve: Place 2 orange wedges and
1 lime wedge onto each skewer. Serve tea
in glasses filled with ice cubes. Add fruit
skewers to each glass.
Makes 6 (6-ounce) servings.

Nutrition facts per serving: 92 cal., 0 g fat, 0 mg chol.,
6 mg sodium, 23 g carbo., 0 g fiber, 1 g pro.

**Winter Orange-
Pomegranate Iced Tea**

Chocolate Eggnog Deluxe

Prep: 25 minutes Cook: 5 minutes Chill: 4 hours

¾ cup granulated sugar
½ cup unsweetened cocoa powder
3 eggs, lightly beaten
3 egg yolks, lightly beaten
1 12-ounce can evaporated milk
2 3-inch pieces stick cinnamon
1 cup whipping cream
¼ cup port wine or Madeira
¼ cup brandy, cognac or rum
1½ teaspoons vanilla
　Whipped Cream
　Chocolate shavings and/or chocolate
　　sprinkles
　Peppermint sticks

1. In a heavy large saucepan, stir together sugar and cocoa powder. Stir in eggs, egg yolks, evaporated milk and cinnamon. Cook, stirring constantly, over medium heat until mixture thickens slightly and an instant-read thermometer registers 165°; do not let boil.

2. Place pan in a sink or bowl of ice water and stir for 2 minutes. Remove stick cinnamon; discard. Whisk in whipping cream, port wine, brandy and vanilla. Cover and chill at least 4 hours or up to 24 hours before serving. Garnish each serving with a dollop of whipped cream and top with chocolate shavings and/or chocolate sprinkles. Add peppermint sticks to each serving. **Makes 8 (4-ounce) servings.**

Nutrition facts per serving: 339 cal., 19 g fat, 211 mg chol., 91 mg sodium, 28 g carbo., 0 g fiber, 8 g pro.

Christmas Brandy Eggnog

Prep: 45 minutes Chill: 4 hours

6 eggs, beaten
1 quart (4 cups) half-and-half, light
　cream or whole milk
¾ cup granulated sugar
¼ to ½ cup brandy or cognac
¼ to ½ cup bourbon
¼ cup light rum
2 teaspoons vanilla

1 cup whipping cream
2 tablespoons powdered sugar
½ teaspoon ground cardamom, nutmeg
　or ground cinnamon

1. In a heavy medium saucepan, stir together eggs, half-and-half and granulated sugar. Cook and stir over medium heat until mixture just coats a metal spoon; do not let boil. (Should take about 20 minutes and register 160° to 165° on instant-read thermometer.) Immediately place pan in a sink or bowl of ice water and stir for 2 minutes. Stir in brandy, bourbon, light rum and vanilla. Cover and chill for at least 4 or up to 24 hours. Meanwhile, chill a mixing bowl and beaters of an electric mixer.

2. Just before serving, in a chilled bowl, combine whipping cream, powdered sugar and cardamom. Beat with chilled beaters on low until soft peaks form. Transfer egg mixture to a punch bowl. Fold in whipped cream. **Makes 10 to 12 (6-ounce) servings.**

Nutrition facts per serving: 357 cal., 23 g fat, 195 mg chol., 91 mg sodium, 21 g carbo., 0 g fiber, 7 g pro.

Coconut-Rum Cream Eggnog

Prep: 20 minutes Chill: 4 hours

4 egg yolks, lightly beaten
1 14-ounce can unsweetened coconut milk
½ cup cream of coconut
⅓ cup sugar
1½ cups whipping cream
¼ to ½ cup light rum, spiced rum,
　coconut-flavor rum or milk
1 tablespoon sugar
¼ teaspoon coconut extract or
　½ teaspoon vanilla
　Toasted flaked coconut

1. In a heavy medium saucepan, stir together egg yolks, coconut milk, cream of coconut and ⅓ cup sugar. Cook and stir over medium heat until mixture just starts to bubble.

2. Place the pan in a sink or very large bowl of ice water and stir for 2 minutes. Stir in 1 cup

of the whipping cream and the rum. Cover and chill for at least 4 or up to 24 hours.

3. Just before serving, in a chilled medium mixing bowl, beat remaining ½ cup whipping cream, 1 tablespoon sugar and the coconut extract with an electric mixer or whisk until soft peaks form. Divide coconut mixture among six serving glasses. Dollop each with whipped cream and sprinkle with toasted coconut. **Makes 6 (5-ounce) servings.**

Nutrition facts per serving: 501 cal., 44 g fat, 219 mg chol., 47 mg sodium, 18 g carbo., 0 g fiber, 5 g pro.

Orange-Eggnog Punch

Prep: 40 minutes Chill: 4 hours

6 egg yolks, lightly beaten
2 cups whole milk
½ cup sugar
1 6-ounce can frozen orange juice
　concentrate, thawed
½ of 6-ounce can (⅓ cup) frozen
　lemonade concentrate, thawed
2 teaspoons vanilla
1 quart (4 cups) French vanilla or vanilla
　ice cream
1 28-ounce bottle ginger ale, chilled
　Ground nutmeg or grated white
　chocolate and orange peel twists

1. In a heavy medium saucepan, stir together egg yolks, milk and sugar. Cook and stir over medium heat until mixture just coats a spoon; do not let boil. (Should take about 25 minutes and register 170° to 175° on instant-read thermometer.)

2. Place the pan in a sink or bowl of ice water and stir for 2 minutes. Stir in orange juice and lemonade concentrates and vanilla. Cover and chill for 4 to 24 hours.

3. Cut ice cream in small chunks; put in a punch bowl. Pour ginger ale over ice cream. Stir in chilled egg mixture. Sprinkle each serving with nutmeg or white chocolate and add an orange twist. **Makes 22 (4-ounce) servings.**

Nutrition facts per serving: 146 cal., 6 g fat, 83 mg chol., 35 mg sodium, 20 g carbo., 0 g fiber, 3 g pro.

Christmas Brandy Eggnog

Coconut-Rum Cream Eggnog

Orange-Eggnog Punch

Chocolate Eggnog Deluxe

Vanilla Bean-Infused
Hot Chocolate

Vanilla Bean-Infused Hot Chocolate

Prep: 20 minutes Chill: 2 hours

4 cups whole milk
2 cups whipping cream or heavy cream
2 4- to 6-inch vanilla beans
14 ounces bittersweet chocolate or semisweet chocolate, coarsely chopped
Sugar (optional)
Whipped cream

1. In a heavy large saucepan, heat milk and cream over medium heat until hot but not boiling. Remove from heat. Using the tip of a paring knife, slit vanilla beans down the center. Using the side of the knife, scrape the seeds. Place seeds and vanilla pods into hot milk mixture. Cover and chill. Allow vanilla pods to infuse flavor into milk for at least 2 hours. Or transfer mixture to a container with a tight-fitting lid and chill in the refrigerator overnight. Remove vanilla pods and press the milk out of the bean to extract all the seeds; discard.

2. When ready to make the hot chocolate, heat the milk mixture over medium heat until hot, but not boiling. Add the chocolate. Whisk until the mixture is smooth and chocolate is melted. Add sugar to sweeten, if you like. Top with whipped cream.
Makes 15 (4-ounce) servings.

Nutrition facts per serving: 311 cal., 27 g fat, 62 mg chol., 42 mg sodium, 18 g carbo., 2 g fiber, 4 g pro.

Hot Coffee Latte Eggnog

Start To Finish: 30 minutes

3 eggs, slightly beaten
2 cups whole milk
1 cup whipping cream
1/2 cup coffee liqueur
2 tablespoons honey
1 tablespoon instant espresso coffee powder or 4 teaspoons instant coffee
Whipped cream (optional)
Ground cinnamon
8 long cinnamon sticks (optional)

1. In a heavy large saucepan, stir together the eggs, milk, whipping cream, coffee liqueur, honey and espresso coffee powder. Cook and stir over medium heat until mixture just coats a metal spoon; do not let boil. (Should take 20 to 25 minutes and register 170° to 175° on instant-read thermometer.)

2. Pour the hot eggnog into heatproof glasses or coffee cups. Top with whipped cream, if you like. Sprinkle each with ground cinnamon and, if you like, serve with cinnamon sticks. Serve immediately.
Makes 8 (4-ounce) servings.

Nutrition facts per serving: 194 cal., 15 g fat, 128 mg chol., 69 mg sodium, 9 g carbo., 0 g fiber, 6 g pro.

Nonalcoholic Coffee Latte Eggnog: Prepare as above, except omit the coffee liqueur. Increase the milk to 2 1/2 cups.

Homemade Ginger Ale Summer Sodas

Prep: 10 minutes Cook: 3 minutes Cool: 1 hour Chill: 24 hours

2 cups water
2 cups sugar
2 cups fresh ginger, peeled and cut into 1/4-inch-thick slices
Ice cubes
1 32-ounce bottle club soda, chilled
Lime wedges

1. For ginger syrup: In a medium saucepan, bring the water, sugar and ginger to boiling over medium-high heat; reduce heat. Simmer, uncovered, for 3 to 5 minutes or until the mixture thickens slightly. Remove from heat; let cool to room temperature. Strain mixture through fine-mesh sieve, discarding solids. Cover and chill for 24 hours or up to 2 weeks.

2. Just before serving, pour 1/4 cup ginger syrup into ice-filled tall glasses. Slowly add 1/2 cup club soda to each glass. Stir gently to mix. Garnish each glass with a lime wedge.
Makes 8 (6-ounce) servings.

Nutrition facts per serving: 186 cal., 0 g fat, 0 mg chol., 14 mg sodium, 48 g carbo., 0 g fiber, 0 g pro.

Summer Wine Punch

Prep: 10 minutes Chill: 2 hours

6 cups water
2 12-ounce cans frozen pink lemonade concentrate, thawed
1 750-milliliter bottle berry wine, such as elderberry, strawberry or raspberry, chilled

1. In two large pitchers or a large punch bowl, stir together the water and lemonade concentrate until well combined. Add wine to lemonade mixture. Cover; chill for 2 to 24 hours. Stir before serving.
Makes 12 (8-ounce) servings.

Tip: Serve over ice and float a few fresh raspberries in the glass.

Nutrition facts per serving: 202 cal., 0 g fat, 0 mg chol., 11 mg sodium, 35 g carbo., 0 g fiber, 0 g pro.

Hot Coffee Latte Eggnog

Apple Pie Pancakes,
page 46

BREAKFAST & BRUNCH

Bacon, Ham and Egg Hash

Bacon, Ham & Egg Hash

Start to finish: 35 minutes

- 4 slices bacon
- 2 large potatoes, peeled and chopped (2½ cups)
  Cooking oil
- 8 ounces smoked ham, coarsely chopped
- 5 eggs, lightly beaten
- ¼ teaspoon salt
- ⅛ teaspoon ground black pepper
- ¼ cup shredded cheddar cheese (1 ounce)

1. In a large skillet, cook bacon until crisp. Remove bacon from skillet, reserving fat. Drain well on paper towels and crumble. Set aside.

2. Add potatoes to the reserved fat and add additional oil if necessary. Cook, uncovered, over medium heat about 10 minutes or until potatoes are almost tender and browned, turning frequently. Add the ham. Cook about 5 minutes more or until potatoes are tender, stirring gently.

3. In a small bowl, combine eggs, salt and pepper. Pour egg mixture over potato-ham mixture. Cook over medium heat, without stirring, until egg mixture begins to set on the bottom and around edge. Using a spatula or a large spoon, lift and fold the partially cooked egg mixture so that the uncooked portion flows underneath.

4. Continue cooking over medium heat until egg mixture is cooked through but is still glossy and moist. Sprinkle with cheese and reserved bacon. Remove from heat. Cover and let stand for 1 to 2 minutes or until cheese is melted. **Makes 4 servings.**

Nutrition facts per serving: 481 cal., 31 g fat, 330 mg chol., 1,338 mg sodium, 25 g carbo., 2 g fiber, 25 g pro.

A Hole-in-One Breakfast

Prep: 25 minutes   Cook: 12 minutes

- 4 ounces bulk pork sausage
- ⅓ cup finely chopped fresh mushrooms
- ⅓ cup finely chopped red, yellow or green sweet pepper
- ¼ cup thinly sliced green onion
- ½ cup shredded cheddar or Monterey Jack cheese (2 ounces)
- 4 slices home-style whole wheat or white bread
- 4 teaspoons butter or margarine, softened
- 4 eggs
  Salt and freshly ground black pepper
  Assorted fresh fruit, such as pineapple chunks, nectarine wedges, strawberries, blackberries, raspberries and/or seedless grapes (optional)

1. In a 12-inch nonstick skillet, cook sausage, mushrooms, sweet pepper and green onion until meat is brown and vegetables are tender, stirring to break up sausage as it cooks. Remove sausage mixture from skillet; drain. In a small bowl, combine sausage mixture and cheese; set aside. Carefully wipe skillet clean with paper towels; set aside.

2. With a 2-inch round cookie cutter, biscuit cutter or a small juice glass, cut out the center of each bread slice. (Use centers in another recipe for bread crumbs.) Spread both sides of the bread slices with the butter.

3. In the same 12-inch skillet, toast bread* on one side over medium heat about 2 minutes or until golden brown. Reduce heat to medium-low. Turn the bread slices over.

4. Break one of the eggs into a 1-cup glass measuring cup with a handle. Holding the lip of the cup as close to the bread as possible, carefully slide egg into the hole. Repeat with remaining three eggs and bread slices. Lightly sprinkle the eggs with salt and pepper. Spoon sausage mixture atop bread slices, avoiding the eggs as much as possible.

5. Cook, covered, for 10 to 15 minutes or until eggs are firm. Using a wide spatula, carefully lift out bread-and-egg slices and transfer to four dinner plates. Serve with assorted fresh fruit, if you like. **Makes 4 servings.**

*Tip: If your bread slices are too large to fit in the skillet at the same time, cook half of them at a time.

Nutrition facts per serving: 317 cal., 22 g fat, 257 mg chol., 558 mg sodium, 12 g carbo., 2 g fiber, 18 g pro.

A Hole-in-One Breakfast

Eggs Flo

Start to finish: 20 minutes

    Basil Hollandaise Sauce (recipe follows)
4 eggs
4 ³/₄-inch slices of challah, brioche or
    egg bread
12 ounces sliced smoked turkey breast
2 cups fresh baby spinach leaves
¹/₄ cup shredded Asiago or Parmesan
    cheese (1 ounce) (optional)

1. Prepare Basil Hollandaise Sauce. Keep warm while preparing eggs.

2. Lightly grease a large skillet. Half fill the skillet with water. Bring water to boiling; reduce heat to simmering (bubbles should begin to break the surface of the water). Break one of the eggs into a dry measuring cup. Carefully slide the egg into the simmering water, holding the lip of the cup as close to the water as possible. Repeat with remaining eggs, allowing each egg an equal amount of space.

3. Simmer eggs, uncovered, for 3 to 5 minutes or until the whites are completely set and yolks begin to thicken but are not hard. Remove eggs with a slotted spoon and place them in a large pan of warm water to keep them warm, if necessary.

4. Meanwhile, place bread slices and turkey slices on a large baking sheet. Broil 3 to 4 inches from the heat for 1 to 2 minutes or until bread is toasted. Turn bread slices and turkey slices over. Broil 1 to 2 minutes more or until bread is toasted and meat is heated through.

5. To serve, top each bread slice with one-fourth of the spinach leaves, one-fourth of the smoked turkey and one poached egg. Spoon Basil Hollandaise Sauce over eggs. Sprinkle with Asiago cheese, if you like. **Makes 4 servings.**

Basil Hollandaise Sauce: Cut ¹/₂ cup butter (1 stick) into thirds and bring to room temperature. (Allow about 45 minutes.) In the top of a double boiler, combine three beaten egg yolks, 1 tablespoon water and 1 tablespoon lemon juice. Add a piece of the butter. Place over gently boiling water (the upper pan should not touch water). Cook, whisking rapidly until butter melts and sauce begins to thicken. (Sauce may appear to curdle at this point but it will smooth out when remaining butter is added.) Add the remaining butter, one piece at a time, stirring constantly until melted. Continue to cook and stir for 2 to 2¹/₂ minutes or until sauce thickens. Immediately remove from heat. If sauce is too thick or curdles, immediately whisk in 1 to 2 tablespoons hot water. Stir in 1 tablespoon snipped fresh basil, ¹/₈ teaspoon salt and ¹/₈ teaspoon white pepper. Makes ³/₄ cup sauce.

Nutrition facts per serving: 910 cal., 72 g fat, 760 mg chol., 1,408 mg sodium, 31 g carbo., 3 g fiber, 36 g pro.

Asparagus Scramble Biscuits

Prep: 20 minutes Cook: 10 minutes
Bake: 5 minutes Oven: 350°

    8 ounces fresh asparagus, trimmed and
        cut into bite-size pieces
1 tablespoon butter

12 eggs, lightly beaten
¹/₂ teaspoon salt
¹/₂ teaspoon cracked black pepper
³/₄ cup roasted red sweet peppers,
    chopped
    Bacon-Cheddar Cornmeal Biscuits, split
    horizontally (recipe follows)
³/₄ cup shredded Swiss cheese (3 ounces)

1. Preheat oven to 350°. In a large skillet, cook asparagus in hot butter over medium heat abut 6 minutes or until crisp-tender. Remove asparagus from skillet.

2. Add eggs, salt and pepper to skillet. Using a spatula, lift and fold cooked egg, letting uncooked egg run underneath. Cook 4 minutes or until almost set; stir in red peppers and asparagus. Remove from heat.

3. Arrange bottoms of biscuits in a 15x10x1-inch baking pan; divide egg mixture and Swiss cheese among biscuit bottoms. Add tops. Bake, uncovered, for 5 to 8 minutes or until heated through and cheese is melted. Makes 8 (two-biscuit) servings.

Open-Face Method: Split biscuits in half and wrap in foil. Reheat in a 350° oven for 20 minutes or until warm. Spoon egg mixture atop split biscuits; top with cheese.

Bacon-Cheddar Cornmeal Biscuits: In a large bowl, mix 1³/₄ cups all-purpose flour, ¹/₂ cup cornmeal and 1 tablespoon baking powder. Using pastry blender, cut ¹/₄ cup butter into flour mixture until pieces are pea-size. Add ³/₄ cup shredded cheddar cheese (3 ounces); four slices bacon, crisp-cooked, drained and crumbled; ²/₃ cup milk; one egg, lightly beaten; and 2 tablespoons snipped fresh chives. Stir until moistened. Turn out onto floured surface. Knead lightly four to six strokes or until dough just holds together. Pat or roll to a ¹/₂-inch-thick 8-inch square. Using sharp knife, cut into sixteen 2-inch squares. Transfer to lightly greased baking sheet; brush with additional milk. Bake in 425° oven 10 to 12 minutes or until golden brown. Remove; cool on a wire rack. Makes 16 biscuits.

Nutrition facts per serving: 434 cal., 24 g fat, 390 mg chol., 635 mg sodium, 32 g carbo., 2 g fiber, 22 g pro.

Eggs Flo

Asparagus Scramble Biscuits

Pasta Frittata

Pasta Frittata

Prep: 40 minutes Cook: 25 minutes
Bake: 40 minutes Oven: 350°

  6 ounces dried spaghetti
    Nonstick cooking spray
  2 tablespoons olive oil
  ³⁄₄ cup chopped onion
  1¹⁄₂ cups sliced fresh mushrooms
  1 medium zucchini, cut into thin bite-size
    strips (1¹⁄₂ cups)
  1 medium red sweet pepper, cut into
    thin bite-size strips (³⁄₄ cup)
  2 cloves garlic, minced
  1 teaspoon salt
  1 teaspoon dried oregano, crushed
  ¹⁄₂ teaspoon freshly ground black pepper
  10 eggs
  1¹⁄₄ cups milk
  ¹⁄₂ cup grated Parmesan cheese
  2 8-ounce packages cream cheese, cut
    into small cubes and softened
  1¹⁄₂ cups shredded sharp cheddar cheese
    (6 ounces)
    Sauteed Tomato Sauce (recipe follows)

1. Cook spaghetti according to package directions. Drain; keep warm.

2. Lightly coat a 3-quart baking dish with cooking spray. Set aside.

3. In a large saucepan, heat olive oil over medium heat. Add onion. Cook and stir over medium heat for 5 minutes or until onion is tender. Add mushrooms, zucchini, sweet pepper and garlic. Cook and stir for 3 minutes more or until vegetables are just tender. Drain off liquid and discard. Stir salt, oregano and pepper into vegetable mixture. Set aside to cool.

4. In a large mixing bowl, beat eggs, milk and Parmesan with an electric mixer on low speed until combined. Add cream cheese pieces. Beat for 30 seconds.

5. Place cooked spaghetti on bottom of prepared baking dish. Add vegetables. Sprinkle with cheddar cheese. Pour egg mixture evenly over mixture in dish. Pat down with a spatula or back of a spoon so most of solids are covered with the liquid.

6. Bake, uncovered, in a 350° oven about 40 minutes or until set and lightly browned on edges. Cut into serving-size pieces. To serve, spoon about ¹⁄₃ cup of Sauteed Tomato Sauce on each plate; place a frittata serving on top of sauce. Serve immediately. Makes 12 servings.

Sauteed Tomato Sauce: In a medium saucepan, melt 2 tablespoons butter or margarine over medium heat. Cook ³⁄₄ cup chopped onion in hot butter for 5 minutes or until onion is tender, stirring often. Add two cloves minced garlic; cook and stir 30 seconds more. Carefully stir in one 28-ounce can whole Italian-style tomatoes in puree, undrained and cut up; half of a 6-ounce can (¹⁄₃ cup) tomato paste; ¹⁄₂ teaspoon sugar; ¹⁄₂ teaspoon kosher or sea salt; and ¹⁄₄ teaspoon freshly ground black pepper. Bring to boiling; reduce heat. Simmer, uncovered, about 15 minutes or to desired consistency. Stir in 1 teaspoon dried oregano, crushed. Cook for 5 minutes more. Makes about 4 cups.

Nutrition facts per serving: 407 cal., 28 g fat, 244 mg chol., 727 mg sodium, 22 g carbo., 2 g fiber, 18 g pro.

Lazy Morning Sausage Pie

Prep: 20 minutes Bake: 25 minutes
Stand: 10 minutes Oven: 400°

  1 pound bulk pork sausage
  1 large onion, chopped (1 cup)
  1 cup shredded American, Swiss or
    cheddar cheese (4 ounces)
  2 eggs, lightly beaten
  1 cup low-fat milk or fat-free milk
  ¹⁄₂ cup packaged biscuit mix or packaged
    low-fat pancake and baking mix
    Salsa
    Dairy sour cream

Lazy Morning Sausage Pie

1. In a large skillet, cook sausage and onion over medium-high heat until meat is brown and onion is tender. Drain sausage mixture on paper towels. Spoon sausage mixture into a greased 9-inch pie plate. Top with shredded cheese.

2. In a small bowl, combine eggs and milk. In another small bowl, place biscuit mix; gradually whisk egg mixture into biscuit mix until combined. Slowly pour egg mixture over the cheese.

3. Bake in a 400° oven for 25 to 30 minutes or until a knife inserted near the center comes out clean. Let stand for 10 minutes before serving. Cut into wedges and serve with salsa and sour cream. **Makes 6 servings.**

Nutrition facts per serving: 416 cal., 31 g fat, 149 mg chol., 1,032 mg sodium, 13 g carbo., 1 g fiber, 21 g pro.

Tomato Benedict

Prep: 20 minutes Cook: 3 minutes Broil: 2 minutes

Water
2 tablespoons lemon juice
Dash kosher salt
8 eggs
Hollandaise Sauce (recipe follows)
4 English muffins, split
¼ cup purchased basil pesto
4 cups loosely packed baby spinach
  leaves
2 large tomatoes, thickly sliced and
  sprinkled with salt and ground black
  pepper (8 slices total)
½ cup bottled roasted red sweet
  peppers, well drained and cut into
  thin bite-size strips

1. For poached eggs: Lightly grease a 12-inch skillet. Half fill the skillet with water; add lemon juice and dash salt. Bring water to boiling; reduce heat to simmer (bubbles should begin to break the surface of the water). Break one of the eggs into a 1-cup measuring cup with a handle. Holding the lip of the cup as close to the water as possible, carefully slide egg into simmering water, taking care to not break the egg. Repeat with remaining eggs, allowing each egg an equal amount of space.

2. Simmer eggs, uncovered, for 3 to 4 minutes or until whites are completely set and yolks begin to thicken but are not hard. Remove eggs with a slotted spoon and place in a pan of warm water to keep them warm.

3. Prepare Hollandaise Sauce. If you like, place the Hollandaise Sauce in a glass measuring cup and place the measuring cup in a pan of gently simmering water to keep warm until ready to serve.

4. Meanwhile, place English muffin halves, cut sides up, on a baking sheet. Broil 3 to 4 inches from the heat about 2 minutes or until toasted. Remove from oven. Evenly spread pesto over muffin halves.

5. To serve, place spinach leaves on top of each pesto-topped muffin half. Top with a tomato slice and a well-drained poached egg. Top eggs with roasted sweet pepper strips. Spoon about 2 tablespoons of the Hollandaise Sauce over each egg. **Makes 4 (or 8) servings.**

Hollandaise Sauce: For clarified butter: In a small saucepan, melt 1 cup butter over very low heat without stirring; cool slightly. Slowly pour off clear layer into a small bowl. Discard milky layer (you should have about ¾ cup of clarified butter). In a 2-quart saucepan, combine three lightly beaten egg yolks and 3 tablespoons cold water. Using a wire whisk, whisk egg mixture about 1 minute or until it becomes light and frothy. Heat mixture, whisking vigorously, over medium heat until egg mixture thickens and you start to see the bottom of the saucepan. Continue whisking 5 seconds more. Remove from heat and continue whisking for 30 seconds more (otherwise the sauce may become overcooked). While gently whisking, add the clarified butter in a thin, steady stream. (When all of the butter is added, the sauce will have a smooth texture.) Whisk in 2 tablespoons lemon juice, ⅛ teaspoon kosher salt and ⅛ teaspoon ground white pepper. Makes 1½ cups sauce.

Nutrition facts per serving: 830 cal., 67 g fat, 707 mg chol., 1,203 mg sodium, 37 g carbo., 4 g fiber, 23 g pro.

Tomato Benedict

Mushroom-Stuffed Chicken

Prep: 45 minutes Bake: 30 minutes Oven: 375°

3 cups finely chopped fresh mushrooms
1 14.5-ounce can reduced-sodium
  chicken broth
1 cup finely chopped onion
1 teaspoon dried thyme, crushed
1 teaspoon dried basil, crushed
1 cup soft bread crumbs (1⅓ slices bread)
6 skinless, boneless chicken breast halves
  (about 2 pounds)
  Salt and ground black pepper
2 tablespoons butter
1 tablespoon olive oil
1 cup purchased marinara sauce
½ cup whipping cream

1. For filling: In a large skillet, combine mushrooms, broth, onion, thyme and basil. Bring to boiling; reduce heat and boil gently, uncovered, about 20 minutes or until chicken broth has almost evaporated, stirring occasionally. Remove from heat; cool for 10 minutes. Stir in bread crumbs.

2. Meanwhile, place a chicken breast half between two pieces of plastic wrap. Using the flat side of a meat mallet, pound chicken lightly to about ¼ inch thick. Remove plastic wrap. Repeat with remaining chicken breast halves. Sprinkle chicken breasts with salt and pepper. Spread about ¼ cup of the filling on each chicken piece. Fold in the bottom and sides; roll up. Press all edges firmly to seal in the filling. Secure with wooden toothpicks.

3. In a 12-inch oven-going skillet, heat butter and oil. Add chicken. Cook over medium-high heat about 5 minutes or until golden brown, turning to brown all sides. Bake in a 375° oven for 30 to 35 minutes or until chicken is no longer pink (170°). Remove toothpicks.

4. Meanwhile, in a small saucepan, stir together marinara sauce and cream; heat through (do not boil). To serve, slice stuffed breasts. Serve with sauce. **Makes 6 servings.**

Nutrition facts per serving: 368 cal., 18 g fat, 126 mg chol., 540 mg sodium, 10 g carbo., 2 g fiber, 39 g pro.

Mushroom-Stuffed Chicken

Farmhouse Cheese Torte

Start to finish: 45 minutes Oven: 375°

2 teaspoons butter, melted
1 15-ounce carton ricotta cheese
2 ounces Fontina or Swiss cheese, shredded (¹⁄₂ cup)
1 egg, lightly beaten
1 egg white, lightly beaten
¹⁄₂ teaspoon snipped fresh oregano
¹⁄₈ teaspoon kosher salt
¹⁄₈ teaspoon freshly ground black pepper
¹⁄₃ cup freshly grated Parmigiano-Reggiano or grated Parmesan cheese
2 cups sliced fresh assorted mushrooms
1 shallot, finely chopped
1 tablespoon minced garlic (6 cloves)
1 tablespoon butter
1¹⁄₂ cups whipping cream
2 ounces Taleggio or Brie cheese, rind removed if necessary, cut up
1 teaspoon snipped fresh oregano
Panko-Breaded Fried Eggs (recipe follows)
Fresh herbs or parsley leaves

1. For tortes: Using the 2 teaspoons melted butter, lightly coat six 6-ounce ramekins, soufflé dishes or custard cups. Set aside.

2. In a medium bowl, combine ricotta, fontina, egg, egg white, ¹⁄₂ teaspoon oregano, salt and black pepper. Spoon cheese mixture into prepared cups, filling each cup just under half full. Sprinkle Parmigiano-Reggiano on top of each.

3. Bake, uncovered, in a 375° oven for 20 to 25 minutes or until set and lightly browned. Set aside and keep warm.

4. For sauce: In a large skillet, cook mushrooms, shallot and garlic in 1 tablespoon hot butter over medium heat about 5 minutes or until tender, stirring occasionally. Stir in the whipping cream. Bring to boiling, stirring often; reduce heat. Add Taleggio cheese; stir until cheese is melted. Stir in 1 teaspoon oregano. Set aside and keep warm.

5. To serve, remove tortes from the ramekins. Place each torte on a dinner plate. Place a Panko-Breaded Fried Egg on top of each torte. Spoon sauce around torte. Garnish with fresh herbs or parsley leaves. **Makes 6 servings.**

Make-Ahead Tip: Prepare tortes as directed above through Step 2. Cover and chill up to 4 hours. To serve, bake and assemble as directed. Prepare sauce as directed in Step 4. Refrigerate in an airtight container up to 24 hours. To serve, place sauce in a small saucepan and heat over low heat until heated through, stirring occasionally. Poach eggs as directed in recipe for Panko-Breaded Fried Eggs. After cooling in ice water, drain. Place eggs on a tray or large platter; cover. Refrigerate up to 4 hours. Coat and fry as directed below. Crumb coating mixture can be made as directed and stored in an airtight container in the refrigerator up to 24 hours.

Panko-Breaded Fried Eggs: For poached eggs: In a large skillet, combine 4 cups water, ¹⁄₄ cup white vinegar and 1 tablespoon salt. Bring to boiling; reduce heat to simmer (bubbles should begin to break the surface of the water). Break one of six eggs into a 1-cup dry measure with a handle. Holding the lip of the cup as close to the water as possible, carefully slide egg into simmering water, taking care not to break the egg. Repeat with remaining eggs, allowing each egg an equal amount of space. Simmer, uncovered, for 3 to 4 minutes or until whites are completely set and yolks begin to thicken but are not hard. Remove with a slotted spoon and place in a large bowl of ice water to cool. For breaded eggs: In a food processor or blender, combine ¹⁄₂ cup panko bread crumbs, 3 tablespoons Parmigiano-Reggiano cheese and leaves from one sprig fresh oregano. Cover and process or blend until finely chopped. Transfer to a shallow dish. In another shallow dish, place ¹⁄₄ cup flour. In another shallow dish, combine one lightly beaten egg and 1 tablespoon water. To bread eggs, coat one of the poached eggs lightly in flour. Dip in egg mixture, then in bread crumbs to coat both sides. Repeat with remaining eggs. In a large skillet, heat 1 inch

cooking oil to 375°. Fry breaded eggs, three at a time, for 1 to 2 minutes or until golden brown and crisp, turning to brown evenly.

Nutrition facts per serving: 815 cal., 63 g fat, 675 mg chol., 968 mg sodium, 23 g carbo., 1 g fiber, 36 g pro.

Blueberry Surprise French Toast Casserole

Prep: 25 minutes Chill: 2 to 24 hours
Bake: 50 minutes Stand: 10 minutes Oven: 375°

12 slices dry white bread, cut into ¹⁄₂-inch cubes (about 8 cups)*
2 8-ounce packages cream cheese, cut into ³⁄₄-inch cubes
1 cup fresh or frozen blueberries
12 eggs
2 cups milk
¹⁄₂ cup maple syrup or maple-flavor syrup
Blueberry-flavor, maple or maple-flavor syrup

1. Cover bottom of a well-buttered 3-quart rectangular baking dish with half the bread cubes. Sprinkle cream cheese and blueberries over bread cubes. Arrange remaining bread cubes over blueberries.

2. In a large mixing bowl, beat eggs; beat in milk and the ¹⁄₂ cup syrup. Carefully pour egg mixture over bread mixture. Cover dish with plastic wrap. Chill for 2 to 24 hours.

3. Preheat oven to 375°. Remove plastic wrap and cover dish with foil. Bake for 25 minutes. Uncover and bake about 25 minutes more or until a knife inserted near the center comes out clean and top is puffed and golden brown. Let stand for 10 minutes. Serve warm with syrup. **Makes 8 servings.**

***Test Kitchen Tip:** To dry bread slices, arrange bread in a single layer on a wire rack; cover loosely and let stand overnight. Or cut bread into ¹⁄₂-inch cubes; spread in a large baking pan. Bake, uncovered, in a 300° oven for 10 to 15 minutes or until dry, stirring twice; cool.

Nutrition facts per serving: 503 cal., 30 g fat, 386 mg chol., 497 mg sodium, 40 g carbo., 1 g fiber, 19 g pro.

Heavenly Hots

Prep: 20 minutes Stand: 2 minutes
Cook: 4 minutes per batch

  4 eggs
  1 16-ounce container dairy sour cream
  ¼ cup sifted cake flour or all-purpose
     flour
  2 tablespoons potato starch or
     corn starch
  3 tablespoons sugar
  ½ teaspoon baking soda
  ½ teaspoon salt
  2 cups assorted fresh fruit, such as
     orange sections, blackberries,
     raspberries or blueberries; pitted
     sweet cherries; and/or sliced bananas,
     strawberries, peaches or pears
     Crème fraîche or sour cream (optional)
     Orange marmalade (optional)

1. In a covered blender container, blend eggs, sour cream, cake flour, potato starch, sugar, baking soda and salt for 30 seconds. Stop the blender. Scrape down the sides of container with a rubber spatula and blend again until smooth. Let sit for 2 to 3 minutes.

2. Pour slightly less than ¼ cup batter into a 3-inch circle onto a hot, lightly greased griddle or heavy skillet. Cook over medium heat about 2 minutes on each side or until pancakes are golden brown, carefully turning (pancakes are very tender) to second side when pancakes have bubbly surfaces and edges are slightly dry. Serve warm with fresh fruit and, if you like, crème fraîche and orange marmalade. **Makes 12 to 13 pancakes.**

Nutrition facts per pancake: 146 cal., 10 g fat, 87 mg chol., 191 mg sodium, 12 g carbo., 1 g fiber, 4 g pro.

Apple Pie Pancakes

Prep: 20 minutes Cook: 4 minutes per batch

  1½ cups all-purpose flour
  2 tablespoons granulated sugar
  1 tablespoon baking powder
  ½ teaspoon apple pie spice or ground
     cinnamon
  ¼ teaspoon salt
  2 eggs, lightly beaten
  1 cup apple juice or ½ cup apple juice
     and ½ cup milk
  3 tablespoons butter, melted
  2 teaspoons vanilla
  ¼ cup snipped dried apple or ½ cup
     chopped fresh apple
     Nonstick cooking spray
     Powdered sugar (optional)
     Pure maple syrup
     Coarsely chopped walnuts or pecans,
     toasted (optional)

1. In a medium bowl, stir together flour, sugar, baking powder, apple pie spice and salt. Make a well in the center of the flour mixture; set aside.

2. In a small bowl, use a fork to combine eggs, apple juice, melted butter and vanilla. Add egg mixture all at once to flour mixture. Stir just until moistened (batter should be slightly lumpy). Stir in apple.

3. For each maple leaf-shape pancake: Lightly coat the inside of a 3- to 4-inch metal maple leaf-shape cookie cutter* or desired-shape pancake ring or metal cookie cutter* with nonstick cooking spray. Place the ring on the hot, lightly greased griddle to preheat for 2 to 3 minutes. Carefully spoon the batter into the ring or cutter, filling about one-third full (use a table knife to spread batter to all edges). Cook over medium heat about 2 minutes or until sides appear dry and start to pull away from ring or cutter. Carefully lift off ring with the handle or carefully lift cookie cutter with tongs. (Use the tip of a table knife to push pancake from ring or cutter, if necessary.) Turn pancake and continue to cook as directed. Recoat ring or cutter with cooking spray as needed and preheat before adding more batter.

4. For each standard-size pancake: Pour about ¼ cup batter onto a hot, lightly greased griddle or heavy skillet, spreading batter to a 4-inch circle. Cook over medium heat for 1 to 2 minutes on each side or until pancakes are golden brown, turning to second side when pancakes have bubbly surfaces and edges are slightly dry.

5. Serve warm. If you like, lightly sprinkle pancakes with powdered sugar. Top with maple syrup and, if you like, toasted walnuts. **Makes about 30 maple leaf-size pancakes or 10 to 12 standard-size pancakes.**

To keep warm: Place cooked pancakes on ovenproof plate in 200° oven while cooking remaining batter.

*Note: Make sure cutter is riveted rather than soldered; solder can melt on the griddle.

Nutrition facts per standard-size pancake: 143 cal., 5 g fat, 51 mg chol., 209 mg sodium, 22 g carbo., 1 g fiber, 2 g pro.

Heavenly Hots

Apple Pie Pancakes

Four-Grain Pancakes

Four-Grain Pancakes

Start to finish: 30 minutes

1¼ cups whole wheat flour
1 cup regular rolled oats
¼ cup yellow cornmeal
¼ cup toasted wheat germ
1 tablespoon flaxseeds (optional)
1 tablespoon baking powder
½ teaspoon salt
¼ teaspoon baking soda
2 eggs, lightly beaten
2 cups buttermilk or sour milk*
¼ cup canola oil or cooking oil
2 tablespoons packed brown sugar or honey
Maple syrup

1. In a large bowl, stir together flour, oats, cornmeal, wheat germ, flaxseeds (if you like), baking powder, salt and baking soda. Make a well in the center of the flour mixture; set aside.

2. In a small bowl, use a fork to combine eggs, buttermilk, oil and brown sugar. Add egg mixture all at once to flour mixture. Stir just until moistened (batter should be slightly lumpy but thick).

3. For each standard-size pancake: Pour about ¼ cup batter onto a hot, lightly greased griddle or heavy skillet, spreading batter to a 4-inch circle. (For dollar-size pancakes, use about 1 tablespoon batter and spread slightly.) Cook over medium heat for 1 to 2 minutes on each side or until pancakes are golden brown, turning to second side when pancakes have bubbly surfaces and edges are slightly dry. Serve warm with maple syrup. **Makes 18 standard-size pancakes or 48 dollar-size pancakes.**

*Tip: For 2 cups of sour milk, place 2 tablespoons lemon juice or vinegar in a glass measuring cup. Add enough milk to make 2 cups total liquid; stir. Let the mixture stand for 5 minutes before using.

Nutrition facts per standard-size pancake: 126 cal., 5 g fat, 25 mg chol., 181 mg sodium, 17 g carbo., 2 g fiber, 5 g pro.

Finnish Baked Pancakes

Prep: 15 minutes Stand: 30 minutes
Bake: 15 minutes Oven: 450°

2 eggs
½ cup all-purpose flour
½ cup milk
¼ cup butter, melted
¼ teaspoon almond extract
¼ teaspoon finely shredded lemon peel
½ cup fresh blueberries, raspberries and/or sliced strawberries
Powdered sugar, honey or maple syrup (optional)

1. Allow eggs to stand at room temperature 30 minutes. In a medium mixing bowl, whisk eggs until frothy. Add flour, milk, 2 tablespoons of the melted butter and almond extract; beat until smooth. Stir in lemon peel.

2. Heat two 6-inch cast-iron skillets, one 8-inch ovenproof skillet or one 8-inch round baking pan in a 450° oven for 2 minutes. Add the remaining 2 tablespoons melted butter to the two skillets or to the 8-inch skillet; swirl to coat pan(s). Pour batter into hot skillet(s). Bake pancake(s) about 15 minutes or until puffed and golden.

3. To serve, remove pancake(s) from oven. Spoon fruit into center of pancake(s). If you like, sprinkle with powdered sugar or drizzle with honey or maple syrup. (Pancake will collapse as it cools.) **Makes 2 servings.**

Nutrition facts per serving: 445 cal., 30 g fat, 278 mg chol., 265 mg sodium, 33 g carbo., 2 g fiber, 12 g pro.

Finnish Baked Pancakes

Mix-and-Match Muffins,
page 58

BREADS

Orange-Honey Sweet Rolls

Prep: 45 minutes Rise: 1 hour 30 minutes
Bake: 25 minutes Oven: 350°

2 packages active dry yeast
1¼ cups warm water (110° to 115°)
½ cup nonfat dry milk powder
⅓ cup butter, softened
⅓ cup honey
2 eggs, lightly beaten
2 tablespoons toasted wheat germ
1 teaspoon salt
3 cups white whole wheat flour or
　　all-purpose flour
2 to 2¼ cups bread flour
1 cup golden raisins
¼ cup butter, softened
¼ cup honey
2 teaspoons finely shredded orange peel
　　Orange Icing (recipe follows)

1. In a large mixing bowl, dissolve the yeast in the warm water; let stand for 5 minutes. Add dry milk, the ⅓ cup butter, ⅓ cup honey, the eggs, wheat germ and salt. Beat with an electric mixer on low speed for 30 seconds, scraping sides of bowl occasionally. Add 2 cups of the white whole wheat flour. Beat on low to medium speed for 30 seconds. Beat on high speed for 3 minutes. Using a wooden spoon, stir in remaining white whole wheat flour and as much of the bread flour as you can.

2. Turn dough out onto a lightly floured surface. Knead in enough of the remaining bread flour to make a moderately soft dough that is smooth and elastic (about 6 minutes). Shape dough into a ball.

3. Place dough in a lightly greased bowl; turn once to coat the top. Cover loosely with plastic wrap and a clean kitchen towel; let rise in a warm place until double in size (about 1 hour).

4. Punch dough down. Turn out onto a lightly floured surface. Cover; let rest for 10 minutes. Meanwhile, lightly grease a 13x9x2-inch baking pan; set aside.

5. For filling: In a small bowl, cover raisins with cold water; let stand for 5 minutes and drain well. In a medium bowl, whisk together the ¼ cup butter, ¼ cup honey and the orange peel until creamy and well combined.

6. Roll dough into an 18x15-inch rectangle. Spread the butter mixture to within ½ inch of the edges. Sprinkle with raisins. Roll up rectangle, starting from a long side. Pinch to seal seams. Slice roll into 15 pieces. Place, cut sides down, in prepared pan.

7. Cover loosely with plastic wrap, leaving room for rolls to rise. Let dough rise in a warm place until nearly double (about 30 minutes).

8. Remove plastic wrap. Bake in a 350° oven about 25 minutes or until lightly browned. Remove from oven. Cool for 1 minute. Invert rolls onto a wire rack. Cool slightly. Invert again onto a serving platter. Drizzle with Orange Icing. **Makes 15 rolls.**

Orange Icing: In a small bowl, combine 1 cup powdered sugar and 1 teaspoon finely shredded orange peel. Stir in enough orange juice (1 to 2 tablespoons) to reach drizzling consistency.

Nutrition facts per roll: 346 cal., 8 g fat, 48 mg chol., 241 mg sodium, 61 g carbo., 4 g fiber, 9 g pro.

Cinnamon Surprise Buns

Prep: 30 minutes Rise: 30 minutes
Bake: 15 minutes Oven: 350°

⅓ cup packed brown sugar
¼ cup finely chopped walnuts or pecans,
　　toasted if desired
1 teaspoon ground cinnamon
1 16-ounce package (12) frozen white
　　roll dough, thawed
2 tablespoons butter, melted
　　Cream Cheese Icing (recipe follows)

1. Lightly grease an 11x7x1½-inch baking pan; set aside. In a small bowl, combine brown sugar, nuts and cinnamon.

2. On a lightly floured surface, pat each thawed roll into a 3½-inch circle. Brush each circle with a little of the melted butter. Place about 1 tablespoon of the nut mixture onto the center of each dough circle. Bring up edges of each roll and pinch to seal and enclose filling. Place filled rolls, seam sides down, in prepared pan. Cover and let rise in warm place until nearly double in size (about 30 minutes).

3. Brush tops of rolls with remaining melted butter. Bake in a 350° oven for 15 to 20 minutes or until rolls are golden. Cool slightly; remove from pan. Generously frost warm rolls with Cream Cheese Icing. Serve rolls warm or cool on a wire rack.
Makes 12 rolls.

Cream Cheese Icing: In a medium mixing bowl, beat 2 ounces cream cheese, softened; 1 tablespoon butter, softened; and ½ teaspoon vanilla until light and fluffy. Beat in 1 tablespoon milk. Gradually add 1¼ cups powdered sugar until icing is of spreading consistency. Makes about 1 cup frosting.

Nutrition facts per roll: 231 cal., 8 g fat, 13 mg chol., 184 mg sodium, 37 g carbo., 1 g fiber, 4 g pro.

Cinnamon Surprise Buns

Peanut Butter-Cinnamon Rolls

Prep: 45 minutes Rest: 10 minutes Rise: 1 hour
Bake: 20 minutes Oven: 375°

    2 cups whole wheat flour
    2/3 cup nonfat dry milk powder
    2 tablespoons sugar
    2 packages active dry yeast
    2 teaspoons salt
    2 1/4 cups hot water (120° to 130°)
    1 cup peanut butter
    3 1/2 to 4 cups bread flour
    1/2 cup sugar
    2 teaspoons ground cinnamon
      Peanut Butter Icing (recipe follows)

1. In a large mixing bowl, combine whole wheat flour, dry milk powder, 2 tablespoons sugar, yeast and salt. Add the hot water and 1/2 cup of the peanut butter. Beat with an electric mixer on low speed for 30 seconds, scraping sides of bowl occasionally. Add 1 cup of the bread flour. Beat on low to medium speed for 30 seconds. Beat on high speed for 3 minutes. Using a wooden spoon, stir in as much of the remaining bread flour as you can.

2. Turn dough out onto a lightly floured surface. Knead in enough of the remaining bread flour to make a moderately soft dough that is smooth and elastic (3 to 5 minutes total). Shape dough into a ball.

3. Place dough in a lightly greased bowl; turn once to coat the top. Cover; let rise in a warm place until double in size (about 30 minutes).

4. Punch dough down. Turn out onto a lightly floured surface. Divide in half. Cover; let rest for 10 minutes. Meanwhile, lightly grease two 9x9x2-inch square baking pans; set aside.

5. For filling: In a small bowl, combine 1/2 cup sugar and cinnamon.

6. Roll each half of dough into a 14x6-inch rectangle. Spread each rectangle with 1/4 cup of the remaining peanut butter to within 1/2 inch of the edges. Sprinkle each with sugar-cinnamon mixture. Roll up each rectangle starting from a long side. Pinch to seal seams. Slice each roll into 9 pieces. Arrange, cut sides down, in prepared pans.

7. Cover loosely with plastic wrap, leaving room for rolls to rise. Let dough rise in a warm place until nearly double (about 30 minutes).

8. Bake in a 375° oven for 20 to 25 minutes or until browned. Remove from oven. Cool for 1 minute. Carefully invert rolls onto a wire rack. Cool slightly. Invert again onto a serving platter. Drizzle with Peanut Butter Icing. **Makes 18 rolls.**

Peanut Butter Icing: In a small bowl, combine 2 cups powdered sugar and 2 tablespoons peanut butter. Stir in enough milk (3 to 4 tablespoons) to reach drizzling consistency.

Nutrition facts per roll: 304 cal., 9 g fat, 1 mg chol., 359 mg sodium, 55 g carbo., 4 g fiber, 11 g pro.

Peanut Butter-Cinnamon Rolls

Pull-Apart Cornmeal Dinner Rolls

Prep: 25 minutes Rise: 1 hour 30 minutes
Bake: 12 minutes Oven: 400°

    1 cup milk
    1/4 cup sugar
    1/4 cup butter
    1/4 cup yellow cornmeal
    1 teaspoon salt
    1 package active dry yeast
    1/4 cup warm water (105° to 115°)
    1 egg, lightly beaten
    3 1/2 to 4 cups all-purpose flour
      Butter, melted
      Yellow cornmeal (optional)

1. In a small saucepan, combine milk, sugar, 1/4 cup butter, 1/4 cup cornmeal and salt; cook and stir until warm (105° to 115°).

2. In a large bowl, dissolve yeast in the warm water. Add egg and milk mixture. Gradually stir in enough flour to make a soft dough. Turn out onto lightly floured surface; knead gently 2 to 3 minutes to make a smooth ball. (Knead in just enough remaining flour so dough is no longer sticky.) Place in greased bowl, turning once to grease surface. Cover; let rise in warm place until double in size (1 hour). Punch dough down; turn out on lightly floured surface. Let dough rest for 10 minutes. Grease 15x10x1-inch baking pan.

3. To shape rolls, roll or pat dough to a 10x8-inch rectangle about 3/4 inch thick. Cut into 2 1/2x1-inch strips. Arrange strips in prepared pan, leaving about 1/2 inch between each strip. Cover and let rise until nearly double in size (about 30 minutes).

4. Brush with melted butter. Sprinkle with additional cornmeal, if you like. Bake in a 400° oven for 12 to 15 minutes or until rolls are golden and sound hollow when lightly tapped. Remove from pan. Serve warm or room temperature. **Makes 32 rolls.**

Nutrition facts per serving: 82 cal., 2 g fat, 12 mg chol., 92 mg sodium, 13 g carbo., 0 g fiber, 2 g pro.

Pull-Apart Cornmeal Dinner Rolls

Cardamom Wreath Bread

Cardamom Wreath Bread

Prep: 45 minutes Rise: 1 hour 45 minutes
Bake: 25 minutes Oven: 375°

- 1/3 cup warm water (105° to 115°)
- 2 packages active dry yeast
- 1/2 cup butter, softened
- 3/4 cup granulated sugar
- 3 eggs
- 1 12-ounce can evaporated milk
- 1/4 cup dairy sour cream
- 1 tablespoon finely shredded orange peel
- 2 1/4 teaspoons ground cardamom
- 2 teaspoons salt
- 7 to 7 1/2 cups all-purpose flour
- 1 egg, lightly beaten
- 1 tablespoon milk
  Sliced almonds or coarse sugar
  Cardamom Butter (recipe follows)

1. In a small bowl, combine the warm water and yeast; set aside for 5 minutes.

2. In a large mixing bowl, beat butter with an electric mixer on medium to high speed for 30 seconds. Add sugar. Beat until combined, scraping sides of bowl occasionally. Add three eggs and beat until combined. Stir in evaporated milk, sour cream, orange peel, cardamom and salt. Stir in yeast mixture (mixture will look curdled). Stir in as much of the flour as you can.

3. Turn dough out onto a lightly floured surface. Knead in enough of the remaining flour to make a moderately stiff dough that is smooth and elastic (6 to 8 minutes total).

4. Shape into a ball. Place in a lightly greased bowl, turning once. Cover; let rise in a warm place until double in size (about 1 hour).

5. Punch dough down. Turn out onto a lightly floured surface. Divide dough into six equal portions. Cover; let rest for 10 minutes.

6. Roll each portion of dough into a rope that is 22 to 24 inches long. Line up three of the ropes, 1 inch apart, on the lightly floured surface. Starting in the middle, braid by bringing left rope underneath center rope; lay it down. Then bring right rope under new center rope; lay it down. Repeat to end. On the other end, braid by bringing outside ropes alternately over center rope to center. (Braid the ropes loosely so the bread has room to expand.) Join ends of braid to form a wreath. Transfer to a greased baking sheet. Repeat with remaining three ropes for a second wreath. Cover; let rise until almost double in size (45 to 60 minutes).

7. Stir together one egg and 1 tablespoon milk. Brush over tops of wreaths. Top with almonds. Bake in a 375° oven 25 minutes or until lightly browned and bread sounds hollow when tapped (if necessary, cover wreaths with foil the last 5 to 10 minutes to prevent overbrowning). Transfer to wire racks to cool. Serve with Cardamom Butter.
Makes 2 wreaths (24 servings).

Cardamom Butter: Combine 1 cup butter, softened; 2 tablespoons powdered sugar; 3/4 teaspoon ground cardamom; 3/4 teaspoon finely shredded orange peel; and 1/4 teaspoon ground nutmeg. Makes 1 cup.

Nutrition facts per serving: 218 cal., 7 g fat, 51 mg chol., 250 mg sodium, 34 g carbo., 1 g fiber, 6 g pro.

Granny's (Slightly Caffeinated) Banana Bread

Guests at the Ann Bean Mansion Bed and Breakfast in Stillwater, Minnesota, love the homey aroma of this bread baking. The hint of coffee offers a twist on a traditional banana bread. Innkeeper Erin Drews uses freshly ground beans (her favorite is Costa Rican). She also waits until the bananas are black and extremely mushy for best results.

Prep: 20 minutes Bake: 1 hour
Stand: 10 minutes plus overnight Oven: 350°

- 2 cups all-purpose flour
- 1 to 2 teaspoons freshly ground coffee beans
- 1/2 teaspoon baking soda
- 1/2 teaspoon salt
- 1 egg, lightly beaten
- 1 cup granulated sugar
- 1 cup mashed ripe bananas (3 medium)
- 1/3 cup butter, melted
- 3 tablespoons milk
- 1 teaspoon vanilla
- 2 tablespoons turbinado sugar

1. Grease and flour bottom and 1/2 inch up the sides of an 8x4x2-inch loaf pan; set aside. In a large bowl, combine flour, coffee, baking soda and salt. Make a well in center of flour mixture; set aside.

2. In a medium bowl, combine egg, granulated sugar, bananas, melted butter, milk and vanilla. Add egg mixture all at once to flour mixture. Stir just until moistened (batter should be lumpy). Spoon batter into prepared pan. Generously sprinkle with raw sugar.

3. Bake in a 350° oven for 60 to 70 minutes or until a wooden toothpick inserted near center comes out clean (if necessary, cover loosely with foil the last 15 minutes of baking to prevent overbrowning).

4. Cool in pan on a wire rack for 10 minutes. Remove from pan. Cool completely on rack. Wrap; store overnight before slicing.
Makes 1 loaf (14 slices).

Nutrition facts per slice: 184 cal., 5 g fat, 27 mg chol., 166 mg sodium, 33 g carbo., 1 g fiber, 3 g pro.

Granny's (Slightly Caffeinated) Banana Bread

Pumpkin-Banana Bread

Prep: 25 minutes Bake: 50 minutes Oven: 350°

2 cups sugar
$^2/_3$ cup cooking oil
4 eggs
3$^1/_3$ cups all-purpose flour
2 teaspoons baking soda
1$^1/_2$ teaspoons salt
1 teaspoon baking powder
1 teaspoon ground cinnamon
$^1/_2$ teaspoon ground ginger
$^2/_3$ cup water
1 15-ounce can pumpkin
$^1/_2$ cup mashed ripe banana (1 large)
$^3/_4$ cup chopped pecans, toasted

1. Grease the bottom and $^1/_2$ inch up the sides of two 9x5x3-inch loaf pans; set aside. In a very large mixing bowl, beat sugar and oil with an electric mixer on medium speed until combined. Add eggs, one at a time, beating well after each addition; set sugar mixture aside.

2. In a large bowl, combine flour, baking soda, salt, baking powder, cinnamon and ginger. Alternately add flour mixture and the water to the sugar mixture, beating on low speed after each addition just until combined. Beat in pumpkin and banana. Stir in pecans. Spoon batter into prepared pans.

3. Bake in a 350° oven for 50 to 60 minutes or until a toothpick inserted near centers comes out clean. Cool in pans on wire racks for 10 minutes. Remove from pans. Cool on wire racks. Wrap and store overnight before slicing. **Makes 2 loaves (32 slices).**

Nutrition facts per slice: 170 cal., 7 g fat, 26 mg chol., 209 mg sodium, 25 g carbo., 1 g fiber, 1 g pro.

Mix-and-Match Muffins

Prep: 20 minutes Bake: 15 minutes
Cool: 5 minutes Oven: 400°

Basic Ingredients:
1 flour option
$^1/_4$ cup granulated sugar or packed brown sugar
1$^1/_2$ teaspoons baking powder
$^1/_2$ teaspoon baking soda
$^1/_4$ teaspoon salt
2 eggs, lightly beaten
1 liquid option
$^3/_4$ cup buttermilk, sour milk or milk
2 tablespoons butter or margarine, melted, or cooking oil
1 stir-in option
1 topping option (optional)

Flour Options:
2 cups all-purpose flour
1$^1/_3$ cups all-purpose flour and $^3/_4$ cup buckwheat flour
1$^1/_2$ cups all-purpose flour and $^3/_4$ cup quick-cooking oats
1 cup all-purpose flour and 1 cup yellow cornmeal
1 cup all-purpose flour and 1 cup rye flour
$^1/_2$ cup all-purpose flour and 1$^1/_2$ cups whole wheat flour

Liquid Options:
Savory: $^3/_4$ cup ricotta cheese, dairy sour cream, plain yogurt or finely shredded unpeeled zucchini

Sweet: $^3/_4$ cup canned pumpkin, unsweetened applesauce or lemon curd

Stir-In Options:
Savory: 2 to 4 tablespoons thinly sliced green onion, snipped fresh chives, snipped fresh parsley, finely chopped onion, finely chopped green or red sweet pepper, finely diced cooked ham, crumbled crisp-cooked bacon, 2 tablespoons Parmesan cheese or 1 tablespoon poppy seeds

Sweet: $^3/_4$ cup fresh or frozen blueberries, raisins, chopped dried cranberries or cherries, snipped pitted dates, snipped dried apricots, snipped dried figs or snipped dried plums

Topping Options:
Savory Chip Topping: Crush 1 cup of your favorite flavored potato chips or dry cereal flakes; measure about $^1/_3$ cup crushed.

Sweet Streusel Topping: In a small bowl, stir together 3 tablespoons all-purpose flour, 3 tablespoons packed brown sugar, and $^1/_4$ teaspoon ground cinnamon or ground ginger. Cut in 2 tablespoons butter until mixture resembles coarse crumbs. Stir in 2 tablespoons chopped pecans, walnuts, almonds or hazelnuts.

1. Lightly coat twelve 2$^1/_2$-inch muffin cups with nonstick cooking spray; set aside. In a medium bowl, combine all-purpose flour or another flour option, granulated sugar, baking powder, baking soda and salt. Make a well in the center of the flour mixture; set aside.

2. In a small bowl, combine eggs, a savory or sweet liquid option, buttermilk, and melted butter. Add egg mixture all at once to flour mixture. Stir just until moistened (batter should be lumpy). Fold in a savory or sweet stir-in.

3. Using a spoon and rubber spatula, spoon muffin batter evenly into prepared muffin cups.

4. Sprinkle the savory or sweet topping, if you like, over batter in cups. Bake in a 400° oven for 15 to 18 minutes or until golden. Cool in muffin cups on a wire rack for 5 minutes. **Makes 12 muffins.**

Mix-and-Match Muffins

Pumpkin-Banana Bread

Overnight Cherry-Chocolate Coffee Cake

Prep: 35 minutes Chill: 4 hours
Stand: 30 minutes Bake: 50 minutes Oven: 350°

- ⅔ cup all-purpose flour
- ⅔ cup rolled oats
- ½ cup packed brown sugar
- ½ teaspoon ground cinnamon
- ⅓ cup butter
- ½ cup semisweet chocolate pieces
- ½ cup dried tart red cherries
- 1 cup all-purpose flour
- ½ cup whole wheat flour
- 1½ teaspoons baking powder
- ¼ teaspoon baking soda
- ¼ teaspoon salt
- ½ cup butter, softened
- ⅔ cup granulated sugar
- 2 eggs
- 1 8-ounce carton dairy sour cream

1. Grease a 9x9x2-inch baking pan; set aside. For streusel topping: In a large bowl, stir together ⅔ cup flour, oats, brown sugar and cinnamon. Using a pastry blender, cut in ⅓ cup butter until mixture resembles coarse crumbs. Stir in chocolate pieces and cherries.

2. In a medium bowl, stir together 1 cup flour, the whole wheat flour, baking powder, baking soda and salt. In a large bowl, beat ½ cup butter on medium for 30 seconds. Add granulated sugar; beat until fluffy. Add eggs and sour cream; beat until combined.

3. Add flour mixture and beat on low speed until just combined. Spread half of the batter into pan. Sprinkle with half of the streusel. Spoon remaining batter over streusel; spread to edges. Top with remaining streusel. Cover and refrigerate for 4 to 24 hours.

4. Uncover. Let stand at room temperature 30 minutes. Bake in a 350° oven for 50 minutes or until a toothpick inserted near the center comes out clean.
Makes 12 servings.

Nutrition facts per serving: 412 cal., 20 g fat, 79 mg chol., 244 mg sodium, 54 g carbo., 3 g fiber, 6 g pro.

Maple Oatmeal Muffins

Prep: 15 minutes Bake: 15 minutes
Cool: 10 minutes Oven: 400°

- 1 cup quick-cooking or regular rolled oats
- ½ cup milk
- 1 cup all-purpose flour
- 2 teaspoons baking powder
- ¼ teaspoon salt
- ¼ teaspoon ground cinnamon
- ¾ cup pure maple syrup
- ¼ cup butter, melted
- 1 egg, lightly beaten
- ½ cup chopped pecans

1. Grease twelve 2½-inch muffin cups or line with paper bake cups; set aside. In a medium bowl, combine oats and milk; let stand for 5 minutes. In a large bowl, combine flour, baking powder, salt and cinnamon. Make a well in center of flour mixture; set aside.

2. Stir maple syrup, melted butter and egg into oats mixture. Add egg mixture all at once to flour mixture. Stir just until moistened (batter should be lumpy). Fold half of the pecans into the batter.

3. Spoon batter into prepared muffin cups, filling each two-thirds full. Sprinkle with remaining nuts. Bake in a 400° oven for 15 to 18 minutes or until tops are golden and a wooden toothpick inserted in centers comes out clean. Cool in muffin cups on a wire rack for 10 minutes. Remove from muffin cups; serve warm. **Makes 12 muffins.**

Nutrition facts per muffin: 218 cal., 9 g fat, 29 mg chol., 149 mg sodium, 31 g carbo., 2 g fiber, 5 g pro.

Maple Oatmeal Muffins

Whole Wheat Apple-Nut Bread

Prep: 25 minutes Bake: 1 hour Cool: 10 minutes
Oven: 350°

1½ cups whole wheat flour
¾ cup all-purpose flour
1 tablespoon baking powder
1 teaspoon salt
1 teaspoon ground cinnamon
½ teaspoon baking soda
2 eggs, lightly beaten
1 cup unsweetened applesauce
1 6-ounce carton plain low-fat yogurt
  (⅔ cup)
½ cup packed brown sugar
⅓ cup cooking oil
1 cup chopped pecans, black walnuts or
  hickory nuts
⅓ cup raisins
2 tablespoons toasted wheat germ

1. Grease the bottom and ½ inch up the sides of a 1½-quart casserole; set aside. In a large bowl, combine whole wheat flour, all-purpose flour, baking powder, salt, cinnamon and baking soda. Make a well in center of flour mixture; set aside.

2. In a small bowl, combine eggs, applesauce, yogurt, brown sugar and oil. Add egg mixture all at once to flour mixture. Stir just until moistened (batter should be lumpy). Fold in nuts and raisins. Spoon batter into the prepared pans. Sprinkle with the wheat germ.

3. Bake, covered, in a 350° oven for 60 to 70 minutes, or until a wooden toothpick inserted near center comes out clean. Cool in casserole on a wire rack for 10 minutes. Remove from casserole. Cool completely on wire rack. Wrap and store overnight before slicing. **Makes 1 loaf (12 servings).**

Note: Bread will be slightly moister the second day.

Nutrition facts per serving: 274 cal., 15 g fat, 36 mg chol., 333 mg sodium, 34 g carbo., 3 g fiber, 6 g pro.

Streusel Apple Bread

Prep: 30 minutes Bake: 55 minutes
Cool: 10 minutes Oven: 350°

2 cups all-purpose flour
1 cup chopped cored apple
½ cup butter, softened
1 cup granulated sugar
2 eggs
1 teaspoon vanilla
1 teaspoon baking soda
½ teaspoon salt
⅓ cup sour milk* or orange juice
⅓ cup chopped fresh cranberries
⅔ cup chopped walnuts
⅓ cup packed brown sugar
2 tablespoons all-purpose flour
1 teaspoon finely shredded lemon peel
1 tablespoon butter, melted

1. Grease bottom and ½ inch up sides of a 9x5x3-inch loaf pan; set aside. In a small bowl, toss 2 tablespoons of the 2 cups flour with the apple; set aside. In a large mixing bowl, beat ½ cup butter with an electric mixer on medium speed for 30 seconds; gradually beat in granulated sugar until combined. Beat in eggs and vanilla. Combine remaining flour with baking soda and salt; add to beaten mixture alternately with milk or orange juice. Stir in apple mixture, cranberries and ⅓ cup of the walnuts. Spoon into prepared pan, spreading evenly.

2. In a medium bowl, combine brown sugar, 2 tablespoons flour, the lemon peel, 1 tablespoon melted butter and the remaining nuts; sprinkle evenly over batter in pan. Bake, uncovered, in a 350° oven for 55 to 60 minutes or until a toothpick inserted near the center comes out clean.

3. Cool in pan on wire rack 10 minutes. Remove from pan and cool completely on wire rack. Wrap and store overnight at room temperature before slicing. **Makes 12 servings.**

*Note: Place 1 teaspoon lemon juice or vinegar in a 1-cup glass measure; add milk to equal ⅓ cup. Let stand 5 minutes.

Nutrition facts per serving: 310 cal., 14 g fat, 59 mg chol., 281 mg sodium, 43 g carbo., 1 g fiber, 3 g pro.

Streusel Apple Bread

Blue-Ribbon Coffee Cake

Prep: 25 minutes Bake: 40 minutes
Cool: 10 minutes Oven: 325°

Nonstick cooking spray for baking
2 cups all-purpose flour
1 teaspoon baking powder
1 teaspoon baking soda
¾ teaspoon salt
2 eggs, lightly beaten
1 cup granulated sugar
½ cup butter or margarine, softened
1 teaspoon vanilla
1 8-ounce carton dairy sour cream
1 cup coarsely chopped walnuts
⅔ cup packed brown sugar
½ cup granulated sugar
2 teaspoons ground cinnamon
2 teaspoons vanilla

1. Spray a 10-inch fluted tube pan with cooking spray; set pan aside. In a medium bowl, stir together flour, baking powder, baking soda and salt; set aside.

2. In a large bowl, stir together eggs, 1 cup granulated sugar, the butter and 1 teaspoon vanilla. Add flour mixture to egg mixture; stir just until moistened. Add sour cream and stir vigorously until batter is smooth.

3. For streusel: In a small bowl, stir together walnuts, brown sugar, ½ cup granulated sugar, the cinnamon and 2 teaspoons vanilla.

4. Spoon one-third of the batter into the bottom of the prepared pan; spread evenly. Sprinkle with one-third of the streusel. Repeat layers with remaining batter and streusel.

5. Bake in a 325° oven for 40 to 50 minutes or until a wooden toothpick inserted near the center comes out clean. Cool cake in pan on a wire rack for 10 minutes. To remove cake from pan, cover with an inverted serving plate and turn cake onto plate. Serve warm. **Makes 12 servings.**

Nutrition facts per serving: 408 cal., 19 g fat, 64 mg chol., 361 mg sodium, 56 g carbo., 1 g fiber, 5 g pro.

Maple Date-Nut Bread

Prep: 20 minutes Bake: 50 minutes
Cool: 10 minutes Oven: 350°

1 cup all-purpose flour
1 cup whole wheat flour
1 teaspoon baking powder
1 teaspoon salt
¾ teaspoon baking soda
1 cup boiling water
1 cup chopped pitted dates
1 tablespoon butter, softened
¾ cup maple syrup
1 egg, lightly beaten
½ cup chopped pecans

Blue-Ribbon Coffee Cake

1. Grease the bottom and ½ inch up the sides of an 8x4x2-inch loaf pan; set aside. In a large bowl, combine flours, baking powder, salt and baking soda. Make a well in center of flour mixture; set aside.

2. In a medium bowl, pour the boiling water over dates and butter; stir until butter melts. Stir maple syrup and egg into date mixture. Add egg mixture all at once to flour mixture. Stir just until moistened (batter should be lumpy). Fold pecans into the batter. Pour batter into the prepared pan; spread evenly.

3. Bake in a 350° oven for 50 to 60 minutes or until a wooden toothpick inserted near center comes out clean (if necessary, cover loosely with foil the last 15 minutes of baking to prevent overbrowning).

4. Cool in pan on a wire rack for 10 minutes. Remove from pan. Cool completely on rack. Wrap; store overnight before slicing. **Makes 1 loaf (16 slices).**

Nutrition facts per slice: 159 cal., 4 g fat, 15 mg chol., 231 mg sodium, 30 g carbo., 2 g fiber, 3 g pro.

Maple Date-Nut Bread

Gingerbread Scones

Prep: 25 minutes Bake: 12 minutes Oven: 375°

- 1 cup all-purpose flour
- 1 cup whole wheat flour
- ⅓ cup packed brown sugar
- 2 teaspoons baking powder
- ¾ teaspoon ground ginger
- ½ teaspoon kosher salt or ¼ teaspoon salt
- ½ teaspoon ground cinnamon
- ¼ teaspoon baking soda
- ¼ cup cold butter
- ½ cup dried currants or raisins
- 1 tablespoon finely chopped crystallized ginger
- 1 egg, lightly beaten
- ½ cup whipping cream
- ¼ cup mild-flavor molasses
- 1 egg white, lightly beaten
- ½ teaspoon water
  Coarse sugar (optional)

1. In a large mixing bowl, combine the flours, brown sugar, baking powder, ground ginger, salt, cinnamon and baking soda. Using a pastry blender, cut in butter until mixture resembles coarse crumbs. Stir in currants and crystallized ginger. Make a well in the center of the mixture.

2. In a small bowl, stir together the egg, whipping cream and molasses; add all at once to flour mixture. Using a fork, stir until ingredients are combined.

3. Turn dough onto a lightly floured surface. Knead dough for 10 to 12 strokes or until nearly smooth. Divide dough in half. Lightly pat or roll each dough portion to a ¾-inch-thick 5- to 5½-inch circle. Cut each circle into six wedges. Place wedges about 2 inches apart on a large ungreased baking sheet. In a small bowl, combine egg white and the water. Brush tops of scones with egg white mixture and, if you like, sprinkle with coarse sugar.

4. Bake in a 375° oven 12 to 15 minutes or until a wood toothpick inserted into a crack in top of scones comes out clean. Serve warm or at room temperature. **Makes 12 scones.**

Make-Ahead Tip: Cool scones completely and wrap in a single layer of foil; place in a freezer bag. Freeze for up to 1 month. To serve, remove from freezer bag. Place frozen, foil-wrapped scones in a 300° oven and heat for 20 minutes or until warm (12 minutes, if thawed).

Nutrition facts per scone: 210 cal., 8 g fat, 42 mg chol., 214 mg sodium, 32 g carbo., 2 g fiber, 4 g pro.

Cedarburg Breakfast Scones

These savory cheese-and-sausage scones are served warm from the oven at The Washington House Inn in Cedarburg, Wisconsin. To reheat leftover scones, wrap in a single layer of foil and heat in a 350° oven for 15 minutes or until heated through.

Prep: 30 minutes Bake: 15 minutes Oven: 425°

- 12 ounces bulk pork sausage
- 3¼ cups all-purpose flour
- ½ cup sugar
- 2½ teaspoons baking powder
- ½ teaspoon salt
- ¾ cup butter
- 1½ cups shredded cheddar cheese (6 ounces)
- ¾ cup buttermilk
  Whipped Maple Butter (recipe follows)

1. In a medium skillet, cook sausage over medium heat until meat is brown; drain off fat. Set aside.

2. In a very large bowl, combine flour, sugar, baking powder and salt. Using a pastry blender, cut in butter until mixture resembles coarse crumbs. Stir in sausage and cheese. Make a well in center of the flour mixture. Add buttermilk all at once to flour mixture. Using a fork, stir just until moistened.

3. Turn dough out onto a lightly floured surface. Knead dough by folding and gently pressing it for 10 to 12 strokes or until dough is nearly smooth. Pat or lightly roll dough until ¾ inch thick. Cut dough with a floured 2½-inch biscuit cutter; reroll dough scraps as necessary and dip cutter into flour between cuts.

4. Place dough circles 1 inch apart on a large ungreased baking sheet. Bake in a 425° oven about 15 minutes or until golden. Remove scones from baking sheet and serve warm. Serve with Whipped Maple Butter. **Makes 13 or 14 scones.**

Whipped Maple Butter: In a mixing bowl, beat ½ cup softened butter with an electric mixer on medium speed for 30 seconds. Gradually add ¼ cup pure maple syrup, beating on medium to high speed until combined. Transfer to a small serving container. Cover and chill until ready to serve. Serve at room temperature. Makes about ¾ cup.

Nutrition facts per scone: 454 cal., 29 g fat, 80 mg chol., 523 mg sodium, 37 g carbo., 1 g fiber, 11 g pro.

Cedarburg Breakfast Scones

Brats & Beer Cheddar
Chowder, page 75

SOUPS, SANDWICHES & MAIN-DISH SALADS

Beef & Bulgur Soup
with Chickpeas

Beef & Bulgur Soup with Chickpeas

Prep: 35 minutes Cook: 1 hour 5 minutes

    2 tablespoons olive oil or cooking oil
    1 teaspoon cumin seeds
    2 cloves garlic, minced
    1 teaspoon salt
    1 teaspoon garam masala
    1 teaspoon grated fresh ginger or
        ½ teaspoon ground ginger
    ½ teaspoon ground turmeric
    ¼ to ½ teaspoon cayenne pepper
    1 pound beef stew meat, cut into 1-inch
        cubes
    3 medium onions, chopped (1½ cups)
    3 14½-ounce cans lower-sodium beef
        broth or 5¼ cups beef stock
    1 14½-ounce can no-salt-added stewed
        tomatoes, undrained and cut up
    1 15-ounce can garbanzo beans
        (chickpeas), rinsed and drained
    1 cup bulgur, cracked wheat or quick-
        cooking barley
    2 medium carrots, thinly sliced (1 cup)
    3 tablespoons snipped fresh parsley

1. In a 5- to 6-quart Dutch oven, heat olive oil over medium heat. Add cumin seeds. Cook and stir for 10 seconds. Add garlic, salt, garam masala, ginger, turmeric and cayenne pepper all at once to oil mixture. Cook and stir for 15 seconds (watch closely to avoid burning).

2. Add half of the meat and half of the onion to spice mixture; cook and stir until browned. Remove meat mixture with a slotted spoon (it's ok if some of the onion remains in the pan). Add remaining meat and onion. Cook and stir until meat is brown (adding more oil if necessary). Return all meat and onions to Dutch oven. Stir in beef broth and undrained tomatoes. Bring to boiling; reduce heat. Simmer, covered, for 45 minutes, stirring occasionally.

3. Stir in the garbanzo beans, bulgur and carrots. Return to boiling; reduce heat. Simmer, covered, for 20 to 25 minutes more or until meat, vegetables and bulgur are tender, stirring occasionally. Stir in parsley just before serving. **Makes 8 main-dish servings.**

Nutrition facts per serving: 270 cal., 7 g fat, 33 mg chol., 795 mg sodium, 34 g carbo., 7 g fiber, 19 g pro.

Chipotle Black-Bean Chili

Prep: 20 minutes Cook: 7 hours on low or 3 hours 30 minutes on high

    1½ pounds ground beef, ground pork,
        bulk pork sausage, uncooked ground
        turkey or uncooked bulk turkey
        sausage
    2 14½-ounce cans reduced-sodium beef
        broth or chicken broth
    1 16-ounce jar chunky salsa
    1 15-ounce can black beans, rinsed and
        drained
    1 15-ounce can golden hominy, rinsed
        and drained
    2 cups loose-pack frozen diced hash
        brown potatoes with onions and
        peppers
    1 to 2 canned chipotle chile peppers in
        adobo sauce, finely chopped*
    2 teaspoons chili powder
    1 teaspoon dried oregano, crushed
    1 teaspoon ground cumin
        Dairy sour cream, chopped avocado
        and/or shredded cheddar cheese
        (optional)
        Tortilla chips or corn bread (optional)

1. In a large skillet, cook ground beef until meat is brown. Drain off fat. Transfer meat to a 4- or 5-quart slow cooker. Stir broth, salsa, beans, hominy, potatoes, chipotle peppers, chili powder, oregano and cumin into meat in cooker.

2. Cover and cook on low-heat setting for 7 to 8 hours or on high-setting for 3½ to 4 hours.

3. Top individual servings with sour cream, avocado and/or cheddar cheese and serve with tortilla chips, if you like.
Makes 6 servings (9½ cups total).

*Test Kitchen Tip: Because hot chile peppers contain volatile oils that can burn your skin and eyes, avoid direct contact with chiles as much as possible. When working with chile peppers, wear plastic or rubber gloves. If your bare hands do touch the chile peppers, wash your hands and fingernails well with soap and water when you are done.

Nutrition facts per serving: 450 cal., 24 g fat, 81 mg chol., 1,287 mg sodium, 34 g carbo., 8 g fiber, 27 g pro.

Chipotle Black-Bean Chili

Kansas City Steak Soup

Prep: 15 minutes Cook: 25 minutes

1½ pounds lean ground beef (sirloin)
 1 large onion, chopped (1 cup)
 2 stalks celery, sliced (1 cup)
 2 14½-ounce cans lower-sodium beef
   broth or 3½ cups beef stock
 1 28-ounce can diced tomatoes,
   undrained
 1 10-ounce package frozen mixed
   vegetables
 2 tablespoons steak sauce
 2 teaspoons Worcestershire sauce
 ¼ teaspoon salt
 ¼ teaspoon ground black pepper
 ¼ cup all-purpose flour

1. In a 4-quart Dutch oven, cook beef, onion and celery over medium heat until meat is brown and vegetables are tender. Drain well; return to Dutch oven.

2. Stir in 1 can of the beef broth, the undrained tomatoes, mixed vegetables, steak sauce, Worcestershire sauce, salt and pepper. Bring to boiling; reduce heat. Cover and simmer 20 minutes.

3. In a medium mixing bowl, whisk together remaining can of beef broth and the flour. Stir into mixture in Dutch oven. Cook until thickened and bubbly. Cook and stir 1 minute more. **Makes 6 main-dish servings.**

Nutrition facts per serving: 290 cal., 11 g fat, 71 mg chol., 713 mg sodium, 21 g carbo., 3 g fiber, 24 g pro.

Kansas City Steak Soup

Bacon & Baked Potato Soup

Prep: 20 minutes Bake: 40 minutes
Cook: 15 minutes Oven: 425°

 2 6- to 8-ounce baking potatoes (such as
   russet or Yukon gold)
 3 tablespoons butter
 ½ cup chopped onion
 ¼ cup chopped celery
 3 tablespoons all-purpose flour
 ½ teaspoon dried thyme, crushed
 ¼ teaspoon salt
 ⅛ teaspoon ground black pepper
 4 cups half-and-half, light cream or milk
1¼ cups shredded American cheese
   (5 ounces)
 1 cup chicken broth
 8 slices bacon, crisp-cooked, drained and
   crumbled
 2 tablespoons thinly sliced green onion
 ¼ cup dairy sour cream

1. Scrub potatoes with a vegetable brush; pat dry. Prick potatoes with a fork. Bake in a 425° oven for 40 to 60 minutes or until tender; cool. Peel potatoes, if desired. Chop potatoes; set aside.

2. In a heavy large saucepan or Dutch oven, melt butter over medium heat. Add onion and celery. Cook and stir about 5 minutes or until crisp-tender. Stir in flour, thyme, salt and pepper. Add half-and-half all at once. Cook and stir for 5 to 6 minutes or until thickened and bubbly. Add potatoes, 1 cup of the cheese and the broth; stir until cheese melts. Slightly mash potatoes with the back of a spoon or a potato masher.

3. Reserve 2 tablespoons of the bacon for the topping. Stir the remaining bacon and 1 tablespoon of the green onion into soup. Heat through.

4. To serve, top each serving with reserved bacon, remaining ¼ cup cheese, green onion and the sour cream.
Makes 6 (1-cup) servings.

Nutrition facts per serving: 510 cal., 40 g fat, 118 mg chol., 1,056 mg sodium, 22 g carbo., 2 g fiber, 17 g pro.

Bacon & Baked Potato Soup

Brats & Beer Cheddar
Chowder

Brats & Beer Cheddar Chowder

Start To Finish: 45 minutes

- 2 tablespoons butter or margarine
- 1 medium onion, finely chopped (½ cup)
- 1 medium carrot, coarsely shredded (½ cup)
- 3 large shallots, chopped
- 1 14-ounce can vegetable broth or 1¾ cups vegetable stock
- ⅓ cup all-purpose flour
- 1 cup whole milk, half-and-half or light cream
- 1 teaspoon caraway seeds, crushed
- ¼ teaspoon ground black pepper
- 10 ounces Wisconsin aged cheddar cheese or sharp cheddar cheese, shredded
- 4 cooked smoked bratwurst, knockwurst or Polish sausage (about 12 ounces total), halved lengthwise and sliced
- 1 12-ounce can beer or 12-ounce bottle ale Rye bread (optional)

1. In a large saucepan, heat the butter over medium heat. Add onion, carrot and shallots; reduce heat to medium-low. Cook, stirring frequently, about 10 to 15 minutes or until the onion is very soft and golden.

2. In a large screw-top jar, combine broth and flour. Cover and shake until combined and smooth. Stir into the onion mixture. Add the milk, caraway seeds and pepper. Cook over medium heat, stirring frequently, about 5 minutes or until the mixture thickens. Gradually stir in the cheese; reduce heat to low. Cook, stirring frequently, until cheese melts, but do not boil. Stir in the bratwurst and beer. Cook, stirring frequently, until heated through. If you like, serve with rye bread. **Makes 4 to 6 main-dish servings (7 cups).**

Nutrition facts per serving: 737 cal., 54 g fat, 162 mg chol., 1,633 mg sodium, 25 g carbo., 1 g fiber, 32 g pro.

Knoephla (Potato Dumpling Soup)

Prep: 25 minutes   Cook: 25 minutes

- 1½ cups all-purpose flour
- 1 teaspoon baking powder
- ¼ teaspoon salt
- 1 egg, lightly beaten
- ½ cup milk
- 2 tablespoons cooking oil
- 2 14½-ounce cans reduced-sodium chicken broth or 3½ cups chicken stock
- 1 1.8-ounce envelope white sauce mix
- 4 medium potatoes, chopped (4 cups)
- 1 large onion, chopped (1 cup)
- 1 cup diced cooked ham or Canadian-style bacon
- 1 12-ounce can evaporated milk
- ½ teaspoon ground white or black pepper
- ¼ cup snipped fresh parsley

1. For dumplings: In a medium mixing bowl, stir together the flour, baking powder and salt. Make a well in the center of the mixture. In a small mixing bowl, stir together the egg, milk and oil. Add egg mixture to the flour mixture; mix well. Cover; set aside.

2. For soup: In a 4-quart Dutch oven, gradually stir chicken broth into white sauce mix until mixture is smooth. Stir in potatoes, onion, ham, evaporated milk and pepper. Bring to boiling; reduce heat. Simmer, covered, for 15 minutes, stirring occasionally.

3. Drop rounded teaspoons of dough into the soup (don't worry if dumplings touch). Return to boiling; reduce heat. Simmer, uncovered, for 10 to 15 minutes more or until potatoes are tender and a toothpick inserted near the center of a dumpling comes out clean. Sprinkle with parsley. **Makes 10 side-dish servings (10 cups).**

Nutrition facts per serving: 241 cal., 8 g fat, 38 mg chol., 671 mg sodium, 33 g carbo., 2 g fiber, 9 g pro.

Knoephla (Potato Dumpling Soup)

Chicken Salsa Chili

2. Just before serving, stir in cilantro and lime juice. If you like, top each serving with sour cream, red onion, cheese and avocado. **Makes 6 main-dish servings.**

Nutrition facts per serving: 190 cal., 2 g fat, 23 mg chol., 1,200 mg sodium, 27 g carbo., 7 g fiber, 17 g pro.

Wild Rice & Turkey Soup

Prep: 25 minutes Cook: 20 minutes

  1 6.2-ounce package quick-cooking long grain and wild rice mix
  2 tablespoons butter or margarine
  4 ounces shiitake mushrooms, stems removed and sliced (about 1½ cups)
  2 stalks celery, sliced (1 cup)
  2 14½-ounce cans reduced-sodium chicken broth or 3½ cups chicken stock
  ¼ teaspoon ground black pepper
  2 cups chopped smoked turkey or chopped cooked turkey or chicken (about 10 ounces)
  1 cup whipping cream
  2 tablespoons dry sherry (optional)

1. Prepare the rice mix (using the seasoning packet) according to package directions, except omit any butter or margarine.

2. In a large saucepan, melt butter over medium heat. Add mushrooms and celery. Cook about 5 minutes or until vegetables are almost tender and most of the mushroom liquid has evaporated, stirring occasionally. Add chicken broth and pepper. Bring to boiling; reduce heat. Simmer, covered, for 5 minutes. Stir in cooked rice mixture, turkey, whipping cream and, if you like, dry sherry. Heat through. **Makes 6 main-dish servings.**

Nutrition facts per serving: 348 cal., 21 g fat, 91 mg chol., 1,519 mg sodium, 28 g carbo., 1 g fiber, 14 g pro.

Chicken Salsa Chili

This off-the-shelf chili relies on jars of salsa, cans of beans and frozen chicken for its super-quick prep.

Prep: 15 minutes Cook: 20 minutes

  1 16-ounce jar thick and chunky salsa
  1 15-ounce can yellow hominy or garbanzo beans (chickpeas), rinsed and drained
  1 15-ounce can dark red kidney beans or black beans, rinsed and drained
  1 14½-ounce can chicken broth
  1 9-ounce package (2 cups) frozen diced cooked chicken
  1 4-ounce can diced green chile peppers
  1 tablespoon chili powder
  2 teaspoons bottled minced garlic or ½ teaspoon garlic powder
  ¼ to ½ teaspoon crushed red pepper
  ¼ cup snipped fresh cilantro
  2 tablespoons lime juice
    Dairy sour cream or plain low-fat yogurt (optional)
    Chopped red onion and/or sliced green onion (optional)
    Shredded sharp cheddar cheese (optional)
    Chopped avocado (optional)

1. In a 4-quart Dutch oven, combine salsa, hominy, beans, chicken broth, chicken, chile peppers, chili powder, garlic and red pepper. Bring to boiling; reduce heat. Simmer, covered, for 20 minutes.

Chicken & Wild Rice Soup

Chicken & Wild Rice Soup

Prep: 25 minutes Cook: 1 hour

- 2 14½-ounce cans reduced-sodium chicken broth or 3½ cups chicken stock
- 1 cup uncooked wild rice, rinsed and drained
- 1 cup chopped celery
- ½ cup chopped onion, sliced leek or green onion
- ¼ to ½ teaspoon ground black pepper
- 1 pound skinless, boneless chicken breast halves
- 1 tablespoon olive oil
- 1 14½-ounce can reduced-sodium chicken broth or 1¾ cups chicken stock or water
- 1 10¾-ounce can condensed cream of chicken with herb soup
  Thin strips of carrot (optional)

1. In a 4-to 5-quart Dutch oven, combine the two cans of chicken broth, uncooked wild rice, celery, onion and pepper. Bring to boiling; reduce heat. Simmer, covered, about 50 minutes or until rice is tender.

2. Meanwhile, cut chicken into ¾-inch pieces. In a large skillet, heat oil over medium-high heat. Add chicken. Cook and stir for 3 to 4 minutes or until chicken is no longer pink.

3. Stir the remaining one can of chicken broth and the soup into wild rice mixture until smooth and creamy. Stir in chicken. Cook, covered, about 10 minutes or until heated through. If you like, garnish each serving with carrot. **Makes 6 (1½-cup) main-dish servings.**

Nutrition facts per serving: 253 cal., 5 g fat, 48 mg chol., 916 mg sodium, 27 g carbo., 3 g fiber, 25 g pro.

Potato-Topped Duck Stew

Prep: 25 minutes Cook: 28 minutes

- 3 boneless duck breast halves (with skin) (about 1½ pounds) or 1¼ pounds skinless, boneless chicken breast halves
- ¼ teaspoon salt
- ¼ teaspoon ground black pepper
- 1 large onion, coarsely chopped (1 cup)
- 2 stalks celery, sliced (1 cup)
- 2 cloves garlic, minced
- 2 14½-ounce cans chicken broth or 3½ cups chicken stock
- 1 8-ounce can tomato sauce
- ¾ cup extra-dry vermouth, dry white wine or chicken broth
- 2 bay leaves
- 1 10-ounce package frozen peas and carrots
- ¾ teaspoon dried sage, crushed
  Potato Topper (recipe follows)
- 2 tablespoons snipped fresh chives

1. Trim excess fat from duck (do not remove skin). Score the skin in a diamond pattern. Season duck breasts with salt and pepper. In a 4-quart Dutch oven, cook duck breasts, skin sides down, over medium heat for 5 minutes. Turn and cook about 5 minutes more or until browned. Drain off fat, reserving 2 tablespoons fat. Remove duck; set aside. (If using chicken, brown chicken on both sides in 2 tablespoons olive oil; set aside.)

2. Add onion, celery and garlic to the Dutch oven. Cook and stir over medium heat for 4 minutes. Add broth, tomato sauce, wine and bay leaves. Bring to boiling; reduce heat. Remove skin from duck and discard. Cut duck or chicken into 1-inch pieces. Add duck or chicken to pan. Simmer, covered, for 20 minutes. Stir in peas and carrots and sage. Cook, uncovered, for 8 to 10 minutes or until peas and carrots are tender, stirring occasionally.

3. Remove bay leaves; discard. Stir half of the Potato Topper into stew until blended. Spoon remaining potato topper into six mounds in shallow soup bowls. Spoon stew around potatoes; sprinkle with chives. **Makes 6 main-dish servings.**

Potato Topper: Peel and quarter 2 pounds (about six medium) Yukon gold potatoes or baking potatoes (such as russet). In a covered medium saucepan, cook potatoes and 1 teaspoon salt in enough boiling water to cover for 20 to 25 minutes or until tender; drain. Mash with a potato masher or beat with an electric mixer on low speed. Add ¼ cup butter, softened. Season to taste with salt and ground black pepper. Gradually beat in ⅓ to ½ cup milk to make potato mixture light and fluffy. Set aside. Makes about 4 cups.

Nutrition facts per serving: 621 cal., 42 g fat, 84 mg chol., 1,415 mg sodium, 34 g carbo., 5 g fiber, 23 g pro.

Potato-Topped Duck Stew

Red Tomato-Garlic Soup

Prep: 15 minutes Cook: 45 minutes

  1 medium fennel bulb with tops
  1 tablespoon olive oil
  1 tablespoon butter or margarine
  1 large onion, quartered and thinly
    sliced
 10 cloves garlic, minced
  1 28-ounce can diced tomatoes,
    undrained
  1 14½-ounce can reduced-sodium
    chicken broth
  1 8-ounce can tomato sauce
  1 cup hot-style vegetable juice or
    vegetable juice
  1 teaspoon dried basil or dried Italian
    seasoning, crushed

1. Reserve some of the fennel leaves to garnish the soup. Remove any tough or bruised outer leaves from the fennel bulb. Trim off the root end and the stems; discard. Thoroughly rinse the trimmed bulb and quarter the bulb lengthwise; remove and discard the core. Chop remaining fennel bulb.

2. In a 4-quart Dutch oven, heat olive oil and butter over medium-high heat. Add fennel, onion and garlic. Reduce heat to medium-low and cook, covered, for 25 minutes or until onions are tender, stirring occasionally. Uncover; cook and stir over medium-high heat for 3 to 5 minutes more or until onion is golden.

3. Add the undrained tomatoes, broth, tomato sauce, vegetable juice and dried basil. Bring to boiling; reduce heat. Simmer, covered, for 15 minutes more. Garnish each serving with the reserved fennel leaves.
Makes 8 side-dish servings.

Nutrition facts per serving: 94 cal., 3 g fat, 4 mg chol., 546 mg sodium, 14 g carbo., 2 g fiber, 2 g pro.

Great Lakes Salmon Chowder

Prep: 20 minutes Cook: 20 minutes

  1 pound fresh skinless salmon fillets
 1½ cups water
  2 14-ounce cans vegetable broth or
    3½ cups vegetable stock
  2 cups frozen whole small onions or
    ½ cup frozen chopped onion
  3 medium red-skin potatoes, cubed
    (2½ cups)
  1 tablespoon snipped fresh dill or
    ½ teaspoon dried dillweed
  1 teaspoon finely shredded lemon peel
  ½ teaspoon salt
  ½ teaspoon ground black pepper
 2½ cups whole milk, half-and-half or
    light cream
  2 tablespoons cornstarch
  1 10-ounce package frozen cut asparagus,
    thawed and well-drained or 2 cups cut-
    up fresh trimmed asparagus
    Fresh dill sprigs (optional)

1. Rinse salmon; pat dry. In a large skillet, bring the water to boiling. Add salmon. Return to boiling; reduce heat. Simmer, covered, for 6 to 8 minutes or until the salmon flakes easily with a fork. Remove salmon from skillet, discarding poaching liquid. Flake salmon into ½-inch pieces; set aside.

2. Meanwhile, in a 4-quart Dutch oven, combine vegetable broth, onions, potatoes, snipped fresh dill, lemon peel, salt and black pepper. Bring to boiling; reduce heat. Simmer, covered, for 15 minutes or until vegetables are tender, stirring occasionally.

3. In a large screw-top jar, combine milk and cornstarch. Cover and shake well; stir into soup. Stir in asparagus. Cook and stir until slightly thickened and bubbly. Cook and stir for 2 minutes more. Gently stir in poached salmon; heat through. If you like, garnish with fresh dill sprigs.
Makes 8 main-dish servings (11 cups).

Nutrition facts per serving: 185 cal., 5 g fat, 37 mg chol., 621 mg sodium, 20 g carbo., 2 g fiber, 17 g pro.

Red Tomato-Garlic Soup

Veggie-Cheese Chowder

Veggie-Cheese Chowder

Prep: 25 minutes Cook: 15 minutes

- 2 tablespoons butter or margarine
- 1 medium onion, chopped
- 1 medium green or red sweet pepper, chopped
- 2 stalks celery, sliced
- 2 cups whole milk or light cream
- 1 15-ounce can cream-style corn
- 1 14-ounce can vegetable broth
- 1 10.75-ounce can condensed nacho fiesta cheese soup
- 8 ounces pasteurized prepared cheese product with jalapeño peppers, cut up, or 1 cup jarred cheese dip (salsa con queso)
- 1 cup shredded sharp cheddar cheese (4 ounces)
- ¾ teaspoon dried oregano, crushed
- ¼ teaspoon ground black pepper

1. In a large saucepan, melt butter over medium heat. Add onion, sweet pepper and celery; cook until vegetables are tender. Stir in milk, corn, broth, soup, cheese product, shredded cheese, oregano and black pepper.

2. Cook, uncovered, over medium heat about 15 minutes or until mixture is almost simmering (do not boil), stirring occasionally. **Makes 6 to 8 main-dish servings.**

Nutrition facts per serving: 393 cal., 25 g fat, 74 mg chol., 1,581 mg sodium, 28 g carbo., 2 g fiber, 16 g pro.

Creamy Brie Soup

Prep: 15 minutes Cook: 23 minutes

- 1½ cups Chardonnay or dry white wine
- ½ cup white wine vinegar
- 4 cups whipping cream or heavy cream
- 1 12-ounce round Brie cheese, rind removed and cut into 1-inch pieces
- 1 clove garlic, minced
- 1 sprig fresh thyme
- 1 sprig fresh basil
  - Salt and ground white pepper
  - Snipped fresh basil and/or fresh thyme (optional)
  - Sliced baguette-style French bread, toasted

1. In a heavy medium saucepan, bring wine and vinegar to boiling; reduce heat. Simmer, uncovered, until liquid is reduced to 1 cup (this should take about 15 minutes). Stir in whipping cream, Brie, garlic, sprig of thyme and basil. Cook and stir about 8 minutes, or until Brie melts.

2. Before serving strain with a fine-mesh sieve and season soup to taste with salt and white pepper. Serve topped with additional snipped basil and/or thyme and bread slices.

3. For Brie Fondue, prepare as directed, except increase the white wine vinegar to 1 cup. Whisk ¼ cup all-purpose flour into the whipping cream before adding to vinegar mixture. Cook and stir until cheese is melted and mixture is thickened. Sprinkle with additional snipped basil and/or thyme. Serve with bread cubes and/or dippers. **Makes 8 appetizer servings.**

Nutrition facts per serving: 690 cal., 57 g fat, 207 mg chol., 595 mg sodium, 23 g carbo., 1 g fiber, 15 g pro.

Creamy Brie Soup

Missouri Apple Soup

Pumpkin Corn Chowder

Prep: 15 minutes Cook: 25 minutes

    2 tablespoons butter
    1 cup thinly sliced leek or 8 large green
      onions, thinly sliced
    2 cloves garlic, minced
 1½ teaspoons ground cumin
    2 cups 1-inch cubes sweet potatoes
      (about 12 ounces)
    1 14-ounce can vegetable broth
  ¼ teaspoon salt
  ¼ teaspoon ground black pepper
    1 15-ounce can pumpkin
    1 14.75-ounce can cream-style corn
    1 10.75-ounce can reduced-fat and
      reduced-sodium condensed cream of
      celery or onion soup
    1 cup milk
    1 tablespoon snipped fresh thyme or
      1 teaspoon dried thyme, crushed
    2 tablespoons pumpkin seeds (pepitas),
      toasted
      Dairy sour cream (optional)
      Assorted crackers (optional)

1. In a 4-quart Dutch oven, melt butter. Add leek and garlic. Cook and stir over medium heat for 5 minutes. Sprinkle in cumin and stir for 30 seconds. Add sweet potatoes, broth, salt and pepper. Bring to boiling; reduce heat. Simmer, covered, for 15 to 20 minutes or until potatoes are tender.

2. Stir pumpkin, corn, soup, milk and thyme into sweet potato mixture. Cook over medium heat until heated through, stirring occasionally. To serve, sprinkle soup with pumpkin seeds. If you like, garnish soup with sour cream and serve with crackers.
Makes 6 servings (8 cups).

Nutrition facts per serving: 226 cal., 8 g fat, 14 mg chol., 806 mg sodium, 37 g carbo., 5 g fiber, 6 g pro.

Missouri Apple Soup

Prep: 25 minutes Cook: 15 minutes

    1 medium onion, thinly sliced
    2 tablespoons butter or margarine
    3 medium Missouri-grown apples or
      desired cooking apples, peeled, cored
      and chopped
    1 tablespoon curry powder
    3 cups chicken stock or broth
    1 cup milk
    1 green onion, thinly sliced
  ⅓ cup slivered almonds, toasted

1. In a large saucepan, cook the onion in hot butter over medium heat for 5 minutes or until tender. Stir in apples and curry powder. Add chicken broth. Bring mixture to boiling; reduce heat. Simmer, uncovered, about 15 minutes or until apples are very tender. Stir in milk. Cook and stir until heated through. If you like, use a potato masher to slightly mash apples.

2. Garnish servings with sliced green onion and almonds. **Makes 4 servings.**

Nutrition facts per serving: 216 cal., 12 g fat, 20 mg chol., 429 mg sodium, 23 g carbo., 4 g fiber, 9 g pro.

Pumpkin Corn Chowder

Sloppy Brisket Sandwiches

Sloppy Brisket Sandwiches

Prep: 20 minutes Marinate: 8 hours
Bake: 4 hours 30 minutes Oven: 325°

- 1 3½- to 4-pound fresh beef brisket
- ½ cup bottled chili sauce
- 2 tablespoons liquid smoke
- 1 tablespoon Worcestershire sauce
- 1 tablespoon steak seasoning blend
- 1 teaspoon garlic salt
- 2 ½-ounce packages dried morel mushrooms (optional)
- 2 large onions, coarsely chopped
- 1 12-ounce bottle or can beer or 1½ cups apple juice or apple cider
- 1½ cups bottled barbecue sauce
- 2 12-ounce loaves ciabatta bread, halved horizontally, or 10 to 12 kaiser rolls or French-style rolls, split and toasted

1. Trim fat from brisket. Place the meat in a large resealable plastic bag set in a large dish. In a small bowl, combine chili sauce, liquid smoke, Worcestershire sauce, steak seasoning and garlic salt. Spread the seasoning mixture on the meat, coating all sides evenly. Seal bag. Marinate brisket in the refrigerator for 8 to 24 hours.

2. In a small bowl, cover the dried mushrooms, if using, with hot water. Let stand 20 minutes. Drain and rinse; drain again. Squeeze out excess moisture. Slice the mushrooms crosswise. Transfer the brisket and marinade to a roasting pan. Top brisket with mushrooms, if you like, and onions. Pour beer over mushrooms and onions.

3. Cover with foil and bake brisket in a 325° oven for 4 to 4½ hours or until very tender. Uncover; pour barbecue sauce over meat. Bake, uncovered, for 30 to 40 minutes or until sauce is heated through and meat is extremely tender, adding a little water if necessary.

4. To serve, remove meat to a cutting board, reserving sauce mixture. Use two forks to gently separate the meat into long, thin strands. Return meat to pan with sauce mixture; stir to moisten. Spoon brisket onto bread or toasted buns. Spoon additional sauce mixture over meat, if you like. **Makes 10 to 12 sandwiches.**

Make-Ahead Tip: Prepare brisket and shred as directed; cool. Store brisket and sauce in an airtight container in the refrigerator for up to 3 days. To reheat, transfer brisket and sauce to a Dutch oven. Cook over medium-low heat, stirring frequently, until warmed through.

Nutrition facts per sandwich: 452 cal., 11 g fat, 92 mg chol., 1,216 mg sodium, 42 g carbo., 3 g fiber, 41 g pro.

Wild Rice & Turkey Loaf Sandwiches

Prep: 50 minutes Cook: 50 minutes
Bake: 1 hour 20 minutes Cool: 1 hour
Chill: 6 hours Oven: 350°

- 2 tablespoons butter or margarine
- 1 cup chopped onion (1 large)
- 1 cup chopped celery (2 stalks)
- 1 cup uncooked wild rice, rinsed and drained
- 1 14½-ounce can chicken broth
- ¼ cup water
- 3 eggs, slightly beaten
- 1 cup shredded Monterey Jack cheese (4 ounces)
- ½ of a 7-ounce jar oil-packed dried tomatoes, drained and chopped, or ½ cup snipped dried cranberries
- 1 teaspoon dried rosemary or leaf sage, crushed
- ½ teaspoon garlic salt
- ½ teaspoon ground black pepper
- 1½ pounds lean uncooked ground turkey or chicken
- 16 to 20 slices firm-texture whole wheat, white or oatmeal bread, toasted if you like
- ½ cup mayonnaise or salad dressing
  Roasted sweet red pepper strips (optional)

1. In a large skillet, melt butter over medium heat. Add onion and celery; cook about 10 minutes or until tender, stirring occasionally. Add wild rice. Cook and stir for 3 minutes more. Carefully add broth and the water. Bring to boiling; reduce heat. Simmer, covered, about 40 minutes or until rice is tender and most of the liquid is absorbed. Remove from heat. Let stand at room temperature about 30 minutes or until cooled.

2. In a large bowl, combine eggs, cheese, dried tomatoes, rosemary, garlic salt and pepper. Stir in cooled wild rice mixture. Add turkey; mix well. (Mixture will be soft.) Lightly pat mixture into a 9x5x3-inch loaf pan (pan will be nearly full). Place pan in a shallow baking pan.

3. Bake in a 350° oven about 1 hour 20 minutes or until no longer pink and the internal temperature registers 165°. Remove from oven. Let cool on a wire rack for 30 minutes. Remove loaf from pan. Wrap in a double thickness of plastic wrap, then in a double thickness of foil, making sure to seal well. Chill for at least 6 hours or up to 3 days.

4. To serve, spread the bread slices with mayonnaise. Cut turkey loaf into eight to 10 slices. Arrange turkey loaf slices on the bread slices. Add pepper strips, if you like. Cover with the remaining bread slices. **Makes 8 to 10 sandwiches.**

Make-Ahead Tip: Prepare turkey loaf as directed through Step 3. Store in an airtight container in the refrigerator for up to 3 days.

Nutrition facts per sandwich: 590 cal., 32 g fat, 178 mg chol., 869 mg sodium, 48 g carbo., 3 g fiber, 29 g pro.

Wild Rice & Turkey Loaf Sandwiches

Applejack Turkey Sandwich

Prep: 30 minutes Grill: 8 minutes Cook: 6 minutes

- 1 medium red sweet pepper, seeded and cut into ¼-inch rings
- 1 medium green sweet pepper, seeded and cut into ¼-inch rings
- 1 medium sweet red or yellow onion, halved and thinly sliced
- 1 tablespoon olive oil
- 8 ½- to ¾-inch-thick slices sourdough bread
- ¼ cup apple butter
- ¼ cup honey mustard
- 4 slices Swiss cheese (3 ounces)
- 4 slices thick-cut bacon, cooked and drained
- 4 slices American or cheddar cheese (3 ounces)
- 8 to 10 ounces sliced cooked turkey breast
- 3 tablespoons olive oil

1. In a large bowl, combine pepper rings and onion slices; drizzle with 1 tablespoon oil and toss to evenly coat. Transfer vegetables to a grill basket.

2. For a charcoal grill, place grill basket directly over medium coals. Grill for 8 to 10 minutes or until vegetables are crisp-tender, turning to brown evenly. (For a gas grill, preheat grill. Reduce heat to medium. Grill as above.)

3. Preheat an electric sandwich press, a covered indoor grill, a grill pan or a large skillet.

4. To assemble sandwiches, spread one side of four bread slices with apple butter and one side of remaining four bread slices with honey mustard. Layer the Swiss cheese, grilled vegetables, bacon, American cheese and turkey on the four bread slices with apple butter. Top with remaining four bread slices, mustard side down. Brush both sides of each sandwich with the 3 tablespoons oil.

5. Place sandwiches (half at a time, if necessary) in the sandwich press; cover and cook about 6 minutes or until bread is toasted. (If using a grill pan or skillet, place sandwiches on grill pan. Weight sandwiches down with a heavy skillet and grill 2 to 3 minutes or until bread is toasted. Turn sandwiches over, weight down and grill until remaining side is toasted.) Serve immediately. **Makes 4 sandwiches.**

Nutrition facts per sandwich: 668 cal., 32 g fat, 74 mg chol., 1,339 mg sodium, 66 g carbo., 4 g fiber, 30 g pro.

Rachel Sandwiches

The Rachel is a twist on the classic Reuben.

Prep: 15 minutes Cook: 4 minutes

- ⅓ cup bottled Thousand Island salad dressing
- 8 slices pumpernickel or dark rye bread
- 12 ounces thinly sliced cooked turkey
- 4 slices baby Swiss cheese
- 1 cup sauerkraut, well drained
- 4 dill pickle spears

1. Spread salad dressing on one side of each bread slice.* With salad dressing side up, top 4 bread slices with turkey, cheese and sauerkraut. Top with remaining bread slices, salad dressing sides down.

2. Preheat a 12-inch skillet over medium heat. Place sandwiches in skillet; reduce heat to medium-low. Cook for 4 to 6 minutes or until cheese is melted and bread is toasted, turning once.

3. To serve, cut sandwiches in half and serve with dill pickle spear. **Makes 4 sandwiches.**

*Note: If you like, spread one side of each bread slice with softened butter or margarine. Spread other side with salad dressing. With buttered sides down, top four slices with meat, cheese and sauerkraut. Top with remaining bread slices, dressing sides down. Cook as above.

Nutrition facts per sandwich: 406 cal., 17 g fat, 63 mg chol., 1,711 mg sodium, 39 g carbo., 6 g fiber, 27 g pro.

Tailgate Ham & Cheese Sandwiches

Prep: 15 minutes Grill: 12 minutes

- 4 kaiser or French-style rolls, split
- ¼ cup bottled barbecue sauce
- 8 1-ounce slices Swiss, mozzarella, provolone and/or Colby and Monterey Jack cheese
- 8 to 12 ounces thinly sliced cooked ham
- 8 slices bacon, crisp-cooked, drained and halved crosswise
- ⅔ cup bottled roasted red pepper strips (optional)
  Pickles (optional)

1. Fold four 18x12-inch pieces of heavy foil in half to make four 9x12-inch pieces. Set aside. Spread roll bottoms and tops evenly with barbecue sauce. Top each roll bottom with cheese, cutting to fit if necessary. Top each with ham. Top with bacon, and, if you like, pepper strips. Place each roll top, sauce side down, over cheese. Wrap in foil.

2. For a charcoal grill, arrange medium-hot coals around bottom edge of grill. Test for medium heat above center of grill. Place foil-wrapped sandwiches on center of grill rack, not over the coals. Cover and grill for 12 to 15 minutes or until heated through and cheese melts, turning once halfway through grilling. (For a gas grill, preheat grill. Reduce heat to medium. Adjust for indirect cooking. Cover and grill as above.) Serve warm. If you like, serve with pickles. **Makes 4 sandwiches.**

Note: To make these in advance, assemble sandwiches as directed through Step 1. Chill wrapped sandwiches up to 8 hours. To tote, place wrapped sandwiches in an insulated cooler with ice packs. At tailgating site, grill sandwiches as directed in Step 2.

Nutrition facts per sandwich: 571 cal., 30 g fat, 101 mg chol., 1,654 mg sodium, 37 g carbo., 2 g fiber, 36 g pro.

Applejack Turkey Sandwich

Rachel Sandwiches

Lobster Egg Salad Brioche Sandwiches

Lobster Egg Salad Brioche Sandwiches

Start to finish: 15 minutes

- 5 Hard-Cooked Eggs (recipe follows)
- 1/3 cup mayonnaise
- 2 teaspoons finely chopped onion or green onion
- 1 teaspoon Dijon-style mustard
- 1 teaspoon prepared horseradish
- 1/2 teaspoon lemon juice
- 1/4 teaspoon salt
- 1/8 teaspoon cayenne pepper
- 1/8 teaspoon paprika
- 1/3 to 1/2 cup finely chopped fresh or frozen cooked lobster or salad-style imitation lobster
- 8 slices brioche or sweet bread (such as Portuguese or Hawaiian sweet bread), toasted
- 4 red-tipped lettuce leaves
- 8 tomato slices

1. Prepare Hard-Cooked Eggs. Finely chop the peeled eggs. Set aside.

2. In a medium mixing bowl, combine mayonnaise, onion, mustard, horseradish, lemon juice, salt, cayenne pepper and paprika. Gently fold in eggs and lobster. Season to taste.

3. Layer four slices of the brioche with lettuce and tomato. Spoon lobster salad on top of tomato slices. Top with remaining bread. **Makes 4 main-dish servings.**

Hard-Cooked Eggs: Place 5 eggs in a single layer in a large saucepan. Add enough cold water to cover the eggs by 1 inch. Bring to a rapid boil over high heat. Remove from heat, cover and let stand for 15 minutes; drain. Run cold water over the eggs or place them in ice water until cool enough to handle; drain. To peel a hard-cooked egg, gently tap it on the countertop. Roll the egg between the palms of your hands. Peel off eggshell, starting at the large end. Makes 5 hard-cooked eggs.

Nutrition facts per serving: 785 cal., 41 g fat, 425 mg chol., 990 mg sodium, 75 g carbo., 3 g fiber, 27 g pro.

Lemon & Dill Walleye Sandwiches with Tartar Sauce

Prep: 1 hour Grill: 10 minutes

- 24 to 36 ounces fresh or frozen skinless, boneless walleye pike, haddock, sole, tilapia or cod fillets, 3/4 inch thick
  Salt
  Freshly ground black pepper
- 2 teaspoons finely shredded lemon peel
- 3 tablespoons lemon juice
- 3 tablespoons olive oil
- 2 tablespoons snipped fresh dill or 1 teaspoon dried dillweed
- 4 cloves garlic, minced
- 1/4 to 1/2 teaspoon bottled hot pepper sauce
- 4 large lemons, cut into 1/4-inch slices
- 12 slices wheat country bread, lightly buttered, or 6 hoagie buns, French-style rolls or other crusty rolls, split and lightly buttered
- 3 cups packaged shredded cabbage with carrot (coleslaw mix) or packaged mixed salad greens
- 6 tomato slices
  Tartar Sauce (recipe follows)

1. Thaw fish, if frozen. Rinse fish; pat dry with paper towels. Sprinkle both sides of fish with salt and black pepper.

2. In a small bowl, combine lemon peel, lemon juice, oil, dill, garlic and hot pepper sauce.

3. For a charcoal grill: Arrange a bed of lemon slices on greased grill rack directly over medium coals. Arrange fish on lemon slices. Brush with the lemon-oil mixture. Cover and grill for 10 to 12 minutes or until fish flakes easily when tested with a fork (do not turn fish). (For a gas grill: Preheat grill. Reduce heat to medium. Arrange lemon slices and fish on greased grill rack over heat [line grill rack with foil if grids are too wide]. Brush with marinade. Cover and grill as above.) Place bread, cut side down, next to fish the last 2 minutes of grilling or until toasted, turning bread slices once.

4. Using a large spatula, transfer fish pieces to six bread slices topped with shredded cabbage mix and tomato slices. Top with Tartar Sauce and cover with remaining bread. Discard lemon slices. **Makes 6 sandwiches.**

Tartar Sauce: In a medium bowl, combine 1 cup mayonnaise or salad dressing, 2 tablespoons finely chopped sweet or dill pickle, 1 tablespoon finely chopped green onion or red onion, 1 tablespoon snipped fresh parsley, 1/2 teaspoon finely shredded lemon peel, 2 teaspoons lemon juice, 1 1/2 teaspoons snipped fresh dill or 1/2 teaspoon dried dillweed,s and 1/2 teaspoon paprika. Store any remaining Tartar Sauce in the refrigerator for up to 1 week. Makes about 1 1/4 cups.

Nutrition facts per serving: 489 cal., 16 g fat, 1,084 mg chol., 645 mg sodium, 57 g carbo., 3 g fiber, 31 g pro.

Lemon & Dill Walleye Sandwiches with Tartar Sauce

Strawberry Spinach Salad with Hickory-Smoked Chicken

Start To Finish: 45 minutes

Orange-Balsamic Vinaigrette (recipe follows)
1 6-ounce package fresh baby spinach or 8 cups fresh baby or torn spinach and/or assorted torn greens
2 cups quartered or sliced strawberries and/or whole blueberries
8 ounces hickory-smoked cooked chicken or turkey, cut into bite-size pieces or 1½ cups chopped cooked chicken or turkey
4 ounces Gruyère, Swiss, Gouda, smoked cheddar and/or Edam cheese, cut into bite-size strips
1 cup fresh enoki mushrooms and/or sliced fresh button mushrooms
½ cup loosely packed fresh Italian (flat-leaf) parsley leaves, snipped
Freshly ground black pepper

1. Prepare Orange-Balsamic vinaigrette. Cover and chill while preparing the salad.

2. For salad: Place spinach on a large serving platter or divide among individual dinner plates. Arrange strawberries, chicken, cheese and mushrooms on spinach. Top with parsley.

3. Shake vinaigrette; pour over salad. Season with pepper. **Makes 4 to 6 main-dish salads.**

Orange-Balsamic Vinaigrette: In a screw-top jar, combine ⅓ cup olive oil or vegetable oil; ¼ cup white balsamic vinegar, white wine vinegar or cider vinegar; 1 teaspoon finely shredded orange peel; ¼ cup orange juice; 1 tablespoon snipped fresh Italian (flat-leaf) parsley; and ⅛ teaspoon salt. Cover and shake well to mix. Serve immediately or cover and store in refrigerator for up to 1 week. Makes about ¾ cup.

Nutrition facts per serving: 413 cal., 29 g fat, 56 mg chol., 810 mg sodium, 19 g carbo., 4 g fiber, 22 g pro.

Harvest Salad with Walnut Oil Vinaigrette

Start To Finish: 30 minutes

Walnut Oil Vinaigrette (recipe follows)
6 cups mesclun or torn mixed salad greens
2 medium tomatoes, sliced or cut into wedges
1 small red onion, thinly sliced or cut into thin wedges
½ cup sliced or chopped celery
½ cup sliced or chopped cucumber
⅓ cup coarsely chopped walnuts, toasted
⅓ cup dried cranberries, dried cherries or dried currants
8 ounces cooked chicken, cut into bite-size strips (optional)

1. Prepare Walnut Oil Vinaigrette. Cover and chill while preparing the salad.

2. In a large salad bowl, combine mesclun, tomatoes, onion, celery, cucumber, walnuts and cranberries. Shake the vinaigrette; pour over the mesclun mixture. Toss gently to coat. If you like, serve with cooked chicken. **Makes 6 side-dish servings or 4 main-dish servings.**

Walnut Oil Vinaigrette: In a medium bowl, combine 3 tablespoons sherry vinegar or white wine vinegar and 1 finely chopped shallot. Let stand for 15 minutes. Whisk in 1 tablespoon Dijon-style mustard, 1 tablespoon honey, ⅛ teaspoon salt and ⅛ teaspoon ground black pepper. Slowly add ¼ cup walnut oil in a steady stream, whisking until mixture is thickened. Makes about ½ cup.

Nutrition facts per serving: 183 cal., 14 g fat, 0 mg chol., 126 mg sodium, 14 g carbo., 2 g fiber, 2 g pro.

Strawberry Spinach Salad with Hickory-Smoked Chicken

Harvest Salad with
Walnut Oil Vinaigrette

Salade Niçoise

Salade Niçoise

Start To Finish: 30 minutes

Balsamic Vinaigrette (recipe follows)
or ¾ cup bottled balsamic vinaigrette
salad dressing

- 1 10-ounce package torn mixed greens (romaine blend) or 8 cups torn romaine
- 2 cups shredded cabbage with carrot (coleslaw mix)
- 1½ cups flaked cooked tuna (8 ounces), chilled, or one 9.25-ounce can chunk white tuna (water pack), chilled, drained and broken into chunks
- 4 ounces mozzarella cheese and/or provolone cheese, cut into ½-inch cubes (1 cup)
- ½ of a 14-ounce can hearts of palm, drained and sliced
- 1 6.5-ounce jar marinated artichoke hearts, drained
- 2 tomatoes, cut into wedges
- 1 small red onion, thinly sliced and separated into rings
- 12 pepperoncini salad peppers, drained
- 12 kalamata olives or pitted ripe olives
- 2 hard-cooked eggs, chilled and sliced or quartered
- 1 2-ounce can anchovy fillets, drained, rinsed and patted dry (optional)

1. Prepare Balsamic Vinaigrette, if using; set aside.

2. To serve, line six chilled dinner plates with torn mixed greens; top with shredded cabbage with carrot. Arrange chilled tuna, cheese cubes, hearts of palm, artichoke hearts, tomatoes, red onion, pepperoncini and olives on greens. Drizzle with Balsamic Vinaigrette. Garnish with egg slices and, if you like, anchovy fillets. **Makes 6 main-dish servings.**

Balsamic Vinaigrette: For dressing, in a blender or food processor, place ⅓ cup white balsamic vinegar or white wine vinegar, ⅓ cup olive oil or salad oil, 1 to 2 teaspoons Dijon-style mustard, 1 to 2 teaspoons sugar, ½ teaspoon dried Italian seasoning, 1 clove garlic or ¼ teaspoon garlic powder, ¼ teaspoon salt and ⅛ teaspoon crushed red pepper. Cover and blend or process about 30 seconds or until thoroughly combined. Transfer to a container with a tight-fitting cover. Makes about ¾ cup.

Nutrition facts per serving: 383 cal., 26 g fat, 101 mg chol., 1,102 mg sodium, 15 g carbo., 3 g fiber, 21 g pro.

Asparagus Salad

Start To Finish: 40 minutes

- 16 fresh large asparagus spears (about 1 pound)
- 3 tablespoons kosher salt or salt
- 4 cups ice cubes
- 1 teaspoon white vinegar
- 4 eggs
- 6 radishes, sliced
- 2 ounces goat cheese, crumbled
Toasted Walnut Vinaigrette (recipe follows)

1. Wash asparagus. Peel or scrape off scales about halfway down on asparagus spears. Break off woody bases where spears snap easily; wash again. Set aside.

2. In a 3- to 4-quart Dutch oven, combine 8 cups water and the salt. Bring to boiling. Meanwhile, in a large bowl, combine another 8 cups cold water and the ice cubes.

3. To blanch, carefully add asparagus to boiling water; cook for 3 to 4 minutes or until just crisp-tender. Cool quickly by plunging asparagus into ice water; drain. Set aside.

4. For poached eggs: Lightly grease a 10-inch skillet. Fill the skillet half full with water; add the white vinegar. Bring water to boiling; reduce heat to simmer (bubbles should begin to break the surface of the water). Break one of the eggs into a 1-cup measuring cup with a handle. Holding the lip of the cup as close to the water as possible, carefully slide egg into simmering water, taking care to not break the egg. Repeat with remaining eggs, allowing each egg an equal amount of space.

5. Simmer eggs, uncovered, 6 minutes or until the yolks are just set. Remove eggs with a slotted spoon and place them on paper towels to drain. Season eggs with salt and ground black pepper. Cut eggs into lengthwise slices; set aside.

6. To serve, place four asparagus spears across four plates. Top with radish slices and egg slices. Add crumbled cheese. Drizzle salads with Toasted Walnut Vinaigrette. **Makes 4 servings.**

Toasted Walnut Vinaigrette: In a small bowl, whisk together ¼ cup walnut oil or extra virgin olive oil, 2 tablespoons sherry vinegar or white wine vinegar, 1½ teaspoons lemon juice and ½ teaspoon salt. Add 2 tablespoons toasted chopped walnuts. Makes about ½ cup.

Nutrition facts per serving: 313 cal., 26 g fat, 226 mg chol., 608 mg sodium, 6 g carbo., 3 g fiber, 14 g pro.

Asparagus Salad

Branding Day Meat Loaf,
page 103

MEAT, POULTRY & FISH

Oven-Roasted Prime Rib
with Dry Rib Rub

Oven-Roasted Prime Rib with Dry Rib Rub

Prep: 15 minutes Roast: 1 hour 45 minutes
Stand: 15 minutes Oven: 350°

¹/₃ cup kosher salt
3 tablespoons dry mustard
4 teaspoons coarsely ground black pepper
1 tablespoon granulated garlic or dried minced garlic or 1¹/₂ teaspoons garlic powder
1 tablespoon onion powder
2 teaspoons dried thyme, crushed
2 teaspoons dried oregano, crushed
2 teaspoons ground coriander
2 teaspoons celery seeds
1 tablespoon olive oil
1 4- to 6-pound beef rib roast or one 4- to 6-pound pork loin center rib roast (backbone loosened)

1. In a small bowl, combine salt, mustard, black pepper, garlic, onion powder, thyme, oregano, coriander and celery seeds. Set aside ¹/₄ cup. (Transfer remaining mixture to small jar or plastic bag. Store in cool, dry place up to 3 months. Shake before using.)

2. Rub oil over meat. Sprinkle the ¹/₄ cup dry rub evenly over meat; rub in with your fingers. Make six 1x¹/₂-inch knife slits into the fat side (the slits allow the seasoning to penetrate the meat). Place meat, fat side up, in a large roasting pan. Insert an oven-going meat thermometer into center without touching bones.

3. Roast beef in a 350° oven for 1³/₄ to 2¹/₄ hours for medium-rare (135°) or 2¹/₄ to 2³/₄ hours for medium (150°). Roast pork in a 325° oven for 1³/₄ to 2¹/₂ hours for medium (150°).

4. Transfer meat to a cutting board. Cover with foil and let stand for 15 minutes before carving. (The temperature of the meat will rise 5° to 10° during standing.)
Makes 12 servings.

Nutrition facts per serving: 318 cal., 21 g fat, 88 mg chol., 934 mg sodium, 0 g carbo., 0 g fiber, 30 g pro.

Peppery Grilled Steak with Summer Tomatoes

Prep: 15 minutes Grill: 10 minutes

4 1-inch-thick beef top loin steaks (New York strip) or ribeye steaks (about 2 pounds)
1 clove garlic, halved
2 to 3 teaspoons peppery steak seasoning
2 cups assorted cherry tomatoes and/or other small tomatoes, whole, halved or quartered
2 tablespoons snipped fresh cilantro
2 tablespoons purchased vinaigrette

1. Trim fat from steaks. Rub steaks with garlic. Sprinkle both sides of steaks with steak seasoning.

2. For charcoal grill, grill steak on the rack of uncovered grill directly over medium coals for 10 to 12 minutes for medium-rare (145°) or for 12 to 15 minutes for medium (160°). (For gas grill, preheat grill. Reduce heat to medium. Place steak on grill rack over heat. Cover and grill as above.)

3. Meanwhile, in a bowl, toss together tomatoes, cilantro and vinaigrette. Serve over grilled steak. **Makes 4 to 8 servings.**

Nutrition facts per serving: 451 cal., 20 g fat, 98 mg chol., 520 mg sodium, 4 g carbo., 1 g fiber, 39 g pro.

Stuffed Beef Tenderloin Filet

Prep: 25 minutes Broil: 20 minutes

1¹/₂ teaspoons butter
1 cup thinly sliced green onion
¹/₂ cup thinly sliced fresh shiitake mushrooms*
1 teaspoon dried thyme, crushed
2 ounces smoked cheddar cheese, shredded (¹/₂ cup)
2 1¹/₄-inch-thick beef tenderloin steaks (about 1 pound total)
Salt and ground black pepper
4 slices bacon

1. Preheat broiler. For stuffing, melt butter in skillet. Add onion, mushrooms and thyme. Cook, uncovered, 3 to 5 minutes or until onion is tender, stirring occasionally. Remove from heat. Stir in cheese; set aside.

2. Cut a 3-inch-wide pocket in the side of each tenderloin filet, cutting to but not through the other side. Spoon stuffing into each pocket. Sprinkle meat lightly with salt and pepper. Wrap two slices of bacon around each filet; secure with toothpicks.

3. Place on unheated rack of broiler pan. Broil 4 to 5 inches from heat 20 to 24 minutes, or until an instant-read thermometer inserted in center of meat and stuffing registers 145° for medium-rare or 160° for medium, turning the beef tenderloins halfway through cooking time. **Makes 2 to 4 servings.**

*Note: Remove and discard stems before slicing shiitake mushrooms.

Nutrition facts per serving: 785 cal., 59 g fat, 211 mg chol., 1,231 mg sodium, 5 g carbo., 2 g fiber, 58 g pro.

Stuffed Beef Tenderloin Filet

Prairie-Style Bean Soup with Beef Ribs

Prep: 30 minutes Bake: 20 minutes Cook: 2 hours
Oven: 350°

- 1 tablespoon olive oil
- 3 to 3½ pounds boneless beef chuck short ribs
- 1 large onion, coarsely chopped (1 cup)
- 2 stalks celery, sliced (1 cup)
- 2 medium carrots, halved lengthwise and cut into ½-inch pieces
- 1 4-ounce can diced green chile peppers
- 2 to 3 teaspoons chili powder
- 2 15-ounce cans Great Northern or pinto beans, rinsed and drained
- 2 14½-ounce cans lower-sodium beef broth or 3½ cups beef stock
- 1 14½-ounce can Mexican-style stewed tomatoes, cut up
- ¼ cup barbecue sauce
  Salt and ground black pepper
  Celery leaves (optional)

Prairie-Style Bean Soup with Beef Ribs

1. In a 4-quart Dutch oven, heat oil over medium-high heat. Add short ribs, half at a time if necessary; cook until browned on all sides, turning to brown evenly. Remove meat and set aside. Add onion, celery, carrots, undrained chile peppers and chili powder. Cook, uncovered, over medium heat for 5 minutes, stirring frequently. Return short ribs to Dutch oven.

2. Add beans and broth. Bring to boiling; reduce heat. Simmer, covered, about 2 hours or until ribs are tender, stirring occasionally. Remove ribs from Dutch oven. Stir in undrained tomatoes. Heat through. Keep warm while meat finishes cooking.

3. Line a shallow roasting pan with a double thickness of foil. Place ribs in pan. Brush with half of the barbecue sauce. Bake in a 350° oven for 10 minutes. Turn ribs; brush with remaining barbecue sauce. Bake about 10 minutes more or until edges of ribs are crisp.

4. Season soup with salt and black pepper to taste. To serve, divide ribs among eight shallow soup dishes and ladle soup over ribs. If you like, garnish with celery leaves. **Makes 8 main-dish servings (10 cups soup plus meat).**

Nutrition facts per serving: 455 cal., 17 g fat, 97 mg chol., 613 mg sodium, 33 g carbo., 8 g fiber, 43 g pro.

Bacon & Cheese-Curd Burger

Prep: 20 minutes Bake: 10 minutes
Chill: 1 hour Grill: 20 minutes Oven: 450°

- 4 thick bacon slices
- ¼ cup packed brown sugar
- 2 pounds 85% lean ground chuck or 90% lean ground sirloin
- ¾ cup cheese curds or string cheese, chopped
  Salt and ground black pepper
- 4 good quality hamburger buns
- 4 ¼-inch-thick slices ripe tomato (optional)
- 4 thin slices white onion (optional)
- 4 iceberg lettuce leaves (optional)

1. Place bacon slices on the unheated rack of a broiler pan. Sprinkle each slice with brown sugar. Bake in a 450° oven for 10 minutes or until crisp. When cool enough to handle, chop bacon; set aside.

2. Divide beef into eight equal portions. Pat beef portions into patties approximately 4 inches in diameter and about ¾ inch thick.

3. Divide the bacon and 3 tablespoons of the cheese curds evenly among the four patties, leaving ½ inch around the edge of the patty. Top each with one of the remaining four patties. Pinch edges of top and bottom patties together to form four large burger patties. Chill, covered, for at least 1 hour.

4. Season burgers with salt and black pepper. For a charcoal grill, place the patties on the well-oiled rack of an uncovered grill directly over medium coals for 10 minutes. Turn with a wide spatula and grill 10 to 12 minutes more, until meat is cooked and an instant-read thermometer inserted into patties registers 160°. Toast buns, cut sides down, on grill during last 1 to 2 minutes of grilling. (For a gas grill, preheat grill. Reduce heat to medium. Place patties on grill rack; cover and grill as above.)

5. To serve, place a cooked burger on bottom half of each bun. If you like, top each with tomato, onion and lettuce.
Makes 4 servings.

Nutrition facts per serving: 743 cal., 41 g fat, 166 mg chol., 686 mg sodium, 35 g carbo., 1 g fiber, 55 g pro.

Bacon & Cheese-Curd Burger

Branding Day Meat Loaf

Branding Day Meat Loaf

This ketchup-glazed meat loaf satisfies the hearty appetites of the hungry crews who work on Triangle Ranch near Badlands National Park. The ranch is also home to the Triangle Ranch Bed and Breakfast.

Prep: 15 minutes Bake: 45 minutes
Stand: 10 minutes Oven: 350°

      2 eggs
    ½ cup ketchup
      1 cup fine dry bread crumbs or crushed
          saltine crackers (28)
      1 envelope (½ of a 2.2-ounce package)
          onion soup mix
      2 pounds lean ground beef
    ¼ cup ketchup
    ¼ cup packed brown sugar
      1 teaspoon dry mustard

1. In a large bowl, beat eggs with a whisk; whisk in the ½ cup ketchup. Stir in bread crumbs and soup mix. Add ground meat; mix well. Lightly pat mixture into an 8x8x2-inch baking pan or an 8x4x2-inch loaf pan, leaving a well around edge for drippings.

2. Bake, uncovered, in a 350° oven for 30 minutes for square pan or 45 minutes for loaf pan. Remove from oven; drain drippings.

3. In a small bowl, combine the ¼ cup ketchup, the brown sugar and dry mustard. Spoon ketchup mixture over meat loaf. Return to oven; bake, uncovered, for 15 to 20 minutes more or until an instant-read thermometer inserted into the center of the meat loaf registers 160°. Let stand for 10 minutes before cutting into slices. **Makes 4 to 6 cowboy servings or 8 to 10 regular-folk servings.**

Nutrition facts per cowboy serving: 668 cal., 27 g fat, 253 mg chol., 1,378 mg sodium, 51 g carbo., 2 g fiber, 54 g pro.

Herb-Crusted Pork Tenderloin with Red Currant Sauce

Prep: 30 minutes Roast: 25 minutes
Stand: 15 minutes Oven: 425°

      1 1- to 1¼-pound pork tenderloin
      2 to 3 teaspoons Dijon-style mustard
          Salt and freshly ground black pepper
      1 tablespoon snipped fresh rosemary
      2 teaspoons snipped fresh thyme
      2 teaspoons snipped fresh sage
      1 tablespoon olive oil
    ⅓ cup red currant jelly
      1 tablespoon white wine vinegar
      2 teaspoons butter, softened
      1 teaspoon prepared horseradish
    ¼ teaspoon finely shredded lemon peel
    ½ teaspoon lemon juice
      3 cups watercress, tough stems removed

1. Trim any fat from meat. Brush meat evenly with Dijon-style mustard. Sprinkle meat with salt and pepper. In a shallow dish, combine rosemary, thyme and sage. Roll meat in the mixed herbs, pressing herbs on all sides of meat.

2. In a very large nonstick skillet, brown tenderloin in hot oil over medium-high heat, turning to brown all sides. Transfer tenderloin to a rack in a shallow roasting pan. Roast in a 425° oven for 25 minutes or until an instant-read thermometer inserted in pork registers 155° and juices run clear. Remove from oven; cover with foil and let stand 15 minutes (temperature will rise to 160°).

3. For currant sauce: In a small saucepan, combine jelly, vinegar and butter. Heat and stir until jelly is melted. Remove from heat. Stir in horseradish, lemon peel and lemon juice.

4. To serve, line a serving platter with watercress. Slice pork and arrange on top of the watercress; spoon some of the currant sauce over pork. Serve remaining sauce on the side. **Makes 4 servings.**

Nutrition facts per serving: 256 cal., 9 g fat, 73 mg chol., 294 mg sodium, 20 g carbo., 1 g fiber, 23 g pro.

Herb-Crusted Pork Tenderloin with Red Currant Sauce

Deluxe St. Louis-Style Grilled Pizza

A thin, crispy crust and shredded Provel cheese instead of mozzarella are what distinguish a St. Louis-style pizza from all others. A tile installer named Ed Imo essentially invented St. Louis-style pizza when he opened Imo's Pizza in 1964. Provel is a processed cheese of cheddar, Swiss and provolone. If you can't find it, use the blend above.

Prep: 30 minutes Grill: 2 minutes to 4 minutes

  Homemade Pizza Crust (recipe follows)
 1 cup Zesty Pizza Sauce (recipe follows)
   or one 8-ounce can pizza sauce
 12 ounces fresh hot or sweet Italian
   sausage links, cut into 1/2-inch pieces
   Olive oil
 2 cups shredded Provel cheese or 3/4 cup
   shredded cheddar, 3/4 cup shredded
   Swiss and 1/2 cup shredded provolone
   cheese (8 ounces)
 1 cup sliced fresh mushrooms
 1/2 cup slivered yellow onion
 1/2 cup thinly sliced green sweet pepper
 3 slices thick-cut bacon, crisp-cooked,
   drained and crumbled

1. Prepare Homemade Pizza Crust and Zesty Pizza Sauce.

2. For topping: In a large skillet, cook sausage until brown; drain fat. Pat with paper towels to remove additional fat. Stir in Zesty Pizza Sauce.

3. For pizza: Remove pizza dough circles from freezer, discarding waxed paper, and brush tops with some olive oil.

4. For a charcoal grill, carefully slide two of the pizza dough circles, oiled sides down, onto a lightly oiled rack of an uncovered grill directly over medium-hot coals. Grill for 1 to 2 minutes or until dough is puffed in some places and starting to become firm. Carefully turn the crusts with tongs, transferring them from rack to the back of a baking sheet. Working quickly and carefully, brush oil over grilled top of crust.

5. For each pizza, sprinkle with one-fourth of the cheese. Top with one-fourth of the sausage mixture and one-fourth of the mushrooms, onion, sweet pepper and bacon. Transfer the pizzas from the baking sheet to the grill rack. Grill for 1 to 2 minutes more or until cheese is melted and crust is crisp. Remove pizzas from grill. (For a gas grill, preheat grill. Reduce heat to medium-hot. Place dough circles on grill rack over heat. Cover and grill as above.)

6. Repeat grilling with remaining two dough circles and toppings. Serve immediately. **Makes four 10- to 12-inch pizzas (6 to 8 servings).**

Homemade Pizza Crust: In a food processor, combine 3 1/4 cups all-purpose flour, 1/4 cup semolina or whole wheat flour and 2 packages active dry yeast. In a small bowl, combine 1 cup warm water (120° to 130°), 3 tablespoons olive oil, 1 tablespoon honey and 1 teaspoon kosher salt or 1/2 teaspoon regular salt. With processor running, pour water mixture through feed tube in a steady stream. Process until dough forms a mass and cleans sides of the bowl. Turn dough out onto a lightly floured surface. Knead for 5 minutes or until smooth and elastic, adding additional flour as needed to keep dough from sticking. Shape into a ball. Place in a lightly greased bowl, turning once to grease top. Cover; let rise in a warm place until double in size (45 to 60 minutes). Punch dough down. Turn dough out onto a lightly floured surface. Cut dough into four equal portions with a serrated knife. Cover; let rest for 10 minutes. Pat each piece of dough into a disk. On a lightly floured surface, roll each dough portion out to a very thin, rough circle that measures 10 to 12 inches in diameter. Separating each pizza dough circle with sheets of waxed paper, stack the circles on a waxed paper-lined baking sheet. Wrap and freeze until firm, about 30 minutes. Makes 4 pizza crusts.

Zesty Pizza Sauce: In a medium saucepan, cook 1/2 cup finely chopped onion, 1/2 cup finely chopped green sweet pepper and 2 teaspoons minced garlic in 1 tablespoon butter over medium heat until vegetables are tender. Stir in one 14 1/2-ounce can diced tomatoes, undrained; one 8-ounce can tomato sauce; 1 1/2 teaspoons oregano, crushed; 1 teaspoon fennel seeds, crushed; 1/2 teaspoon sugar; 1/4 teaspoon salt; 1/4 teaspoon cayenne and 1/4 teaspoon chili powder. Bring to boiling; reduce heat. Simmer, uncovered, for 20 to 25 minutes or until desired consistency, stirring occasionally. Remove from heat. Let cool before using. Cover and refrigerate or freeze sauce in an airtight container. Makes about 2 1/4 cups.

Nutrition facts per serving: 776 cal., 42 g fat, 84 mg chol., 1,209 mg sodium, 68 g carbo., 4 g fiber, 29 g pro.

Frozen Bread Dough Crust: Use 1 pound of frozen whole wheat or white bread dough, thawed. Turn dough out onto a lightly floured surface. Cut dough into four equal portions. Roll out and proceed as directed in Homemade Pizza Crust.

Italian Bread Shell Crust: Use four 12-inch (10-inch) thin Italian bread shells (such as Boboli). Proceed as directed in Step 5 of Deluxe St. Louis-Style Grilled Pizza.

Deluxe St. Louis-Style Grilled Pizza

Two-Pocket Stuffed Chops

Two-Pocket Stuffed Chops

Prep: 20 minutes Bake: 45 minutes Oven: 375°

- ¾ cup coarsely chopped fresh roasted and peeled chestnuts,* or canned vacuum-packed whole peeled chestnuts
- ¼ cup chopped hazelnuts (filberts)
- 2 tablespoons butter, melted
- ¼ cup finely chopped apple
- 2 tablespoons finely chopped onion
- ½ teaspoon ground sage
- ¼ cup finely chopped green sweet pepper
- 1 teaspoon Cajun seasoning or Jamaican jerk seasoning
- 4 boneless pork loin chops, cut 1¼ to 1½ inches thick (about 2 pounds total)
- ½ cup apple jelly

1. In a small bowl, combine chestnuts and hazelnuts. Drizzle with melted butter; toss to coat. Evenly divide nut mixture between two small bowls.

2. For stuffings: In one of the small bowls, stir in apple, 1 tablespoon of the onion and sage. In the other bowl, stir in sweet pepper, remaining 1 tablespoon onion and the Cajun seasoning.

3. Trim fat from meat. Make two pockets in each chop by cutting horizontally from the fat side, starting just off center for each pocket and working the knife through the chop almost to the other side. Spoon a generous 3 tablespoons of each stuffing into one pocket of each pork chop. If necessary, secure opening with a wooden toothpick.

4. Place chops on a rack in a shallow roasting pan. Bake in a 375° oven about 45 minutes or until done (160°) and juices run clear.

5. In a small saucepan, melt apple jelly over low heat. Brush chops with jelly. Before serving, discard toothpicks.
Makes 4 servings.

*Note: To roast chestnuts, using a sharp knife, cut an X in the flat side of 12 whole fresh chestnuts. (This allows the shell to peel easily and prevents the nut from exploding during cooking.) Arrange nuts in a single layer in an ungreased baking pan. Bake in a 425° oven for 15 minutes or until shells curl, tossing once or twice. Cool slightly; peel while warm. (Make-ahead: Roast and peel chestnuts up to 2 days before using. Store, covered, in the refrigerator.)

Nutrition facts per serving: 613 cal., 26 g fat, 160 mg chol., 214 mg sodium, 46 g carbo., 4 g fiber, 49 g pro.

Rolled Spinach Pork Loin

Prep: 40 minutes Roast: 1 hour 30 minutes
Stand: 15 minutes Oven: 325°

- 1 tablespoon olive oil
- 1 medium onion, chopped
- 2 cloves garlic, minced
- 1 10-ounce package frozen chopped spinach, thawed and well drained
- 8 slices bacon, crisp-cooked, drained and crumbled
- 1 cup grated Parmesan cheese
- 1 3½-pound boneless pork center loin roast

1. For filling: In a large skillet, heat oil over medium-hot heat. Add onion and garlic and cook until onion is tender but not brown. Remove skillet from heat. Stir in spinach, bacon and Parmesan cheese; set aside.

2. Trim excess fat from pork. To pinwheel the pork loin, start cutting lengthwise ½ inch under the fat cap on the roast. As you cut the roast, gently rotate the roast at the same time. This will allow the roast to "unroll" as you cut it. When the roast is completely cut, it should be a rectangular piece of meat between ½ and 1 inch thick.

3. Spread spinach mixture over cut side. Roll up the loin tightly from a long side to resemble the initial roast. Tie securely with 100%-cotton kitchen string. Place the roast on a rack in a roasting pan; insert an oven-going meat thermometer into thickest part.

4. Roast in 325° oven for 1½ to 1¾ hours or until meat thermometer registers 150°. Transfer roast to a serving platter. Cover loosely with foil and let stand for 15 minutes before carving. (The temperature of the meat after standing should be 160°.) Remove string; cut into 1-inch-thick slices. **Makes 10 servings.**

Nutrition facts per serving: 308 cal., 13 g fat, 103 mg chol., 368 mg sodium, 3 g carbo., 1 g fiber, 41 g pro.

Rolled Spinach Pork Loin

Vegetable-Pork Oven Stew

Prep: 20 minutes Cook: 10 minutes
Bake: 2 hours Oven: 325°

1½ pounds boneless pork shoulder or pork
    stew meat, cut into ¾-inch cubes
1 tablespoon cooking oil
3 medium onions, coarsely chopped
    (1½ cups)
2 14½-ounce cans lower-sodium chicken
    broth or vegetable broth or
    3½ cups chicken stock
1 teaspoon dried thyme, crushed
1 teaspoon dried oregano, crushed
1 teaspoon lemon-pepper seasoning
½ teaspoon salt
¼ cup all-purpose flour
1 16-ounce package frozen whole kernel
    corn
1 pound tiny new potatoes, halved
2 cups fresh green beans, cut into 2-inch
    pieces, or frozen cut green beans
    Warm corn bread muffins (optional)

1. In a 4-quart Dutch oven, brown half of the meat in hot oil. Remove meat from Dutch oven. Brown remaining meat, adding chopped onions. Return all meat to Dutch oven. Reserve ½ cup of the chicken broth. Stir in remaining chicken broth, the thyme, oregano, lemon-pepper seasoning and salt. Bring to boiling; remove from heat. Cover tightly and bake in a 325° oven for 1 hour.

2. In a small bowl, combine the reserved ½ cup chicken broth and flour; stir into stew. Stir in corn, potatoes and beans. Bake, covered, for 1 hour more or until meat and vegetables are tender and mixture is thickened. If you like, serve with warm corn bread muffins.
Makes 6 main-dish servings (9 cups).

Nutrition facts per serving: 308 cal., 8 g fat, 46 mg chol., 625 mg sodium, 41 g carbo., 6 g fiber, 20 g pro.

Cashew Chicken Stir-Fry

Start To Finish: 35 minutes

12 ounces skinless, boneless chicken
    breast halves
1 tablespoon soy sauce
    Dash ground white pepper
3 tablespoons water
2 tablespoons sugar
2 tablespoons soy sauce
2 tablespoons oyster sauce
2 teaspoons to 2 tablespoons red chili
    paste
2 tablespoons canola oil or cooking oil
1 small red onion, halved lengthwise and
    thinly sliced
6 green onions, bias-sliced into 2-inch
    pieces
4 cloves garlic, minced
1 8-ounce can sliced water chestnuts,
    drained
1 to 2 large dried poblano or ancho chile
    peppers, broken into large pieces and
    seeds discarded, or ½ to 1 teaspoon
    crushed red pepper (optional)
1 cup lightly salted roasted cashews
2 cups hot cooked jasmine, basmati or
    long-grain rice

1. Cut chicken into ½-inch pieces. Place chicken in a medium bowl. Add 1 tablespoon soy sauce and white pepper; toss gently to coat. Set aside.

2. For sauce: In a small bowl, combine the water, sugar, 2 tablespoons soy sauce, the oyster sauce and chili paste. Set aside.

3. Pour oil into a wok or large skillet. (If necessary, add more oil during cooking.) Heat over medium-high heat. Add red onion, green onions and garlic to wok; cook and stir for 2 minutes or until just tender. Remove vegetables from wok.

4. Add chicken to wok; cook and stir for 2 to 3 minutes or until no longer pink. Push chicken to sides of wok. Stir sauce; add to center of wok. Cook and stir until bubbly. Return cooked vegetables to wok. Add water chestnuts and dried chile peppers, if you like. Cook and stir about 1 minute more or until heated through. Remove large pieces of chile pepper, if using. Stir in cashews. Serve with rice. **Makes 4 servings.**

Nutrition facts per serving: 524 cal., 24 g fat, 49 mg chol., 1,576 mg sodium, 54 g carbo., 3 g fiber, 30 g pro.

Vegetable-Pork Oven Stew

Cashew Chicken Stir-Fry

Maple-Glazed Roast Turkey

Maple-Glazed Roast Turkey

Prep: 30 minutes Roast: 3 hours
Stand: 15 minutes Oven: 325°

- 1 12- to 14-pound whole turkey
- ¼ cup olive oil
- 2 tablespoons finely snipped fresh parsley
- 1 tablespoon finely snipped fresh sage leaves
- 1 tablespoon snipped fresh thyme
- 3 large cloves garlic, minced
- 1 teaspoon kosher salt or ½ teaspoon salt
- ¼ teaspoon freshly ground black pepper
- 1 medium apple, quartered and seeded
- 1 lemon, quartered and seeded
- ¼ cup pure maple syrup or honey
- 2 tablespoons butter
   Apple Cider Sauce (recipe follows)

1. Thaw turkey if frozen. If necessary, release turkey legs from leg clamp by pushing down on the legs or band of skin crossing the tail. If desired, remove leg clamp. Remove neck and giblets. Rinse turkey cavity with cold tap water; drain well and pat dry with paper towels.

2. In a small bowl, combine the olive oil, parsley, sage, thyme, garlic, salt and pepper. Rub some of the herb mixture into the body cavity of the turkey. Loosen skin from breast and rub some of the remaining mixture over meat under breast skin. Rub any remaining herb mixture over skin. Place the apple and lemon quarters into the body cavity.

3. Skewer turkey neck skin to back. Tie legs to tail with 100%-cotton kitchen string or tuck the ends of the drumsticks under the band of skin across the tail. Twist the wing tips under the back.

4. Place the turkey, breast side up, on a rack in a shallow roasting pan. Insert an oven-going meat thermometer into the center of one of the inside thigh muscles, being careful not to touch the bone. Cover turkey loosely with foil, leaving some space between the bird and the foil. Loosely press foil over legs and neck. Roast in a 325° oven for 2 hours.

5. For glaze: In a small saucepan, heat and stir maple syrup and butter until butter is melted.

6. Remove turkey from oven. Cut the string between the drumsticks so the thighs will cook evenly. Remove the foil to let the bird brown. Brush about one-third of the glaze over turkey. Return turkey to oven and roast for 60 to 90 minutes more, brushing two more times with remaining glaze, or until thermometer registers 180° and juices run clear after piercing the thickest part of the inner thigh.

7. Remove turkey from oven and cover loosely with foil. Let stand for 15 minutes before carving. Carve turkey into thin slices and serve with Apple Cider Sauce. **Makes 18 servings.**

Apple Cider Sauce: In a medium saucepan, combine one 14½-ounce can chicken broth; 1 cup apple cider or apple juice; 1 large onion, chopped; ⅓ cup pure maple or maple-flavor syrup; 2 tablespoons cider vinegar; and two bay leaves. Bring to boiling; reduce heat. Simmer, covered, for 15 minutes or until onion is very soft. Remove the bay leaves; discard. In a large saucepan, melt 3 tablespoons butter over medium heat. Stir in 3 tablespoons all-purpose flour and ¼ teaspoon ground white pepper or freshly ground black pepper. Carefully add hot cider mixture all at once. Cook and stir over medium heat until thickened and bubbly. Add 1 teaspoon snipped fresh sage or fresh oregano. Makes 3¼ cups.

Nutrition facts per serving: 393 cal., 15 g fat, 191 mg chol., 320 mg sodium, 9 g carbo., 1 g fiber, 51 g pro.

Grilled Turkey Breast with Spiced Almond Butter

Prep: 30 minutes Freeze: 10 minutes
Grill: 1 hour 45 minutes Stand: 10 minutes

- ⅓ cup butter, softened
- ⅓ cup finely chopped slivered almonds or chopped pine nuts
- ¼ cup snipped fresh parsley
- 1 teaspoon finely shredded lemon, orange or tangerine peel
- 1 tablespoon lemon, orange or tangerine juice
- 2 large cloves garlic, minced
- ½ teaspoon ground allspice or ground ginger
- ½ teaspoon freshly ground black pepper
- 1 5- to 6-pound whole turkey breast with bone (thawed, if frozen)

1. In a small bowl, combine butter, almonds, parsley, lemon peel and juice, garlic, allspice and pepper. Cover and chill in freezer for 10 minutes or in refrigerator for 20 minutes or until easy to handle.

2. Starting at the breast bone, slip your fingers between skin and meat to loosen skin, leaving skin attached at the sides to make a pocket. Lift skin and spread the chilled butter mixture under skin of turkey.

3. Place the turkey, breast side up, on a rack in a shallow roasting pan. (To protect your roasting pan and keep it from darkening on the grill, cover the outside of the pan with heavy foil.) Insert an oven-going meat thermometer into the thickest part of the breast without touching the bone.

4. For a charcoal grill, arrange medium-hot coals around edges of grill. Test for medium heat in center of grill. Place turkey in roasting pan on grill rack in center of grill. Cover; grill for 1¾ to 2 hours or until thermometer registers 170°. (For a gas grill, preheat grill. Reduce heat to medium. Adjust for indirect cooking. Grill as above.)

5. Remove turkey from grill and cover loosely with foil. Let stand for 10 minutes before carving. Carve turkey into thin slices.
Makes 8 to 10 servings.

Nutrition facts per serving: 485 cal., 26 g fat, 185 mg chol., 168 mg sodium, 2 g carbo., 1 g fiber, 57 g pro.

Herbed-Tomato Pesto Turkey Breast

Prep: 30 minutes Roast: 1 hour 35 minutes
Stand: 10 minutes Oven: 400°/350°

Nonstick cooking spray
1 3- to 3½-pound bone-in turkey
    breast half
¼ cup purchased dried tomato pesto
3 tablespoons snipped fresh flat-leaf
    (Italian) parsley
2 tablespoons finely chopped walnuts
    or pecans
2 teaspoons snipped fresh rosemary
¼ teaspoon salt
¼ teaspoon freshly ground black pepper

1. Coat a large roasting pan and rack with cooking spray. Place turkey breast portion, bone side down, on rack.

2. In a small bowl, combine dried tomato pesto, parsley, walnuts, rosemary, salt and black pepper; mix well.

3. Starting at the breast bone, slip your fingers between skin and meat to loosen skin, leaving

Herbed-Tomato Pesto Turkey Breast

skin attached at top. Rub pesto over meat. Insert an oven-going meat thermometer into thickest part of breast, without touching bone.

4. Roast, uncovered, in a 400° oven for 20 minutes. Reduce oven temperature to 350°. Roast 1¼ to 1½ hours more or until thermometer registers 170°, juices run clear and turkey is no longer pink. Cover with foil the last 30 to 45 minutes, if necessary, to prevent overbrowning. Let stand, covered with foil, for 10 minutes before slicing. (Pictured with Brined Skillet-Roasted Brussels Sprouts with Lemony Mushrooms, page 128; and Chipotle Smashed Potatoes, page 123.) **Makes 6 to 8 servings.**

Nutrition facts per serving: 338 cal., 14 g fat, 140 mg chol., 316 mg sodium, 3 g carbo., 1 g fiber, 49 g pro.

Turkey Burgers with Poblano Pesto Aïoli

Prep: 25 minutes Grill: 14 minutes

Poblano Pesto Aïoli (recipe follows)
2 egg whites, lightly beaten
2 tablespoons olive oil
1 tablespoon whipping cream
1 teaspoon kosher salt
1 teaspoon curry powder
1 teaspoon chili powder
1 teaspoon ground black pepper
1 teaspoon minced garlic
2 pounds ground uncooked turkey
⅓ cup finely chopped red onion
¼ cup fine dry bread crumbs or ¾ cup
    soft bread crumbs
3 fresh jalapeño peppers, seeded and
    finely chopped (see Tip, page 71)
3 tablespoons snipped fresh chives
6 slices Monterey Jack cheese with
    jalapeño peppers
6 large hamburger buns, split and
    buttered
1½ cups shredded iceberg lettuce
6 dill pickle spears

1. Prepare Poblano Pesto Aïoli. Store, covered, in the refrigerator.

2. In a medium bowl, combine egg whites, oil, whipping cream, salt, curry, chili powder, black pepper and garlic; stir to combine.

3. In a large bowl, combine turkey, onion, bread crumbs, jalapeño peppers and chives. Fold egg white mixture into turkey mixture; mix well. Shape into six ¾-inch-thick patties.

4. For a charcoal grill, grill patties on the rack of an uncovered grill directly over medium coals for 14 to 18 minutes or until no longer pink (165°), turning once halfway through grilling. Top burgers with cheese and grill buns, buttered sides down, directly over medium heat for 30 seconds to 1 minute or until just lightly toasted. (For a gas grill, preheat grill. Reduce heat to medium. Place patties on the well-oiled rack over heat. Cover; grill as above.)

5. To serve, spread about 2 tablespoons of Poblano Pesto Aïoli on each bun top and top with about ¼ cup shredded lettuce. Place a burger on each bun bottom and secure top to bottom with a long pick and serve with a pickle spear. **Makes 6 sandwiches.**

Poblano Pesto Aïoli: Quarter one poblano pepper, removing seeds and membranes. Place pepper pieces on a foil-lined baking sheet. Bake, uncovered, in a 450° oven for 20 to 25 minutes or until pepper skins are charred. Bring up the edges of foil and seal around the pepper pieces. Let pepper stand for 20 minutes to steam. Peel pepper pieces and coarsely chop. In a food processor or blender, combine poblano pepper, ⅓ cup grated Parmesan cheese, ¼ cup fresh cilantro leaves, 3 tablespoons lemon juice, 1 tablespoon toasted pine nuts, 1 clove garlic, ½ teaspoon kosher salt and ¼ teaspoon freshly ground black pepper. Cover and process or blend with on/off pulses until almost smooth. With the processor or blender running, slowly add 2 tablespoons vegetable oil in a thin, steady stream. Transfer mixture to a medium bowl. Stir in 1½ cups mayonnaise. Cover and chill for at least 30 minutes. Store, covered, for up to 1 week. Makes 2 cups.

Nutrition facts per serving: 740 cal., 50 g fat, 167 mg chol., 1,465 mg sodium, 30 g carbo., 2 g fiber, 41 g pro.

Turkey Burgers with
Poblano Pesto Aïoli

Oven-Baked Pheasant Stew with Pastry

Prep: 1 hour 30 minutes Bake: 15 minutes
Cook: 1 hour 15 minutes Stand: 10 minutes
Oven: 450°

- 1 2½- to 3-pound pheasant or whole broiler-fryer chicken
- 3 cups water
- 1 medium onion, cut into wedges
- 1 stalk celery, cut up
- 3 bay leaves
- 6 peppercorns
- 1 teaspoon dried marjoram or oregano, crushed
- ½ teaspoon salt
- ½ teaspoon dried sage, crushed, or poultry seasoning
- ¾ cup dry white wine or chicken broth
- 1 15-ounce package rolled refrigerated unbaked piecrust (2 crusts)
- 1 cup whipping cream
- ⅓ cup all-purpose flour
- 2 egg yolks, lightly beaten
- 4 cups quartered fresh cremini mushrooms
- 2 small yellow summer squash or zucchini, halved lengthwise and thinly sliced (2 cups)
- 1 9-ounce package frozen artichoke hearts, thawed and halved
- 1 egg, lightly beaten
- 1 tablespoon water

1. In a 4-quart Dutch oven, combine pheasant or chicken, 3 cups water, the onion, celery, bay leaves, peppercorns, marjoram, salt and sage. Bring to boiling; reduce heat. Simmer, covered, until poultry is tender (about 1¼ hours for pheasant or 1 hour for chicken).

2. Remove poultry from broth. Skim fat from broth. Discard bay leaves. Strain broth, reserving 1¾ cups (reserve an additional ¾ cup if not using wine); stir in wine or reserved broth. When poultry is cool enough to handle, remove skin and bones and discard. Chop poultry. Set aside.

3. Let piecrusts stand at room temperature for 15 minutes. Unroll piecrusts. On a lightly floured surface, roll each to a 14-inch circle. Using a 14-ounce au gratin dish or an individual casserole as a guide, cut out six circles or ovals measuring 1 inch larger than the top of the dish. Make slits or tiny cutouts in the piecrust circles or ovals. (To make cutouts, use small hors d'oeuvre cutters.) Roll pastry scraps to have enough pastry to cover all six dishes. Set aside.

4. For filling: Transfer broth mixture to a large saucepan. Bring to boiling; reduce heat. Simmer, covered, for 5 minutes. Meanwhile, in a medium bowl, combine whipping cream, flour and egg yolks. Gradually stir about 1 cup of the hot broth mixture into the egg yolk mixture, then return egg yolk mixture to the remaining hot broth mixture. Cook, stirring constantly, until mixture is thickened and bubbly. Stir in chopped poultry, mushrooms, yellow squash and artichokes. (Mixture will become saucier after baking.) Divide filling among six 14-ounce au gratin dishes or individual casseroles.

5. Place a pastry oval or circle over each dish. Fold under the extra pastry; flute the pastry to the edge of the dish. In a small bowl, stir together the whole egg and 1 tablespoon water. Brush pastry with egg glaze. (If you like, place the tiny cutouts on top of the piecrusts and brush the cutouts with the egg glaze.)

6. Bake in a 450° oven about 15 minutes or until the edges of the piecrust are lightly browned and the centers are golden brown. Let stand for 10 minutes before serving.
Makes 6 main-dish servings.

Nutrition facts per serving: 741 cal., 44 g fat, 232 mg chol., 580 mg sodium, 51 g carbo., 4 g fiber, 29 g pro.

Zesty Skillet Turkey

Start To Finish: 30 minutes

- 2 turkey breast tenderloins
- 1 tablespoon olive oil
- 1 cup salsa
- ¼ cup raisins
- 1 tablespoon honey
- ½ teaspoon ground cumin
- ¼ teaspoon ground cinnamon
- 1 cup water
- ¼ teaspoon salt
- ¾ cup quick-cooking couscous
- ¼ cup slivered almonds, toasted

1. Cut each turkey tenderloin in half horizontally. In a large skillet, heat oil over medium-high heat. Add turkey pieces; cook in hot oil about 2 minutes per side or until brown.

2. In a medium bowl, stir together salsa, raisins, honey, cumin and cinnamon. Add salsa mixture to skillet. Bring to boiling; reduce heat. Simmer, covered, for 10 to 12 minutes or until turkey is no longer pink (170°).

3. Meanwhile, in a medium saucepan, bring the water and salt to boiling. Stir in couscous. Cover; remove from heat. Let stand for 5 minutes. Fluff with a fork before serving. Serve turkey and salsa mixture over couscous. Sprinkle with almonds. **Makes 4 servings.**

Nutrition facts per serving: 447 cal., 8 g fat, 105 mg chol., 598 mg sodium, 44 g carbo., 4 g fiber, 49 g pro.

Zesty Skillet Turkey

Black Walnut-Crusted Catfish with Maple Butter Sauce

Start to finish: 25 minutes

4 fresh or frozen catfish fillets, about
    1/2 inch thick (about 1 1/2 pounds)
    Salt
    Ground black pepper
1/4 cup milk
1 egg
2 cups cornflakes, finely crushed
1/4 cup finely chopped black walnuts or
    English walnuts
1 tablespoon butter
1/4 cup pure maple syrup
1/4 cup butter, softened

1. Thaw fish, if frozen. Rinse fish; pat dry with paper towels. Season fish with salt and black pepper. Measure thickness of fish fillets. Set aside.

2. In a shallow dish, beat together milk and egg with a fork. In another shallow dish, combine the cornflakes and walnuts. Dip fish fillets in milk mixture, allowing excess to drip off. Dip coated fish fillets in walnut mixture, turning to coat evenly.

3. In a large skillet, melt 1 tablespoon butter over medium heat. Cook fish, half at a time, in hot butter for 4 to 6 minutes per 1/2-inch thickness or until golden and fish flakes easily when tested with a fork, turning once. (Reduce heat as necessary to prevent overbrowning.)*

4. Meanwhile, for sauce, in a small saucepan, bring syrup to boiling. Remove from heat and whisk in 1/4 cup butter until well combined. Serve with fish.
Makes 4 servings.

*To bake fish: Prepare fish as directed above through Step 2. Place fish on a greased baking sheet. Bake, uncovered, in a 450° oven for 4 to 6 minutes per 1/2-inch thickness or until golden and fish flakes easily when tested with a fork. Serve with maple sauce as directed above.

Nutrition facts per serving: 533 cal., 33 g fat, 172 mg chol., 496 mg sodium, 27 g carbo., 1 g fiber, 32 g pro.

Misto Mare

Prep: 35 minutes Stand: 45 minutes

8 large fresh or frozen shrimp in shells
    (5 ounces)
8 fresh or frozen sea scallops (1 pound)
1 6- to 8-ounce package frozen lump
    crabmeat or one 6-ounce can
    crabmeat, drained, flaked and
    cartilage removed
8 mussels in shells (3 ounces)
6 tablespoons salt
1 cup shucked clams or one 10-ounce can
    whole baby clams, drained
12 ounces dried linguine or fettuccine
1 14.5-ounce can diced tomatoes
1 cup sliced fresh mushrooms
1/2 cup snipped fresh Italian (flat-leaf)
    parsley
1/2 cup dry white wine or chicken broth
4 cloves garlic, minced
1 teaspoon crushed red pepper
1 teaspoon lemon juice
1 cup loosely packed small fresh basil
    leaves
2 teaspoons snipped fresh oregano
    Salt and freshly ground black pepper
1/2 cup finely shredded Parmesan cheese
    (2 ounces)

1. Thaw shrimp, scallops and crabmeat, if frozen. Peel and devein shrimp, leaving tails intact, if desired. Rinse shrimp; pat dry with paper towels. Cut any large scallops in half. Set shrimp, scallops and crabmeat aside.

2. Scrub live mussels under cold running water. Using your fingers, pull out the beards that are visible between the shells. In a very large bowl, combine 2 quarts (8 cups) cold water and 2 tablespoons of the salt. Add the mussels; soak for 15 minutes. Drain and rinse, discarding water. Repeat twice. Set aside.

3. Strain shucked clam juice to remove bits of shell. Set clams and clam juice aside.

4. Cook pasta according to package directions. Drain; keep warm.

5. For sauce: In a 4-quart Dutch oven, combine undrained tomatoes, mushrooms, parsley, wine, garlic, crushed red pepper and lemon juice. Bring to boiling; reduce heat. Simmer, uncovered, for 5 minutes.

6. Add shrimp, scallops, mussels and shucked clams and juice (if using) to tomato mixture. Return to simmer. Cook, covered, about 5 minutes or until shrimp turn pink, scallops are opaque, mussel shells are open and mussels are cooked through (discard any mussels that do not open). Stir in crabmeat, canned clams (if using), basil and oregano; heat through. Remove from heat. Season to taste with additional salt and black pepper.

7. Serve sauce over warm pasta. Sprinkle with Parmesan cheese. Serve immediately.
Makes 6 servings.

Note: To simplify the recipe, use 1 1/2 pounds any combination of shrimp, scallops, crabmeat and clams; omit the mussels.

Nutrition facts per serving: 450 cal., 6 g fat, 120 mg chol., 1,124 mg sodium, 53 g carbo., 4 g fiber, 42 g pro.

Black Walnut-Crusted Catfish with Maple Butter Sauce

Misto Mare

Crispy Beer-Batter Fried Walleye with
Mango Sweet-and-Sour Sauce

Crispy Beer-Batter Fried Walleye with Mango Sweet-and-Sour Sauce

Prep: 30 minutes Cook: 2 minutes per batch

1½ to 2 pounds fresh or frozen boneless, skinless walleye, lake trout, tilapia or sole fillets, ½ to ¾ inch thick
1½ cups all-purpose flour
3 tablespoons paprika
1 tablespoon kosher salt or 2 teaspoons salt
1 tablespoon ground black pepper
2 cups beer
½ cup all-purpose flour
Shortening or cooking oil for deep-fat frying
Mango Sweet-and-Sour Sauce (recipe follows)
½ of a medium red, green and/or yellow sweet pepper, finely chopped
4 green onions (green tops only), cut into thin diagonal slices

1. Thaw fish, if frozen. Rinse fish; pat dry with paper towels. Cut fillets into finger-size strips.

2. For beer batter: In a large bowl, whisk the 1½ cups flour, the paprika, salt and black pepper together until well combined. Whisk in beer to make a thin batter, not much thicker than buttermilk.

3. In a shallow dish or a 9-inch pie plate, place the ½ cup flour. Coat (dredge) fish strips in flour and shake off excess. Dip fish into beer batter; allow excess batter to drip off fish.

4. Carefully add fish strips, three or four at a time, into deep hot fat (375°). Fry about 2 minutes or until golden brown and crisp. Drain on wire racks or on several layers of paper towels. Keep cooked fish warm on a baking sheet in a 300° oven while frying remaining fish.

5. To serve, cover the bottom of six warmed dinner plates with ⅓ cup of Mango Sweet-and-Sour Sauce. Sprinkle the red pepper and green onion tops over sauce. Place fish strips on top. Serve immediately. **Makes 6 servings.**

Mango Sweet-and-Sour Sauce: In a medium saucepan, combine 1 cup sugar and 4 teaspoons cornstarch. Stir in 1¼ cups rice wine vinegar, 1 tablespoon fish sauce (nam pla), 2 teaspoons minced garlic, and 2 teaspoons Asian chili sauce with garlic or 1 teaspoon crushed red pepper. Cook and stir until thickened and bubbly. Cook and stir for 2 minutes more or until reduced and flavor reaches desired intensity. Remove from heat. Stir in half of a peeled and seeded mango cut into ¼-inch pieces (about ½ cup). (Other fruits such as fresh peaches, raspberries, wild blueberries, or strawberries or a combination of fruits may be substituted for mango.) Serve sauce warm with fried walleye. (Cover and chill any leftovers for up to 2 days.) Makes about 2 cups.

Nutrition facts per serving: 638 cal., 19 g fat, 98 mg chol., 1,055 mg sodium, 80 g carbo., 4 g fiber, 27 g pro.

Tilapia Tacos with Chipotle Cream

Start To Finish: 30 minutes

1 pound fresh or frozen skinless tilapia fillets or other white fish
½ cup dairy sour cream
1 teaspoon finely chopped chipotle chile pepper in adobo sauce (see Tip, page 71)
⅛ teaspoon salt
½ cup finely chopped onion
½ cup chopped tomato
3 tablespoons snipped fresh cilantro
4 cloves garlic, minced, or 2 teaspoons bottled minced garlic
1 teaspoon ground cumin
½ teaspoon salt
½ teaspoon ground cinnamon
2 tablespoons butter
1 teaspoon finely shredded lime peel
1 tablespoon lime juice
4 9- to 10-inch flour tortillas, warmed according to package directions
Fresh lime wedges

1. Thaw fish, if frozen. Rinse fish; pat dry with paper towels and set aside. In a small bowl, combine sour cream, chipotle chile and ⅛ teaspoon salt; set aside. In another bowl, combine onion, tomato and cilantro; set aside.

2. In another small bowl, combine garlic, cumin, ½ teaspoon salt and the cinnamon. Rub evenly over both sides of fish using your fingers.

3. In a 12-inch nonstick skillet, melt butter over medium heat. Add fish and cook for 3 minutes. Turn fish and cook for 2 minutes more. Break fish into bite-size chunks; sprinkle with lime peel and juice. Cook 1 to 2 minutes more or until fish begins to flake when tested with a fork. Remove from heat. Remove fish from skillet with a slotted spoon, discarding liquid.

4. Fill each tortilla with ½ cup of the fish and ¼ cup of onion mixture. Top each serving with 2 tablespoons of the chipotle-sour cream mixture. Fold in half or roll up. Serve with lime wedges. **Makes 4 servings.**

Nutrition facts per serving: 370 cal., 16 g fat, 83 mg chol., 667 mg sodium, 29 g carbo., 2 g fiber, 27 g pro.

Tilapia Tacos with Chipotle Cream

Asian Coleslaw, page 132

SIDES

Dressing & Stuffing

Potatoes

Salads & Slaws

Vegetable Sides

Roasted Baby Potatoes with Herbs

Roasted Baby Potatoes with Herbs

Prep: 10 minutes Roast: 55 minutes Oven: 325°

1 pound small potatoes, such as baby Dutch yellow, fingerlings, baby purple and/or new red or yellow potatoes or 3 medium round red or white potatoes, halved (1 pound), cut into 1-inch pieces
1 medium onion, cut into thin wedges or coarsely chopped
1 clove garlic, minced
½ teaspoon kosher salt, sea salt or coarse salt
¼ teaspoon coarsely ground black pepper
2 tablespoons olive oil
1 tablespoon snipped fresh thyme, rosemary and/or flat-leaf Italian parsley
1 5.2-ounce package semisoft cheese with garlic and herbs or ½ of an 8-ounce tub soft-style cream cheese (optional)
  Snipped fresh chives (optional)

1. Wash potatoes. In a greased 9x9x2-inch baking pan or shallow baking pan, combine potatoes, onion and garlic. Sprinkle with salt and pepper. Drizzle with oil; toss to coat.

2. Roast, uncovered, in a 325° oven for 45 minutes. Stir potato mixture; bake for 10 to 20 minutes more or until potatoes are tender and brown on the edges. Stir in fresh herbs. If you like, top with cheese, allowing it to melt slightly, and garnish with snipped chives.

Nutrition facts per serving: 157 cal., 7 g fat, 0 mg chol., 249 mg sodium, 22 g carbo., 2 g fiber, 3 g pro.

Roasted Veggies: Prepare as above, except stir in 2 cups packaged peeled baby carrots or four medium carrots, halved lengthwise and cut into 2-inch pieces, with potatoes and onion. Continue as directed. Makes 4 side-dish servings.

Chipotle Smashed Potatoes

Prep: 20 minutes Bake: 30 minutes
Cook: 15 minutes Oven: 350°

3 large Yukon gold potatoes or other yellow potatoes (6 to 8 ounces each), peeled and quartered
3 large sweet potatoes (6 to 8 ounces each), peeled and quartered
1 3-ounce package cream cheese, softened
¼ cup butter, softened
½ teaspoon salt
¼ teaspoon ground black pepper
½ cup dairy sour cream
1 canned chipotle chile pepper in adobo sauce, finely chopped, plus 1 to 2 teaspoons adobo sauce (see Tip, page 71)
3 slices bacon, crisp-cooked, drained and crumbled

1. In a large saucepan, cook potatoes in enough lightly salted boiling water to cover for 15 to 20 minutes or until tender; drain. Mash with a potato masher or electric mixer. Add cream cheese, butter, salt and black pepper. Mash the potato mixture until combined. Gently stir in the sour cream, chipotle chile pepper and adobo sauce.

2. Lightly grease a 2-quart casserole or an 8x8x2-inch baking dish; spoon in mixture.

3. Bake, uncovered, in 350° oven for 30 to 35 minutes or until heated through. Top with bacon. **Makes 6 to 8 servings.**

Nutrition facts per serving: 276 cal., 18 g fat, 47 mg chol., 433 mg sodium, 25 g carbo., 3 g fiber, 5 g pro.

Fire-Roasted Dilled Potato Medley

Prep: 25 minutes Grill: 25 minutes

3 medium Yukon gold, Yellow Finn or other yellow-fleshed potatoes (about 1 pound), peeled and cut into 1-inch pieces
1½ cups packaged peeled baby carrots, baby carrots with tops trimmed or
3 medium carrots, halved lengthwise and cut into 2-inch pieces
1 cup frozen pearl onions, peeled and halved purple boiling onions, cippolini onions and/or shallots
¼ cup olive oil
2 tablespoons snipped fresh dill or 1 teaspoon dried dillweed
1 teaspoon kosher or sea salt or ¾ teaspoon salt
½ teaspoon coarsely ground black pepper
1 lemon, thinly sliced and seeded

1. Stack two 13x9x2-inch disposable foil pans to make a double thickness. Place potatoes, carrots and onions in pan. In a small bowl, combine oil, dill, salt and pepper. Add to vegetables; toss to coat. Place lemon slices atop vegetables.

2. For a charcoal grill, place foil pan on the rack of an uncovered grill directly over medium coals for 25 to 30 minutes or until vegetables are tender, stirring every 5 to 10 minutes to prevent overbrowning. (For a gas grill, preheat grill. Reduce heat to medium. Place foil pan on grill rack over heat. Cover; grill as above.) Discard lemon slices before serving. **Makes 6 servings.**

Nutrition facts per serving: 153 cal., 9 g fat, 0 mg chol., 253 mg sodium, 17 g carbo., 2 g fiber, 2 g pro.

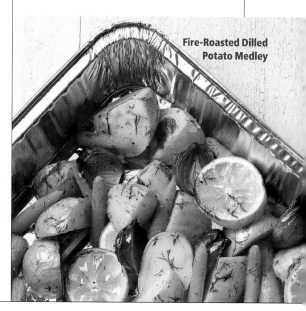

Fire-Roasted Dilled Potato Medley

Grilled Sweet Potato Wedges with Dipping Sauces

Prep: 30 minutes Grill: 8 minutes

6 medium sweet potatoes or russet
   potatoes (about 2 pounds)
¼ cup olive oil
1 teaspoon kosher or sea salt or
   ¾ teaspoon salt
¼ teaspoon freshly ground black pepper
   Honey Sesame Sauce (recipe follows)
   Creamy Chive Sauce (recipe follows)

1. Scrub potatoes with a soft vegetable brush under running water. Cut each unpeeled potato in half lengthwise, then cut each half lengthwise into four wedges. In a covered 4-quart Dutch oven, cook potato wedges in boiling lightly salted water for 8 minutes or until just tender. Drain and cool slightly. Place potatoes in a large bowl; drizzle with oil and sprinkle with salt and pepper. Toss gently to coat.

2. For a charcoal grill, grill potato wedges on the greased rack of an uncovered grill directly over medium coals for 8 to 10 minutes or until edges begin to brown, turning occasionally. (For a gas grill, preheat grill. Reduce heat to medium. Place potato wedges on grill rack over heat. Cover and grill as above.)

3. Transfer potatoes to a serving dish; serve with Honey Sesame Sauce and/or Creamy Chive Sauce. Serve immediately or at room temperature. **Makes 8 servings.**

Nutrition facts per serving: 323 cal., 24 g fat, 14 mg chol., 749 mg sodium, 25 g carbo., 3 g fiber, 3 g pro.

Honey Sesame Sauce: In a small bowl, combine ¼ cup reduced-sodium soy sauce; ¼ cup rice vinegar, sake or white wine vinegar; 3 tablespoons honey; 2 tablespoons finely chopped green onion; 2 tablespoons toasted sesame seeds; and 1 tablespoon toasted sesame oil. Stir until honey dissolves. Makes about ¾ cup.

Creamy Chive Sauce: In a small bowl, combine ½ cup dairy sour cream or plain yogurt, ½ cup mayonnaise or salad dressing, 2 tablespoons snipped fresh chives, and 1 teaspoon desired steak seasoning. Stir in 3 tablespoons finely shredded Asiago cheese, 2 tablespoons grated Parmesan cheese or 1 tablespoon crumbled blue cheese. Makes about 1 cup.

Smokin' Hot Potato Kabobs with Rosemary-Chipotle Butter

Prep: 25 minutes Grill: 8 minutes

1½ pounds small potatoes such as baby
   Dutch yellow, fingerlings, round red
   and/or round white
16 baby sunburst squash, green baby
   pattypan squash or 1 medium
   zucchini or yellow summer squash, cut
   into 1-inch slices
8 medium fresh mushrooms
⅓ cup butter or margarine, melted
1 to 2 tablespoons snipped fresh
   rosemary or oregano
½ teaspoon ground chipotle chile pepper
   or chili powder
   Coarse kosher or sea salt

1. Scrub potatoes. Cut any large potatoes in half. In a covered medium saucepan, cook potatoes in a large amount of boiling lightly salted water for 10 minutes, adding the squash and mushrooms for the last 1 minute of cooking time. Drain and cool slightly.

2. On eight 10- to 12-inch metal skewers, alternately thread potatoes, squash and mushrooms, leaving a ¼-inch space between pieces. In a small bowl, combine butter, rosemary and chipotle chile pepper. Brush over vegetables. Sprinkle kabobs with salt.

3. For a charcoal grill, grill kabobs on the rack of an uncovered grill directly over medium coals for 8 to 10 minutes or until vegetables are tender and brown, turning and brushing occasionally with butter mixture. (For a gas grill, preheat grill. Reduce heat to medium. Place kabobs on grill rack over heat. Cover; grill as above.) **Makes 8 servings.**

Nutrition facts per serving: 139 cal., 8 g fat, 20 mg chol., 123 mg sodium, 16 g carbo., 2 g fiber, 3 g pro.

Smokin' Hot Potato Kabobs with Rosemary-Chipotle Butter

Grilled Sweet Potato Wedges
with Dipping Sauces

Mix-and-Match
Bread Dressing

Mix-and-Match Bread Dressing

Prep: 45 minutes Bake: 55 minutes
Oven: 300°/325°

1 1-pound bread loaf, such as white,
   French, Italian, sourdough, whole
   wheat, honey wheat, pumpernickel,
   seeded rye or artisan
½ cup butter or margarine
1½ cups finely chopped vegetables, such
   as celery with leaves, red or yellow
   sweet pepper, fresh mushrooms,
   fennel bulb, peeled sweet potatoes or
   peeled butternut squash
1 cup finely chopped onion
2 large cloves garlic, minced
1 cup cooked meat, such as bulk pork
   sausage, hot Italian sausage, chorizo
   sausage, cubed ham or crumbled
   bacon (optional)
1 tablespoon snipped fresh sage or
   1 teaspoon dried rubbed sage,
   ground sage or poultry seasoning
2 teaspoons dried herb, crushed, such as
   thyme, oregano, rosemary or basil
¼ teaspoon ground black pepper or
   cayenne pepper
½ cup snipped fresh parsley
⅔ cup chopped and toasted nuts, such as
   pecans, walnuts, almonds or pine nuts
   (optional)
⅔ cup dried fruit, such as cranberries, tart
   red cherries, raisins, golden raisins,
   currants, snipped apricots, snipped
   peaches or snipped apples (optional)
1⅓ to 2 cups turkey stock or chicken broth

1. For dry bread cubes: Cut fresh bread into
½-inch cubes. Measure 12 cups bread cubes.
Place bread cubes in a single layer in two
15x10x1-inch baking pans. Bake in a 300°
oven for 10 to 15 minutes or until cubes are
dry, stirring twice; cool. (Cubes will continue
to dry and crisp as they cool.)

2. In a large skillet, melt butter over medium
heat. Add desired chopped vegetables,
onion and garlic; cook until onion is tender
but not brown. Remove from heat.

3. If you like, stir in desired meat. Stir in sage,
desired dried herb and the pepper.

4. In a very large bowl, toss bread cubes,
onion mixture and parsley. If you like, add
nuts and/or dried fruit. Drizzle with enough
broth to moisten; toss lightly to combine.
Transfer mixture to 2½- to 3-quart casserole.

5. Bake, covered, in a 325° oven for
45 minutes or until heated through. Uncover;
bake for 10 minutes more to crisp top slightly.
Makes 12 to 14 servings (about 10 cups).

Nutrition facts per serving: 189 cal., 9 g fat, 21 mg chol.,
356 mg sodium, 22 g carbo., 2 g fiber, 4 g pro.

Mix-and-Match Corn Bread Dressing:
Prepare recipe as above, except use half of
a bread loaf (8 ounces) or 6 cups dry bread
cubes. Add 5 cups of ¾-inch cubed or
crumbled corn bread (from one prepared
corn bread mix). Makes about 11 cups.

Mix-and-Match Rice Dressing: Prepare recipe
as above, except use half of a bread loaf
(8 ounces) or 6 cups dry bread cubes. Add
5 cups cooked long grain white rice, brown
rice or wild rice. Makes about 15 cups.

Five-Herb Roasted Carrots & Potatoes

Prep: 25 minutes Bake: 45 minutes Oven: 400°

2 pounds tiny new potatoes
3 medium carrots, cut into bite-size
   pieces
2 tablespoons snipped fresh chives
2 tablespoons butter, melted
2 tablespoons olive oil
1 tablespoon snipped fresh oregano
1 tablespoon snipped fresh parsley
2 teaspoons snipped fresh rosemary
1½ teaspoons bottled minced garlic
   (3 cloves) (optional)
1 teaspoon snipped fresh sage
½ teaspoon salt
¼ teaspoon freshly ground black pepper

1. Cut unpeeled potatoes into quarters.
Place in greased 13x9x2-inch baking pan.
Add carrots.

2. In a small bowl, combine chives, melted
butter, oil, oregano, parsley, rosemary, garlic
(if desired), sage, salt and pepper. Drizzle
over potato mixture; toss gently to coat.

3. Cover and bake in a 400° for 30 minutes.
Stir potato mixture. Bake, uncovered, for
15 to 20 minutes more or until potatoes are
tender. **Makes 6 to 8 servings.**

Grilling Directions: Tear off two 22x18-inch
pieces of heavy foil; stack foil. Place potatoes
and carrots in center of foil; drizzle with herb
mixture. Bring up two opposite edges of foil;
seal with double fold. Fold remaining ends to
completely enclose vegetables, leaving space
for steam to build. Place foil packet on rack
of uncovered grill directly over medium to
medium-hot coals. Grill for 35 to 45 minutes
or until potatoes are tender, turning packet
after 20 minutes.

Nutrition facts per servings: 202 cal., 9 g fat, 11 mg chol.,
254 mg sodium, 28 g carbo., 3 g fiber, 4 g pro.

**Five-Herb Roasted
Carrots and Potatoes**

Brined Skillet-Roasted Brussels Sprouts with Lemony Mushrooms

Prep: 25 minutes Stand: 1 hour Roast: 30 minutes Cook: 5 minutes Oven: 350°

1½ pounds Brussels sprouts
 8 cups cold water
 ½ cup kosher salt
 ¼ cup olive oil
 2 tablespoons butter
 2 cups sliced cremini, shiitake or button mushrooms (about 4 ounces)
 2 tablespoons snipped fresh chives
 1 tablespoon lemon juice
 ¼ teaspoon lemon-pepper seasoning

1. Trim stems and remove any wilted outer leaves from Brussels sprouts; wash. Halve any large Brussels sprouts; set aside. In a very large mixing bowl or deep container, stir together the cold water and kosher salt until salt is completely dissolved. Add Brussels sprouts to brine mixture, making sure the sprouts are completely submerged (weight down with a plate, if necessary, to keep sprouts submerged). Let stand for 1 hour.

2. Drain Brussels sprouts; rinse well. In a very large cast-iron skillet or roasting pan, toss Brussels sprouts with olive oil to coat. Roast Brussels sprouts, uncovered, in a 350° oven for 30 to 35 minutes or until tender, stirring once.

3. Meanwhile, in a medium skillet, melt butter over medium heat. Add mushrooms and chives and cook over medium heat about 5 minutes or until mushrooms are tender and golden brown, stirring occasionally. Add lemon juice and lemon-pepper seasoning to mushroom mixture.

4. Remove from heat. Pour mushroom mixture over cooked Brussels sprouts, tossing well. **Makes 6 side-dish servings.**

Nutrition facts per serving: 165 cal., 13 g fat, 10 mg chol., 711 mg sodium, 10 g carbo., 4 g fiber, 5 g pro.

Grilled Green Beans with Shallots & Sesame Seeds

Prep: 15 minutes Grill: 25 minutes

 1 pound fresh green beans and/or yellow wax beans, trimmed
 2 large shallots, coarsely chopped, or ¼ cup chopped onion
 2 tablespoons water
 1 tablespoon canola oil or vegetable oil
 1 teaspoon reduced-sodium soy sauce or light teriyaki sauce
 2 tablespoons shredded or coarsely snipped fresh basil
 1 tablespoon shredded or coarsely snipped fresh mint
 1 tablespoon sesame seeds, toasted
   Sea salt
 2 tablespoons pine nuts or slivered almonds, toasted, or 2 tablespoons chopped pistachio or cashew nuts (optional)

1. In a large bowl, toss together beans, shallots, water, oil and soy sauce; set aside.

2. Fold a 36x18-inch piece of heavy foil in half to make an 18-inch square. Place bean mixture in center of foil. Bring together two opposite edges of foil; seal with a double fold. Fold remaining edges together to enclose the beans, leaving space for steam to build.

3. For a charcoal grill: Place bean packet on the rack of an uncovered grill directly over medium coals. Grill for 20 minutes, turning once. Remove packet from the grill and cool slightly. Carefully open packet (some steam will escape). Return open foil packet to the grill rack. Continue grilling 5 minutes more or until beans are just browned and crisp-tender, stirring occasionally. (For a gas grill, preheat grill. Reduce heat to medium. Place packet on grill rack. Cover and grill beans as above.)

4. Transfer beans to a large bowl. Add basil, mint and sesame seeds. Toss to combine. Season to taste with sea salt. Top with nuts, if you like. **Makes 6 side-dish servings.**

Nutrition facts per serving: 55 cal., 3 g fat, 0 mg chol., 104 mg sodium, 6 g carbo., 3 g fiber, 2 g pro.

Baked Stuffed Vegetables Provençal

Prep: 30 minutes Bake: 10 minutes Oven: 400°

 2 medium-firm plum tomatoes (8 to 9 ounces total)
 1 medium zucchini* (8 ounces)
 1 medium Japanese eggplant* (about 6 ounces)
 ⅔ cup olive oil
 ⅓ cup snipped fresh basil
 3 tablespoons minced shallot
 4 cloves garlic, minced
 ¼ teaspoon coarse kosher salt
1¼ cups fine dry bread crumbs

1. For vegetables: Halve tomatoes lengthwise; scoop out seeds. Cut zucchini into 3-inch lengths; hollow out halfway down one end with a melon baller. Cut Japanese eggplant into thirds; halve and slightly scoop out; set aside.

2. For stuffing: In a small bowl, combine oil, basil, shallot, garlic and salt. Stir in bread crumbs; mix well.

3. Fill each vegetable with a few spoonfuls of filling. Arrange the vegetables in a 15x10x1-inch baking pan. Bake in a 400° oven for 10 to 15 minutes or until the vegetables are tender but hold their shape and the bread crumbs begin to brown. If necessary, remove tomatoes after 10 minutes of baking, as they may get done sooner than the other vegetables. **Makes 6 servings.**

Nutrition facts per serving: 322 cal., 26 g fat, 0 mg chol., 688 mg sodium, 21 g carbo., 3 g fiber, 4 g pro.

*Note: If you like, use 8 ounces baby zucchini in place of the one medium zucchini or one baby eggplant in place of the Japanese eggplant. Cut baby zucchini lengthwise and use a paring knife to cut out a thin wedge of pulp lengthwise from each half. Cut each baby eggplant lengthwise and slightly scoop out.

Grilled Green Beans with
Shallots and Sesame Seeds

Broccoli Grape Salad

Triangle Ranch
Scalloped Corn

Baked Beans 'n' Bacon

Triangle Ranch Scalloped Corn

Prep: 15 minutes Bake: 35 minutes
Stand: 10 minutes Oven: 350°

- 2 eggs, lightly beaten
- 1 14.75- to 16-ounce can cream-style corn
- 4 ounces American cheese, shredded (1 cup), or 4 ounces pasteurized prepared cheese product, finely cut up
- ⅔ cup milk
- 10 saltine crackers, coarsely crushed (⅓ cup)
- ½ of a 4-ounce can diced green chile peppers, drained (3 tablespoons)
- 1 teaspoon sugar
- ¼ teaspoon salt
- ⅛ teaspoon ground black pepper

1. In a large bowl, stir together eggs, corn, cheese, milk, crushed crackers, chile peppers, sugar, salt and black pepper.

2. Transfer to a greased 1½-quart au gratin or shallow baking dish. Bake, uncovered, in a 350° oven for 35 to 40 minutes or until the center appears set. Let stand for 10 minutes before serving. **Makes 6 servings.**

Nutrition facts per serving: 185 cal., 9 g fat, 90 mg chol., 692 mg sodium, 19 g carbo., 1 g fiber, 9 g pro.

Baked Beans 'n' Bacon

Prep: 30 minutes Bake: 50 minutes Oven: 350°

- 1 pound bacon, cut into 1-inch pieces
- 1 medium onion, chopped
- 1 31-ounce can or two 15-ounce cans pork and beans in tomato sauce
- ½ cup packed brown sugar
- ½ cup ketchup
- 2 teaspoons yellow mustard
- ¼ teaspoon garlic powder
- ¼ teaspoon chili powder

1. In a large skillet, cook bacon over medium heat until crisp. Drain bacon pieces on paper towels, reserving 1 tablespoon drippings in skillet.

2. Cook onion in reserved hot bacon drippings about 5 minutes or until tender.

3. In a greased 2-quart casserole, combine pork and beans, bacon and onion. In a small bowl, combine brown sugar, ketchup, mustard, garlic powder and chili powder. Pour ketchup mixture over bean mixture; stir gently to coat.

4. Bake, uncovered, in a 350° oven for 50 to 60 minutes or until heated through and desired consistency. Stir gently before serving. **Makes 8 servings.**

Nutrition facts per serving: 235 cal., 6 g fat, 18 mg chol., 854 mg sodium, 39 g carbo., 5 g fiber, 9 g pro.

Broccoli Grape Salad

Prep: 30 minutes Chill: 1 hour

- 1 pound bacon, cut into 1-inch pieces
- 1 cup mayonnaise or salad dressing
- 1 cup red and/or green seedless grapes, halved
- ½ cup finely chopped red onion
- ¼ cup sugar
- 7 cups fresh broccoli florets (1 large head)

1. In a large skillet, cook bacon over medium heat until crisp. Drain bacon on paper towels and set aside.

2. In a large bowl, stir together mayonnaise, grapes, red onion and sugar. Add broccoli and two-thirds of the bacon; stir to coat. Cover and chill in the refrigerator for at least 1 hour or up to 24 hours. Store remaining cooked bacon, covered, in the refrigerator. Sprinkle remaining bacon over salad just before serving. **Makes 10 to 12 side-dish servings.**

Nutrition facts per serving: 282 cal., 23 g fat, 22 mg chol., 443 mg sodium, 13 g carbo., 2 g fiber, 7 g pro.

Corn & Broccoli Bake

Prep: 15 minutes Bake: 35 minutes Oven: 350°

- 1 10-ounce package frozen cut broccoli
- 1 beaten egg
- 1 14- to 15-ounce can cream-style corn
- ⅔ cup crushed rich round crackers
- ⅛ teaspoon seasoned pepper
- 3 ounces sliced process cheese
- 2 tablespoons butter, melted
- 1 cup crushed potato chips

1. In a colander, run cold water over broccoli to separate. Let drain.

2. In a mixing bowl, combine the egg, corn, cracker crumbs and pepper.

3. In a 1½-quart casserole, layer half of the broccoli, then half of the corn mixture. Top with the cheese slices.

4. Layer with the remaining broccoli, then the corn mixture. Drizzle butter over the top. Sprinkle with potato chips.

5. Bake in a 350° oven for about 35 minutes. Serve warm. **Makes 6 servings.**

Nutrition Facts per serving: 244 cal., 14 g fat, 55 mg chol., 528 mg sodium, 25 g carb., 2 g dietary fiber, 7 g pro.

Corn & Broccoli Bake

Asian Coleslaw

Cover and shake well. Drizzle the dressing over salad; toss gently to coat. Cover and chill for at least 1 hour or up to 3 hours. **Makes 6 side-dish servings.**

Nutrition facts per serving: 98 cal., 7 g fat, 0 mg chol., 283 mg sodium, 8 g carbo., 2 g fiber, 1 g pro.

Buttery Mixed Veggie Kabobs

Prep: 25 minutes Grill: 15 minutes

    1 small zucchini, halved lengthwise and
       cut into eight 1-inch slices
    8 baby sunburst squash, halved or
       quartered, or 1 small yellow squash,
       halved lengthwise and cut into eight
       1-inch slices
    8 red boiling onions, halved, or 2 small
       red onions, cut into 8 wedges each
    2 fresh ears sweet corn, husked, cleaned
       and cut crosswise into 4 pieces each
  1/3 cup butter, melted
  1/4 teaspoon garlic powder
  1/4 teaspoon onion powder
  1/4 teaspoon ground chipotle chile
       powder or cayenne pepper
  1/4 teaspoon dried oregano, crushed

1. On eight 10- to 12-inch metal skewers, alternately thread the zucchini, sunburst squash, onions and corn. In a small bowl, combine butter, garlic powder, onion powder, chipotle chile powder and oregano. Brush over vegetables.

2. For a charcoal grill, grill kabobs on the rack of an uncovered grill directly over medium coals for 15 to 18 minutes or until vegetables are tender and brown, turning and brushing occasionally with butter mixture. (For a gas grill, preheat grill. Reduce heat to medium. Place kabobs on grill rack over heat. Cover; grill as above.) **Makes 4 servings.**

Nutrition facts per serving: 194 cal., 16 g fat, 40 mg chol., 121 mg sodium, 13 g carbo., 2 g fiber, 3 g pro.

Asian Coleslaw

Prep: 20 minutes Chill: 1 hour

    1 cup shredded red cabbage
    3 cups shredded green cabbage
    1 medium tart apple, cored and chopped
  1/4 cup thinly sliced green onion (2)
  1/4 cup rice vinegar
    3 tablespoons sesame or peanut oil
    2 tablespoons snipped fresh cilantro
    2 tablespoons finely chopped pickled
       ginger or 1 teaspoon grated fresh
       ginger

    1 tablespoon soy sauce
  1/2 teaspoon ground ginger
  1/4 teaspoon celery salt
  1/4 teaspoon crushed red pepper flakes
  1/8 teaspoon salt
  1/8 teaspoon freshly ground black pepper

1. Rinse red cabbage; pat dry. In a large bowl, combine red cabbage, green cabbage, apple and green onions.

2. For vinaigrette: In a screw-top jar, combine vinegar, oil, cilantro, pickled ginger, soy sauce, ground ginger, celery salt, red pepper flakes, salt and black pepper.

Buttery Mixed Veggie Kabobs

Fennel-Apple Salad

Fennel-Apple Salad

Start To Finish: 30 minutes

  1 fennel bulb
  2 Granny Smith apples, cored and thinly
    sliced
  1 head radicchio, cored and thinly sliced
  1 teaspoon finely shredded orange peel
  ½ cup orange juice
  ¼ cup olive oil
  2 tablespoons lemon juice
  1 large shallot, finely chopped
  2 teaspoons Dijon-style mustard
  ¼ teaspoon salt
  ⅛ teaspoon freshly ground black pepper
  1 ounce Parmesan cheese

1. Trim and core fennel bulb. Thinly slice fennel. Finely chop some reserved fronds for garnish; set aside.

2. In a very large bowl, combine fennel, apple slices and radicchio.

3. In a screw-top jar, combine orange peel, orange juice, olive oil, lemon juice, shallot, mustard, salt and pepper. Pour dressing over fennel mixture. Toss to coat. Using vegetable peeler, shave Parmesan cheese into shards. If you like, cover and chill for up to 24 hours. If chilled, let stand for 30 minutes before serving. Garnish salad with Parmesan cheese shards and reserved fronds.
Makes 12 (1-cup) servings.

Nutrition facts per serving: 78 cal., 5 g fat, 2 mg chol., 117 mg sodium, 7 g carbo., 1 g fiber, 2 g pro.

Garden Slaw with Spicy Asian Dressing

Prep: 25 minutes Chill: 2 hours

  4 cups shredded green and/or red
    cabbage
  2 carrots, cut into julienne strips or
    coarsely shredded (about 1 cup)
  ¾ cup bite-size strips green, red, yellow
    and/or orange sweet pepper
  ½ cup coarsely chopped radishes
  ¼ cup snipped fresh cilantro leaves
  ¼ cup thinly sliced green onion (2)
    Spicy Asian Dressing (recipe below)

1. In a large bowl, combine cabbage, carrots, sweet pepper, radishes, cilantro and green onion. Pour the dressing over cabbage mixture. Toss to coat. Cover and chill for 2 to 24 hours before serving. Toss slaw before serving.
Makes 6 to 8 side-dish servings.

Spicy Asian Dressing: In a screw-top jar, combine 3 tablespoons rice vinegar or white wine vinegar, 3 tablespoons canola oil or vegetable oil, 2 to 3 tablespoons sugar, 1 tablespoon toasted sesame oil (optional), 2 teaspoons grated fresh ginger, ½ teaspoon dry mustard, ¼ teaspoon salt and ¼ teaspoon crushed red pepper. Cover and shake well to mix. Makes about ½ cup.

Easy Garden Slaw: Prepare the slaw as directed above, except substitute 5 cups packaged shredded cabbage with carrot (coleslaw mix) for the cabbage and carrot.

Nutrition facts per serving: 110 cal., 7 g fat, 0 mg chol., 126 mg sodium, 11 g carbo., 2 g fiber, 1 g pro.

**Garden Slaw with
Spicy Asian Dressing**

BLT Salad

Prep: 25 minutes Bake: 18 minutes Oven: 400°

8 ounces hickory-smoked bacon, cut into ½-inch pieces
4 cups torn romaine lettuce
  Homemade Croutons (recipe follows)
1 cup grape or cherry tomatoes, halved
½ cup bottled ranch salad dressing
½ to 1 teaspoon Kansas City-style or Montreal steak seasoning or dry rib or pork rub

1. In a 10-inch skillet, cook bacon until almost crisp. Remove bacon from skillet; discard fat. Drain bacon on paper towels. Set aside.

2. In a large salad bowl, combine romaine, Homemade Croutons and tomatoes. In a small bowl, combine salad dressing and steak seasoning. Drizzle over salad; gently toss to coat. **Makes 4 to 6 side-dish servings.**

BLT Salad

Homemade Croutons: Spread 2 cups cubed sourdough, Italian or French bread in a single layer in a shallow baking dish. Stir together 2 tablespoons olive oil, ¼ teaspoon freshly ground black pepper and ⅛ teaspoon kosher salt; pour over bread cubes, tossing to coat. Bake in a 350° oven for 10 minutes. Stir; bake for 8 to 10 minutes more or until crisp and brown. Makes 2 cups.

Make-Ahead Tip: Store cooled croutons in airtight container in refrigerator up to 3 days.

Nutrition facts per serving: 468 cal., 34 g fat, 38 mg chol., 908 mg sodium, 16 g carbo., 3 g fiber, 10 g pro.

Persimmon, Blood Orange & Pomegranate Salad

Start To Finish: 50 minutes

  Pine Nut-Persimmon Vinaigrette (recipe follows)
1 pomegranate
2 large ripe Fuyu persimmons
5 cups mesclun, arugula, baby arugula or mixed salad greens
3 green onions, thinly sliced
4 medium blood and/or navel oranges, peeled and thinly sliced*

1. Prepare Pine Nut-Persimmon Vinaigrette; set aside.

2. Score an X in the top of the pomegranate. Break apart into quarters. Working in a bowl of cool water, immerse each quarter and loosen the seeds from the white membrane with your fingers. Discard peel and membrane. Drain the seeds. Set aside.

3. Cut each persimmon in half; remove core. Slice into ¼- to ½-inch-thick slices.

4. In a large bowl, combine mesclun and green onions. Drizzle ½ cup of the vinaigrette over mesclun; toss to coat.

5. To serve, arrange mesclun mixture on six chilled salad plates. Arrange persimmons and oranges atop salad, tucking a few in and under leaves. Sprinkle the reserved pomegranate seeds on top. Pass the remaining vinaigrette. **Makes 6 side-dish servings.**

Pine Nut-Persimmon Vinaigrette: Remove core from one large ripe Fuyu persimmon; cut in half. Scoop out pulp (should have about ⅓ cup), discarding skin. Place pulp in a blender or food processor. Cover and blend or process until smooth. Add ⅓ cup extra virgin olive oil; ¼ cup red or white wine vinegar; 3 tablespoons toasted pine nuts; 1½ teaspoons finely shredded blood orange or orange peel; 2 tablespoons blood orange or orange juice; 1 tablespoon honey; half of a chopped large shallot; ½ teaspoon Dijon-style mustard; dash ground cinnamon or ground allspice, and dash freshly ground black pepper. Cover and blend or process until smooth. Makes about 1¼ cups.

Note: Short, squatty Fuyu persimmons are the ones to use in this salad. (The acorn-shape Hachiya must ripen to a gelatinous softness to be edible and are more often used in baking.) Fuyu persimmons are at peak season October through December. Substitute sliced and seeded papayas or mangoes if persimmons are unavailable.

Make-Ahead Tip: Vinaigrette can be made ahead and stored in an airtight container in the refrigerator up to 3 days.

***Tip:** If desired, substitute two pink or red grapefruit for the oranges. Or use a combination of oranges and grapefruit.

Quick Tip: Use 2 to 3 cups jarred, sectioned citrus fruit in place of the four oranges. Drain the fruit before adding it to the salad.

Nutrition facts per serving: 238 cal., 15 g fat, 0 mg chol., 18 mg sodium, 26 g carbo., 3 g fiber, 2 g pro.

Persimmon, Blood Orange
& Pomegranate Salad

Heirloom Tomato Salad with Blue
Cheese Dressing

Heirloom Tomato Salad with Blue Cheese Dressing

Start to finish: 30 minutes

Creamy Maytag Blue Cheese Dressing (recipe follows)
1¾ pounds assorted heirloom tomatoes, sliced; red or yellow tomatoes, sliced or cut into thin wedges; roma tomatoes, cut into wedges; yellow pear tomatoes, halved; and/or cherry tomatoes, halved
Sea salt or coarse salt
Freshly ground black pepper
1 medium cucumber, halved lengthwise, seeded and coarsely chopped
½ of a small red onion, thinly sliced and separated into rings
¼ cup loosely packed small basil leaves or shredded basil leaves
Snipped fresh chives (optional)

1. Prepare blue cheese dressing. Cover; store in refrigerator while preparing salad.

2. Arrange tomatoes on six individual salad plates. Sprinkle with salt and black pepper. Top with cucumber and onion. Drizzle with dressing. Top with basil leaves. Garnish with chives, if you like. Serve immediately. Makes 6 side-dish salads.

Creamy Maytag Blue Cheese Dressing: In a blender or food processor, combine ⅓ cup mayonnaise or salad dressing; ⅓ cup plain yogurt or dairy sour cream; ¼ cup crumbled blue cheese, other blue cheese, goat cheese or feta cheese (1 ounce); 2 to 3 tablespoons buttermilk or milk; 1 teaspoon lemon juice; and ½ teaspoon minced garlic or ¼ teaspoon garlic powder. Cover; blend or process until smooth. Transfer mixture to a small bowl; stir in ¼ cup crumbled blue cheese, goat cheese or feta cheese (1 ounce) and 1 tablespoon snipped fresh chives (optional). Serve immediately or cover and store in refrigerator for up to 1 week. If necessary, stir in additional buttermilk or milk to make a dressing of desired consistency. Makes about 1 cup.

Nutrition facts per serving: 171 cal., 14 g fat, 14 mg chol., 316 mg sodium, 9 g carbo., 2 g fiber, 5 g pro.

Tomato Salad with Queso Fresco, Pan-Roasted Green Onions & Guajillo Chile Dressing

This recipe comes from chef Rick Bayless of Frontera Grill in Chicago. He describes this delicious salad as a way of recasting salsa ingredients, with smoky dried guajillo chiles standing in for fresh jalapeño or serrano chiles. He only makes this salad in the summer, when a rainbow of ripe, juicy tomatoes is available.

Prep: 25 minutes   Cook: 5 minutes   Cool: 5 minutes

¾ cup olive oil
2 medium dried guajillo or New Mexico chile peppers, stemmed and seeded (about ½ ounce) (see Tip, page 71)
2 cloves garlic, cut into quarters
¼ cup sherry vinegar or white wine vinegar
¾ teaspoon salt
6 green onions, trimmed (roots and wilted leaves removed)
2 large ripe tomatoes, cored and sliced ¼-inch thick (about 1¼ pounds)
Sea salt
½ cup crumbled queso fresco (Mexican farmer cheese), goat cheese, blue cheese or shredded Monterey Jack cheese (2 ounces)

1. For chile dressing: In a medium skillet, heat oil over medium heat. When warm, add chiles and garlic. Stir, turning constantly, about 30 seconds or until insides of chiles have lightened in color and smell toasty. Remove skillet from the heat. Transfer chiles to a blender, leaving oil and garlic in the skillet to cool for 5 to 10 minutes.

2. Add vinegar and ¾ teaspoon salt to blender. Cover; blend for 30 seconds. When oil and garlic are cool, add to blender. (Set skillet aside without washing.) Cover; blend chile mixture for 1 to 2 minutes more or until nearly smooth. Transfer dressing to a screw-top jar. Season to taste, if you like. Cover; set aside.

3. Return same skillet to medium heat, adding a little oil if necessary. Lay green onions in skillet. Cook, turning often, about 4 minutes or until onions are wilted and browned in places. Remove from skillet; cut crosswise into ¼-inch slices.

4. To serve, arrange sliced tomatoes on four salad plates. Sprinkle tomatoes with additional sea salt. Top with green onion slices. Shake chile dressing to combine thoroughly; drizzle some of the dressing over tomatoes. (Cover and store remaining dressing in refrigerator.) Sprinkle salad with cheese. **Makes 4 servings.**

Nutrition facts per serving: 430 cal., 42 g fat, 5 mg chol., 67 mg sodium, 11 g carbo., 3 g fiber, 7 g pro.

Tomato Salad with Queso Fresco, Pan-Roasted Green Onions & Guajillo Chile Dressing

Goat Cheese & Roasted Beet Salad with Lemon Vinaigrette

Goat Cheese & Roasted Beet Salad with Lemon Vinaigrette

Prep: 20 minutes Roast: 40 minutes
Broil: 2 minutes Oven: 425°

 1 pound red, yellow and/or candy-
  striped beets, rinsed and trimmed
 2 tablespoons extra virgin olive oil
 9 cups arugula, watercress, baby spinach
  and/or mesclun
 1 8-ounce log fresh goat cheese
 1/3 cup broken walnuts, toasted
  Lemon Vinaigrette (recipe follows)

1. Cut beets in half. Place beets in a single layer in a shallow baking pan. Drizzle with the olive oil; toss to coat. Cover with foil and roast in a 425° oven for 25 minutes. Uncover and roast 15 minutes more or until fork-tender. Cool; peel and slice 1/4 inch thick. Set aside.

2. Arrange greens on four salad plates. Top with beets and crumbled goat cheese. Drizzle with half of the Lemon Vinaigrette. Sprinkle with walnuts. Serve immediately. Pass remaining vinaigrette.
Makes 4 side-dish servings.

Lemon Vinaigrette: In a screw-top jar, combine 1/3 cup extra virgin olive oil; 1/2 teaspoon finely shredded lemon peel; 1/4 cup lemon juice; 1 tablespoon snipped fresh tarragon or 1/2 teaspoon dried tarragon, crushed; 1 tablespoon honey; 1 teaspoon Dijon-style mustard; 1/4 teaspoon salt; and 1/8 teaspoon ground black pepper. Cover and shake well. Serve immediately or cover and store in refrigerator for up to 3 days if using fresh herbs. If using dried herbs, store covered in refrigerator for up to 1 week. Shake before serving. Makes about 2/3 cup.

Nutrition facts per serving: 516 cal., 43 g fat, 26 mg chol., 481 mg sodium, 20 g carbo., 5 g fiber, 15 g pro.

Roasted Beet Salad

Prep: 20 minutes Roast: 55 minutes Oven: 425°

 8 small fresh beets, 2 to 21/2 inches in
  diameter (about 11/2 pounds)
 2 tablespoons olive oil
 1/2 teaspoon salt
 1/4 teaspoon ground black pepper
 1/3 cup olive oil
 3 tablespoons frozen orange juice
  concentrate, thawed
 2 tablespoons snipped fresh tarragon or
  1 teaspoon dried tarragon, crushed
 1/4 teaspoon salt
 1/8 teaspoon ground black pepper
 6 cups torn mixed salad greens
 1/2 cup coarsely chopped walnuts, toasted
  (optional)
  Orange sections (optional)

1. Thoroughly wash beets, but avoid using a brush because beets have very thin skins. Cut off roots and all but 1 inch of the stems. Place the beets in a 2-quart baking dish. Drizzle with 2 tablespoons olive oil. Sprinkle with 1/2 teaspoon salt and 1/4 teaspoon black pepper. Roast, uncovered, in a 425° oven for 55 to 60 minutes or until beets are tender. (A small knife or toothpick should slip in easily.) Let the beets stand until cool enough to handle, then peel the beets by slipping off the skins. Cut beets into small wedges; transfer to a medium bowl.

2. For dressing: In a screw-top jar, combine 1/3 cup olive oil, orange juice concentrate, tarragon, the 1/4 teaspoon salt and 1/8 teaspoon black pepper. Cover and shake well. Pour dressing over beets. Let stand for 20 minutes to allow beets to soak up flavor.

3. To serve, remove beets from dressing using a slotted spoon; reserve dressing. Toss greens with reserved dressing. Divide greens among six salad plates; top with beet wedges. Sprinkle each serving with nuts, if you like. Garnish with orange slices, if you like. **Makes 6 servings.**

Nutrition facts per serving: 198 cal., 17 g fat, 0 mg chol., 353 mg sodium, 12 g carbo., 3 g fiber, 2 g pro.

Roasted Beet Salad

Spiced Pecan Apple Salad

Winter Orange Salad

Start To Finish: 15 minutes

- 1 6-ounce package fresh baby spinach or 8 cups fresh baby spinach and/or assorted torn greens
- 2 oranges or 3 tangerines, peeled, seeded and sectioned
- ½ of a small red onion, thinly sliced and separated into rings
- ⅓ cup dried cranberries
  Walnut Croutons or Pecan Croutons (recipes follow)
  Bottled Italian salad dressing or your favorite vinaigrette

1. Place spinach on a large serving platter or divide among individual salad plates. Cut orange sections into bite-size pieces. Arrange oranges, onion, cranberries and Walnut Croutons on spinach. Drizzle dressing over spinach mixture. **Makes 6 side-dish servings.**

Walnut Croutons: In a 10-inch skillet, melt 2 teaspoons butter over medium heat. Stir in ⅔ cup English walnut halves or large pieces. Cook for 2 to 3 minutes or until browned and toasted, stirring occasionally. Watch carefully to avoid overbrowning nuts. Cool to room temperature. Store in a tightly covered container. Add to salad just before serving. Makes ⅔ cup.

Nutrition facts per serving: 232 cal., 18 g fat, 3 mg chol., 519 mg sodium, 17 g carbo., 3 g fiber, 3 g pro.

Pecan Croutons: Lightly coat a 10-inch skillet with nonstick cooking spray. Add ¼ cup sugar. Heat over medium-high heat until sugar begins to melt, shaking skillet occasionally to heat sugar evenly. Reduce heat to low and cook until sugar is nearly all melted. Add ⅔ cup pecan halves or large pieces and cook over low heat for 2 to 3 minutes more or until browned and glazed, stirring constantly. Watch carefully to avoid overbrowning nuts. Spread on a piece of foil coated with cooking spray, separating nuts. Cool to room temperature. Store in a tightly covered container. Add to salad just before serving. Makes ⅔ cup.

Spiced Pecan Apple Salad

Prep: 15 minutes Bake: 10 minutes Oven: 350°

- 1⅔ cups pecan pieces
- 3 tablespoons butter
- 1 teaspoon ground cinnamon
- ½ teaspoon salt
- ¼ teaspoon cayenne pepper
- ½ cup extra virgin olive oil or salad oil
- 2 tablespoons sherry wine vinegar
- 1 tablespoon Dijon-style mustard
- 1 large Red Delicious apple
- 2 teaspoons lemon juice
- 1 head red leaf lettuce, torn into bite-size pieces
- 1 cup crumbled feta cheese (8 ounces)
  Butterhead lettuce (Bibb or Boston) leaves
  Cracked black pepper (optional)

1. For pecans: Line a 15x10x1-inch baking pan with foil. Spread pecans in an even layer. In a small saucepan, heat and stir butter, cinnamon, salt and cayenne pepper over low heat until melted. Drizzle butter mixture over pecans; stir gently to coat the nuts. Bake in a 350° oven for 10 to 15 minutes or until pecans are golden brown and aromatic. Cool in pan on a wire rack.

2. For vinaigrette: In a screw-top jar, combine oil, vinegar and mustard. Cover and shake well; set aside.

3. Core and chop the apple; place in a large bowl. Sprinkle lemon juice over apple; stir gently to coat the pieces. Add leaf lettuce and feta cheese to apple in bowl; toss to combine. Shake vinaigrette; drizzle vinaigrette over salad. Toss to coat. Line bowls with Butterhead lettuce leaves. Top with apple mixture. Top with spiced pecans and sprinkle with cracked black pepper, if you like. Serve immediately. **Makes 8 to 10 servings.**

Nutrition facts per serving: 385 cal., 38 g fat, 28 mg chol., 442 mg sodium, 8 g carbo., 3 g fiber, 6 g pro.

Winter Orange Salad

Italian Rice Salad

Prep: 30 minutes Chill: 1 hour

    Garlic Vinaigrette (recipe follows)
3 cups cooked, slightly warm basmati
    rice*
1 cup chopped red, green and/or orange
    sweet pepper
1 6-ounce jar quartered marinated
    artichoke hearts, drained
⅓ cup chopped red onion
¼ cup raisins
2 tablespoons drained capers
    Organic mixed salad greens, mesclun
    or torn romaine
    Fresh basil leaves (optional)

1. Prepare the Garlic Vinaigrette; set aside.

2. In a large bowl, combine rice, sweet pepper, artichokes, red onion, raisins and capers. Stir vinaigrette and drizzle over rice mixture; toss gently to coat. Cover and chill for at least 1 hour or up to 24 hours. Serve rice salad on a bed of salad greens. If you like, garnish with basil. **Makes 6 servings.**

Garlic Vinaigrette: In a small bowl, whisk together ½ cup canola oil or safflower oil; ⅓ cup snipped fresh Italian (flat-leaf) parsley; ¼ cup white wine vinegar; 3 tablespoons snipped fresh dill or 2 teaspoons dried dillweed; 1 teaspoon sea salt; 1 teaspoon freshly ground black pepper; 1 teaspoon snipped fresh basil or ¼ teaspoon dried basil, crushed; 1 teaspoon snipped fresh oregano or ¼ teaspoon dried oregano, crushed; and 2 cloves garlic, minced. Use immediately or cover and store in the refrigerator for up to 3 days. Makes about ¾ cup.

*Tip: To cook rice, place 1 cup uncooked basmati or long grain white rice in a fine-mesh sieve. Run cool water over the rice for several minutes; drain well. In a medium saucepan, bring 2 cups water to boiling. Slowly add rice and return to boiling; reduce heat. Simmer, covered, for 15 to 20 minutes or until liquid is absorbed and rice is tender. Remove from heat and let cool about 15 minutes. Makes 3 cups.

Nutrition facts per serving: 325 cal., 20 g fat, 0 mg chol., 447 mg sodium, 33 g carbo., 2 g fiber, 4 g pro.

Spicy Rice & Red Bean Salad

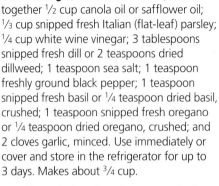

Prep: 30 minutes Chill: 4 hours
Stand: 30 minutes

3 tablespoons lemon juice or apple cider
    vinegar
3 tablespoons olive oil, canola oil or
    salad oil
2 to 3 teaspoons chili powder
1 teaspoon ground cumin
½ to 1 teaspoon bottled hot pepper
    sauce
½ teaspoon all-purpose seasoning blend
¼ teaspoon salt
⅛ teaspoon garlic powder
¼ teaspoon freshly ground black pepper
2 cups cooked brown rice or basmati
    rice, chilled (about ¾ cup uncooked)
1 15-ounce can red beans, rinsed and
    drained
1 large tomato, seeded and chopped
½ cup chopped red sweet pepper
½ cup chopped red onion
¼ cup snipped fresh cilantro or parsley
1 fresh jalapeño chile pepper, seeded
    and finely chopped (see Tip,
    page 71)
    Toasted pita bread wedges (optional)

1. For dressing: In a screw-top jar, combine lemon juice, oil, chili powder, cumin, pepper sauce, all-purpose seasoning, salt, garlic powder and black pepper. Cover and shake well. Set aside.

2. In a large bowl, combine rice, beans, tomato, sweet pepper, onion, cilantro and jalapeño. Shake dressing; pour dressing over the rice mixture. Toss lightly to coat. Cover and chill for 4 to 24 hours. Let salad stand at room temperature 30 minutes before serving. Serve with pita wedges, if you like. **Makes 8 side-dish servings.**

Nutrition facts per serving: 159 cal., 6 g fat, 0 mg chol., 386 mg sodium, 23 g carbo., 5 g fiber, 4 g pro.

Italian Rice Salad

Spicy Rice & Red Bean Salad

White-Chocolate Cheesecake
with Triple-Raspberry Sauce,
page 167

DESSERTS

Chocolate Mocha Gooey
Butter Cake

Chocolate Mocha Gooey Butter Cake

Prep: 20 minutes Bake: 50 minutes Oven: 350°

  1 egg, lightly beaten
  ½ cup butter, melted and cooled
  1 2-layer-size package chocolate cake mix
  1 8-ounce package cream cheese, softened
  2 eggs
  1 16-ounce package powdered sugar
  ½ cup butter, melted and cooled
  ¼ cup chocolate fudge topping
  2 tablespoons very strong brewed coffee or espresso
  1 teaspoon vanilla
    Powdered sugar (optional)

1. Grease a 13x9x2-inch baking pan; set aside.

2. For crust: In a medium bowl, stir together one egg and ½ cup melted butter. Stir in dry cake mix until combined (may need to work together by hand; mixture will be thick). Press evenly into the bottom of prepared pan. Bake in 350° oven for 15 minutes.

3. Meanwhile, for topping: In a large mixing bowl, beat cream cheese with an electric mixer until fluffy. Add two eggs, one at a time, beating on low speed after each addition just until combined. Gradually add 16 ounces powdered sugar, 1 cup at a time, beating on low speed until smooth. Slowly add ½ cup melted butter, chocolate topping, coffee and vanilla, continuing to beat on low speed until just combined. Pour batter over baked crust.

4. Bake in a 350° oven for 35 minutes more (center will not appear to be set). Cool completely in pan on a wire rack before serving. If you like, sprinkle with additional powdered sugar. Cut into bars.
Makes 24 bars.

Nutrition facts per bar: 278 cal., 13 g fat, 57 mg chol., 259 mg sodium, 39 g carbo., 1 g fiber, 3 g pro.

Whimsical German Chocolate-Nut Cake

Prep: 30 minutes Bake: 30 minutes Oven: 350°

  1½ cups broken pecans
  ¾ cup sugar
  ⅓ cup coarsely chopped sweet baking chocolate
  ¼ cup Dutch-process or unsweetened cocoa powder
  1 teaspoon baking powder
  ¼ teaspoon baking soda
  5 eggs
  1½ teaspoons vanilla
    Toasted Coconut-Pecan Caramel Sauce (recipe follows)

1. Grease a 9x1½-inch round cake pan; line bottom with waxed paper. Grease waxed paper; set pan aside. In a blender or food processor, combine pecans, sugar, chopped chocolate, cocoa powder, baking powder and baking soda. Cover; blend or process until nuts are ground. Add eggs and vanilla. Blend or process until nearly smooth.

2. Spread nut mixture in the prepared pan. Bake in a 350° oven about 30 minutes or until a toothpick inserted near center of cake comes out clean.

3. Remove from oven. Cool in pan on wire rack for 10 minutes. Remove cake from pan; cool completely on wire rack.

4. To serve, cut into 16 wedges. Place one wedge on each dessert plate, drizzle with sauce. Place another wedge on top at a different angle. Drizzle with more sauce.
Makes 8 servings.

Toasted Coconut-Pecan Caramel Sauce:
Spread ½ cup flaked coconut and ½ cup chopped pecans in a thin layer in a shallow baking pan. Bake in a 350° oven for 6 to 8 minutes or until the coconut is toasted and the nuts are golden brown, stirring once or twice. Remove from oven. In a medium bowl, stir together one 12.25-ounce jar caramel ice cream topping (room temperature), coconut and pecans. Serve immediately or heat slightly in microwave before serving.
Makes about 1½ cups.

Nutrition facts per serving: 526 cal., 28 g fat, 133 mg chol., 269 mg sodium, 63 g carbo., 4 g fiber, 8 g pro.

Whimsical German Chocolate-Nut Cake

Chocolate Picnic Cake

Lyndy Ireland, owner of Triangle Ranch Bed and Breakfast in South Dakota, says this is her family's version of no-egg Crazy Cake or Sheepherder's Cake. They serve it warm with vanilla ice cream and drizzled with Grandma Betty's Chocolate Sauce.

Prep: 20 minutes Bake: 30 minutes Oven: 350°

2¼ cups all-purpose flour
1½ cups sugar
 ⅓ cup unsweetened cocoa powder
1½ teaspoons baking soda
 ½ teaspoon salt
1½ cups water or strong brewed coffee, cooled
 ½ cup canola oil or cooking oil
4½ teaspoons vinegar
1½ teaspoons vanilla
   Picnic Topping (recipe follows)
   Vanilla ice cream
   Grandma Betty's Chocolate Sauce (recipe follows)

1. Grease and flour a 13x9x2-inch baking pan; set aside. In a large mixing bowl, stir together flour, sugar, cocoa powder, baking soda and salt. Stir in the water, oil, vinegar and vanilla. Beat mixture with a fork until smooth. Pour into prepared pan. Sprinkle with Picnic Topping.

2. Bake in a 350° oven for 30 to 40 minutes or until a wooden toothpick inserted near the center comes out clean. Cool cake slightly in pan on a wire rack. Serve warm with a scoop of vanilla ice cream and drizzle with Grandma Betty's Chocolate Sauce. **Makes 12 servings.**

Picnic Topping: In a bowl, combine 1 cup chopped walnuts, 1 cup semisweet chocolate pieces and ½ cup sugar.

Grandma Betty's Chocolate Sauce: In heavy small saucepan, combine 1½ cups sugar, 3 tablespoons unsweetened cocoa powder and a dash of salt. Stir in ½ cup whipping cream or heavy cream and ¼ cup milk. Bring to a gentle boil, stirring constantly, then reduce heat. Cook and stir for 2 minutes. Remove from heat. Stir in 1 teaspoon vanilla. Transfer to bowl; cover surface with plastic wrap. Cool to room temperature before using. Makes about 1⅔ cups.

Nutrition facts per serving: 722 cal., 32 g fat, 46 mg chol., 334 mg sodium, 107 g carbo., 4 g fiber, 8 g pro.

Heavenly Devil's Food Cake

Prep: 25 minutes Stand: 30 minutes
Bake: 30 minutes Oven: 350°

 ½ cup unsalted butter
 3 eggs
2½ cups all-purpose flour
 ½ cup unsweetened cocoa powder or Dutch-process cocoa powder
1½ teaspoon baking soda
 ¼ teaspoon salt
 1 cup granulated sugar
 1 cup packed brown sugar
 2 teaspoons vanilla
 1 cup buttermilk or sour milk*
 ½ cup boiling water
   Whipped cream (optional)
   Red raspberries or small whole strawberries (optional)

1. Allow butter and eggs to stand at room temperature for 30 minutes. Meanwhile, grease a 13x9x2-inch baking pan. In a medium bowl, stir together flour, cocoa powder, baking soda and salt. Set aside.

2. In a large mixing bowl, beat butter with an electric mixer on medium to high speed for 30 seconds. Add granulated sugar, brown sugar and vanilla. Add eggs, one at a time, beating well after each addition. Alternately add flour mixture and buttermilk to butter mixture, beating on low speed after each addition just until combined. Add the boiling water; beat until smooth. Pour batter into prepared pan.

3. Bake in a 350° oven for 30 to 35 minutes or until a wooden toothpick inserted near center comes out clean. Cool thoroughly in pan on wire rack.

4. Serve with whipped cream and raspberries, if you like, or your favorite flavor ice cream. Or frost with desired cake frosting. **Makes 12 to 16 servings.**

*Note: If you don't have buttermilk on hand when preparing baked goods, substitute sour milk in the same amount. For each cup of sour milk needed, place 1 tablespoon lemon juice or vinegar in a glass measuring cup. Add enough milk to make 1 cup total liquid; stir. Let mixture stand for 5 minutes before using.

Nutrition facts per serving: 340 cal., 10 g fat, 74 mg chol., 254 mg sodium, 57 g carbo., 1 g fiber, 6 g pro.

Heavenly Devil's Food Cake

Chocolate Picnic Cake

Fabulous Red Velvet Cake

Fabulous Red Velvet Cake

Prep: 50 minutes Bake: 25 minutes
Cool: 10 minutes Oven: 350°

- 1 2-layer-size package German chocolate cake mix
- 1 8-ounce container dairy sour cream
- 3/4 cup water
- 1/3 cup cooking oil
- 3 eggs
- 1 1-ounce bottle red food coloring (2 tablespoons)
- White Chocolate-Cream Cheese Frosting (recipe follows)
- 1 1/2 cups coconut shards, purchased coconut chips or flaked coconut, toasted
- Sugared cranberries (optional)

1. Grease and flour two 9x1 1/2-inch round cake pans or two 8x8x2-inch square baking pans or coat with nonstick spray for baking; set aside.

2. In a large mixing bowl, beat cake mix, sour cream, the water, oil, eggs and food coloring with an electric mixer on low speed for 30 seconds. Scrape down sides of bowl. Beat mixture on medium speed for 2 minutes more, scraping down the sides again if needed. Spread batter evenly into prepared pans. Bake in a 350° oven for 25 to 30 minutes for 9-inch pans or 30 to 35 minutes for square pans or until a toothpick inserted near centers comes out clean. Cool cakes in pans on wire racks for 10 minutes. Remove cakes from pans. Cool thoroughly on wire racks.

3. Spread White Chocolate-Cream Cheese Frosting between layers and over sides and top of cake. Sprinkle with coconut. Cover and chill cake. **Makes 12 to 16 servings.**

White Chocolate-Cream Cheese Frosting: In a small saucepan, melt 4 ounces white baking chocolate over low heat, stirring frequently; cool 10 minutes. In a very large mixing bowl, beat 1/3 cup butter, softened; half of an 8-ounce package cream cheese, softened; and 1 1/2 teaspoons vanilla with an electric mixer on medium speed for 30 seconds

or until smooth. Gradually beat in 2 cups powdered sugar. Beat in 1 tablespoon milk. Gradually beat in an additional 2 cups powdered sugar. Beat in melted white chocolate until well combined. If needed, beat in additional milk, 1 teaspoon at a time, to make frosting spreading consistency. Makes about 2 2/3 cups.

Nutrition facts per serving: 648 cal., 31 g fat, 87 mg chol., 463 mg sodium, 89 g carbo., 1 g fiber, 7 g pro.

Our Best-Ever Chocolate Cake

Prep: 50 minutes Stand: 30 minutes
Bake: 35 minutes Cool: 10 minutes Oven: 350°

- 3/4 cup butter
- 3 eggs
- 2 cups all-purpose flour
- 3/4 cup unsweetened cocoa powder
- 1 teaspoon baking soda
- 3/4 teaspoon baking powder
- 1/2 teaspoon salt
- 2 cups sugar
- 2 teaspoons vanilla
- 1 1/2 cups milk
- Chocolate-Sour Cream Frosting (recipe follows)

1. Allow butter and eggs to stand at room temperature for 30 minutes. Meanwhile, lightly grease bottoms of two 8x8x2-inch square or 9x1 1/2-inch round cake pans. Line bottom of pans with waxed paper. Grease and lightly flour waxed paper and sides of pans. Or grease one 13x9x2-inch baking pan. Set pan(s) aside.

2. In a mixing bowl, stir together the flour, cocoa powder, baking soda, baking powder and salt; set aside.

3. In a large mixing bowl, beat butter with an electric mixer on medium to high speed for 30 seconds. Add sugar, about 1/4 cup at a time, beating on medium speed until well combined (3 to 4 minutes). Scrape sides of bowl; continue beating on medium speed for 2 minutes. Add eggs, one at a time, beating after each addition. Beat in vanilla.

4. Alternately add flour mixture and milk to beaten mixture, beating on low speed just until combined after each addition. Beat on medium to high speed for 20 seconds more. Spread batter evenly in prepared pan(s).

5. Bake in a 350° oven for 35 to 40 minutes for 8-inch pans and the 13x9x2-inch pan, 30 to 35 minutes for 9-inch pans or until a wooden toothpick inserted in the center(s) comes out clean. Cool cake layers in pans for 10 minutes. Remove from pans. Peel off waxed paper. Cool on wire racks. Or place 13x9x2-inch cake in pan on a wire rack; cool thoroughly. Frost with Chocolate-Sour Cream Frosting. **Makes 12 to 16 servings.**

Chocolate-Sour Cream Frosting: In a large saucepan, melt one 12-ounce package (2 cups) semisweet chocolate pieces and 1/2 cup butter over low heat, stirring frequently. Cool for 5 minutes. Stir in one 8-ounce carton dairy sour cream. Gradually add 4 1/2 to 5 cups powdered sugar (about 1 pound), beating with an electric mixer until smooth. This frosts tops and sides of two 8- or 9-inch cake layers. (Halve recipe to frost top of a 13x9x2-inch cake.) Cover; store in refrigerator.

Nutrition facts per serving: 729 cal., 33 g fat, 115 mg chol., 394 mg sodium, 107 g carbo., 3 g fiber, 9 g pro.

Our Best-Ever Chocolate Cake

Sour Cream-Walnut Date Bundt Cake with Tangerine Glaze

Prep: 25 minutes Bake: 45 minutes
Stand: 10 minutes Oven: 350°

  1/3 cup all-purpose flour
  3 tablespoons packed brown sugar
  3 tablespoons butter or margarine
  2/3 cup finely snipped pitted dates
  1/2 cup finely chopped walnuts or pecans
  1 yellow cake mix
  1 8-ounce carton dairy sour cream
  3/4 cup water
  3 eggs
  1/2 cup cooking oil
  3/4 teaspoon ground cardamom or ground
    nutmeg
    Tangerine Glaze (recipe follows)

1. Grease and flour a 10-inch fluted tube pan (Bundt); set aside.

2. For filling: In a small bowl, stir together flour and brown sugar. Cut in the butter until crumbly. Stir in dates and walnuts; set aside.

3. For batter: In a large mixing bowl, beat cake mix, sour cream, the water, eggs, oil and cardamom with an electric mixer on low speed until moistened. Beat for 2 minutes at medium speed. Pour half of the batter into prepared pan. Sprinkle the filling over batter in pan. Pour the remaining batter over filling, spreading evenly.

4. Bake in a 350° oven for 45 to 55 minutes or until a wooden toothpick inserted in the center(s) of cake comes out clean. Meanwhile, prepare Tangerine Glaze.

5. When the cake is done, do not remove from the pan. Place on a wire rack. Prick holes over the cake's surface with tines of a fork. Slowly spoon about half of the Tangerine Glaze over hot cake. Let stand for 10 minutes, allowing the glaze to soak in. Loosen sides. Invert onto a serving platter; remove the pan. Prick holes in the top of the cake with tines of fork. Slowly spoon the remaining Tangerine Glaze over cake. Cool thoroughly. **Makes 1 cake (12 servings).**

Tangerine Glaze: In a small saucepan, combine 1/2 cup granulated sugar, 1/2 cup tangerine or orange juice, and 2 tablespoons butter or margarine. Bring to boiling; reduce heat. Simmer, uncovered, for 3 minutes, stirring frequently. Remove from heat; set aside.

Nutrition facts per serving: 472 cal., 25 g fat, 74 mg chol., 344 mg sodium, 60 g carbo., 1 g fiber, 6 g pro.

Poppy Seed Torte

Prep: 45 minutes Stand: 1 hour Bake: 25 minutes
Cool: 1 hour Chill: 2 hours Oven: 375°

  1/3 cup poppy seeds (about 1 1/2 ounces)
  3/4 cup milk
  1 1/2 teaspoons vanilla
  5 eggs
  3/4 cup butter
  1 3/4 cups all-purpose flour
  1 teaspoon baking powder
  1 teaspoon salt
  1/2 cup sugar
  1 tablespoon cornstarch
  1 1/2 cups milk
  1 teaspoon vanilla
  1 1/2 cups sugar
  1 1/2 cups whipping cream
  1/2 cup sugar

1. In a small bowl, soak poppy seeds in 3/4 cup milk and 1 1/2 teaspoons vanilla for 1 hour. Meanwhile, separate eggs. Let butter and egg whites stand at room temperature for 30 minutes. Set egg yolks aside. Grease the bottoms of two 8x1 1/2- or 9x1 1/2-inch round cake pans. Line pans with waxed paper; grease and lightly flour. Set pans aside. In a medium bowl, combine flour, baking powder and salt; set aside.

2. For filling: In a heavy medium saucepan, combine 1/2 cup sugar and the cornstarch. Gradually stir in 1 1/2 cups milk and the egg yolks. Cook and stir over medium-high heat until mixture is thickened and bubbly. Cook and stir for 2 minutes more. Stir in 1 teaspoon vanilla. Pour filling into a bowl. Cover the surface with clear plastic wrap. Chill until completely cooled. Do not stir.

3. For cake: In a large mixing bowl, beat butter with an electric mixer on medium speed for 30 seconds. Gradually add 1 1/2 cups sugar to butter, about 2 tablespoons at a time, beating on medium to high speed until sugar is nearly dissolved. Alternately add flour mixture and poppy seed mixture to butter mixture, beating on low to medium speed after each addition just until combined. Thoroughly wash beaters.

4. In another large mixing bowl, beat egg whites with an electric mixer until stiff peaks form (tips stand straight). Gently fold beaten egg whites into batter. Evenly divide batter between prepared cake pans. Bake in a 375° oven for 30 to 35 minutes for 8-inch pans or 25 to 30 minutes for 9-inch pans or until a wood toothpick inserted near the centers of the layers comes out clean.

5. Cool cakes in pans on wire racks for 10 minutes. Remove cakes from pans. Cool thoroughly on wire racks.

6. To assemble, split each cake layer horizontally in half. Place one cake layer, cut side up, on a serving plate. Spread with one-third of the filling. Top with second cake layer, rounded side up. Spread with one-third of the filling. Top with one more cake layer, cut side up; spread with remaining filling. Top with remaining cake layer, rounded side up.

7. For frosting: In a chilled large mixing bowl, beat whipping cream and 1/2 cup sugar with chilled beaters of an electric mixer until soft peaks form. Spread top and sides of cake with frosting. Chill up to 2 hours, or until ready to serve. **Makes 12 servings.**

Nutrition facts per serving: 512 cal., 27 g fat, 163 mg chol., 356 mg sodium, 61 g carbo., 1 g fiber, 7 g pro.

Sour Cream-Walnut Date Bundt Cake
with Tangerine Glaze

Sweet Potato Cranberry Cake

Sweet Potato Cranberry Cake

Prep: 35 minutes Bake: 55 minutes
Cool: 15 minutes Oven: 350°

  3 cups all-purpose flour
  2 tablespoons ground cinnamon
  1 tablespoon baking powder
  1 tablespoon baking soda
1½ teaspoons ground ginger
  1 teaspoon salt
  ½ teaspoon ground cloves
  ½ teaspoon ground nutmeg
  2 cups cooked, mashed plain sweet
    potatoes*
1½ cups cooking oil
  4 eggs
1½ teaspoons vanilla
1½ cups sugar
  1 cup chopped walnuts and/or pecans,
    toasted
  ¾ cup chopped cranberries
  4 ounces semisweet chocolate, melted
    and cooled slightly
    Powdered sugar (optional)

1. Grease and lightly flour a 10-inch fluted tube pan. In a large bowl, combine flour, cinnamon, baking powder, baking soda, ginger, salt, cloves and nutmeg. Set aside.

2. In a very large bowl, beat sweet potatoes and oil with an electric mixer on medium speed until combined. Beat in eggs and vanilla until well combined. Beat in sugar. Add flour mixture, beating until combined. Fold in walnuts and cranberries.

3. Transfer one-third (about 2½ cups) of the batter to a large bowl; stir in melted chocolate. Spoon half of the remaining plain batter into the prepared tube pan. Spoon chocolate batter atop batter in pan. Spoon remaining plain batter atop chocolate batter. Using a thin metal spatula, swirl batter slightly to create a marbled appearance.

4. Bake in a 350° oven for 55 to 65 minutes or until a wooden skewer inserted in center of cake comes out clean. Cool cake in pan on a wire rack for 15 minutes; invert cake onto a wire rack. Cool completely.

5. If desired, sprinkle top of cake with powdered sugar just before serving. **Makes 16 servings.**

Tip: This cake makes a great morning coffee cake. If serving it in the morning, make it the day before. Wrap and store the cooled cake overnight for easier slicing.

*Note: For 2 cups mashed, plain sweet potatoes, peel 1 pound sweet potatoes. Cut into 2- to 3-inch pieces. Cook potato pieces, covered, in enough boiling water to cover for 20 to 25 minutes or until potatoes are tender. Drain well. Mash with a potato masher or beat with an electric mixer until smooth.

Nutrition facts per serving: 478 cal., 29 g fat, 53 mg chol., 456 mg sodium, 51 g carbo., 3 g fiber, 4 g pro.

Fresh Apple Cake

Prep: 30 minutes Bake: 50 minutes Cool: 1 hour
Oven: 350°

  3 cups all-purpose flour
  2 cups sugar
  1 teaspoon baking soda
  1 teaspoon salt
  1 teaspoon ground cinnamon
  2 eggs, lightly beaten
1¼ cups canola oil or cooking oil
  2 teaspoons vanilla
  3 medium Granny Smith apples, peeled
    and chopped (3 cups)
  1 cup chopped pecans or walnuts,
    toasted
    Sweetened whipped cream (optional)
    Apple slices (optional)

1. Grease a 13x9x2-inch baking pan; set aside. In a very large bowl, combine flour, sugar, baking soda, salt and cinnamon; make a well in center of dry mixture and set aside.

2. In a medium bowl, combine eggs, oil and vanilla; stir in apples and nuts. Add egg mixture to flour mixture, stirring just until moistened (batter will be thick). Spread batter in prepared pan.

3. Bake in a 350° oven for 50 to 55 minutes or until a toothpick inserted in center comes out clean. Cool in pan on a wire rack for at least 1 hour. Serve slightly warm or at room temperature. If you like, top each serving with sweetened whipped cream and an apple slice. **Makes 20 servings.**

Nutrition facts per serving: 324 cal., 18 g fat, 21 mg chol., 187 mg sodium, 38 g carbo., 2 g fiber, 3 g pro.

Fresh Apple Cake

Pretty Pastel Angel Cake

Pretty Pastel Angel Cake

Prep: 20 minutes   Bake: according to package

 1 16-ounce package angel food cake mix
1/2 of a 0.16- to 0.23-ounce envelope dry
    unsweetened soft drink mix, such as
    tropical punch, pink lemonade, black
    cherry or your favorite flavor (about
    3/4 teaspoon)
 4 cups powdered sugar
 3 tablespoons hot water
 1 tablespoon grenadine syrup,
    maraschino cherry liquid or
1/4 teaspoon unsweetened soft drink mix
    White baking chocolate curls

1. In a large mixing bowl, combine angel food cake mix and 3/4 teaspoon soft drink mix. Prepare cake mix according to package directions.

2. In a medium bowl, combine powdered sugar, the hot water, grenadine syrup, and the 1/4 teaspoon soft drink mix. If necessary, add additional water, 1 teaspoon at a time, to make icing drizzling consistency. Drizzle icing over cake. Top with white chocolate curls. **Makes 12 servings.**

Nutrition facts per serving: 293 cal., 0 g fat, 0 mg chol., 259 mg sodium, 71 g carbo., 0 g fiber, 3 g pro.

Honey-Glazed Buttermilk Oatmeal Coffee Cake

*Prep: 30 minutes   Bake: 25 minutes   Oven: 375°
Cool: 10 minutes*

1/2 cup honey
1/3 cup butter, melted
 2 tablespoons light-color corn syrup
 2 teaspoons finely shredded lemon peel
 4 teaspoons lemon juice
1/2 cup chopped pecans
1 1/2 cups rolled oats
 1 cup all-purpose flour
3/4 cup packed brown sugar
1/2 cup chopped pecans
 1 teaspoon baking powder
1/2 teaspoon baking soda
1/2 teaspoon salt
2/3 cup buttermilk or sour milk*
 2 eggs, lightly beaten
1/4 cup butter, melted
1 1/2 teaspoons vanilla
    Honey (optional)

1. Generously grease a 9x1 1/2-inch round cake pan. In a small bowl, combine 1/2 cup honey, 1/3 cup melted butter, corn syrup, lemon peel and lemon juice. Stir in 1/2 cup chopped pecans. Pour into prepared pan; set aside.

2. For cake: In a blender or food processor, blend or process oats until finely ground. Transfer to a large bowl. Stir in flour, brown sugar, 1/2 cup pecans, baking powder, baking soda and salt. Make a well in the center of the flour mixture. In a medium bowl, combine buttermilk, eggs, 1/4 cup melted butter and vanilla. Add the milk mixture all at once to the flour mixture. Stir just until moistened (batter should be lumpy).

3. Spoon batter evenly over honey mixture in pan. Bake in 375° oven about 25 minutes or until a wooden toothpick inserted in center comes out clean. Remove from oven and immediately invert cake onto a serving plate. Cool about 10 minutes. If desired, serve warm drizzled with additional honey. **Makes 9 servings.**

*Test Kitchen Tip: To make 2/3 cup sour milk, place 2 teaspoons lemon juice or vinegar in a glass measuring cup. Add enough milk to equal 2/3 cup; stir. Let the mixture stand for 5 minutes before using.

Nutrition facts per serving: 450 cal., 23 g fat, 79 mg chol., 357 mg sodium, 58 g carbo., 3 g fiber, 6 g pro.

Honey-Glazed Buttermilk
Oatmeal Coffee Cake

Kansas Sunflower Cupcakes

Kansas Sunflower Cupcakes

Prep: 30 minutes Stand: 30 minutes
Bake: 20 minutes Cool: 1 hour Oven: 350°

 2 egg whites
 1 cup all-purpose flour
 1/2 teaspoon baking powder
 1/4 teaspoon baking soda
   Dash salt
 1/4 cup butter, softened
 1 cup sugar
 1 teaspoon vanilla
 2/3 cup buttermilk or sour milk
 2 tablespoons toasted wheat germ
   Lemon Butter Frosting (recipe follows)
   Shelled sunflower seeds
   Yellow colored sugar (optional)

1. Let egg whites stand at room temperature for 30 minutes. Meanwhile, grease twelve 2½-inch muffin cups; set aside.

2. In a small bowl, stir together the flour, baking powder, baking soda and salt; set aside. In a large mixing bowl, beat butter with an electric mixer for 30 seconds. Add sugar and vanilla; beat until well combined. Add egg whites, one at a time, beating well after each addition.

3. Alternately add flour mixture and buttermilk to butter mixture, beating on low speed after each addition just until combined. Stir in the wheat germ. Spoon batter into prepared muffins cups.

4. Bake in a 350° oven about 20 minutes or until a toothpick inserted in center of a cupcake comes out clean. Cool in pan on wire rack for 10 minutes. Remove from pan and cool on wire rack.

5. Prepare Lemon Butter Frosting. Spread or pipe frosting over cupcakes, sprinkle with shelled sunflower seeds and colored sugar, if you like. If you like, serve in paper bake cups. **Makes 12 servings.**

Lemon Butter Frosting: In a mixing bowl, beat 1/4 cup softened butter until smooth. Gradually add 1 cup powdered sugar, beating well. Beat in 2 tablespoons buttermilk or milk and 1 teaspoon vanilla. Gradually beat in 2 cups powdered sugar, adding additional milk if needed to make spreading consistency. Stir in 1/4 teaspoon finely shredded lemon peel. Makes 1½ cups frosting.

Nutrition facts per serving: 313 cal., 9 g fat, 21 mg chol., 140 mg sodium, 55 g carbo., 1 g fiber, 3 g pro.

Amish Apple Butter Cakelets with Caramel Sauce

Prep: 30 minutes Bake: 18 minutes
Cool: 5 minutes Oven: 350°

   Nonstick cooking spray
 2 cups all-purpose flour
 1½ teaspoons baking powder
 3/4 teaspoon ground cinnamon
 1/2 teaspoon baking soda
 1/4 teaspoon salt
 3/4 cup butter, softened
 1/2 cup granulated sugar
 1/2 cup packed brown sugar
 2 eggs
 1 cup apple butter or pumpkin butter
 1 tablespoon vanilla
 2 tablespoons vinegar or lemon juice
 1 5-ounce can evaporated milk (2/3 cup)
 1/2 cup chopped walnuts, toasted if you like
   Caramel Sauce (recipe follows)
   Walnut pieces, toasted if you like (optional)

1. Lightly coat twenty-four 2½-inch muffin cups with cooking spray; set aside. In a medium bowl, combine the flour, baking powder, cinnamon, baking soda and salt; set aside.

2. In a large mixing bowl, beat butter with an electric mixer on medium speed for 30 seconds. Add granulated and brown sugars; beat until fluffy. Beat in eggs. Beat in apple butter and vanilla.

3. Stir vinegar into evaporated milk (mixture will curdle). Add flour mixture and milk mixture alternately to apple butter mixture, beating on low speed after each addition just until combined. Stir in chopped walnuts.

4. Spoon batter evenly into prepared muffin cups, filling each about three-fourths full. Bake in a 350° oven for 18 to 20 minutes or until a wooden toothpick inserted near the centers comes out clean. Cool in muffin cups on wire racks for 5 minutes. Remove from pans. Cool slightly. Serve warm or cool.

5. To serve, place each cake on a dessert plate. Spoon about 1½ tablespoons of the warm Caramel Sauce over each cake. If you like, garnish with walnut pieces. **Makes 24 servings.**

Caramel Sauce: In a heavy medium saucepan, combine 1 cup packed brown sugar and 2 tablespoons cornstarch. Stir in 1/2 cup water. Stir in 1 cup half-and-half or light cream and 1/3 cup light-color corn syrup. Cook and stir until bubbly (mixture may appear curdled). Cook and stir for 2 minutes more. Remove saucepan from heat; stir in 2 tablespoons butter and 1 teaspoon vanilla. Serve warm over cakes. Makes about 2⅓ cups sauce.

Nutrition facts per serving: 285 cal., 10 g fat, 41 mg chol., 145 mg sodium, 46 g carbo., 1 g fiber, 3 g pro.

Amish Apple Butter Cakelets with Caramel Sauce

Molten Chocolate Lava Cakes

*Prep: 15 minutes Bake: 12 minutes Cool: 2 minutes
Oven: 425°*

2 tablespoons butter
8 ounces bittersweet chocolate, coarsely
    chopped
¾ cup butter
3 eggs
3 egg yolks
⅓ cup granulated sugar
1 teaspoon vanilla
1 tablespoon all-purpose flour
    Powdered sugar

1. Using the 2 tablespoons butter, grease six
8- to 10-ounce ramekins, soufflé dishes or
custard cups. Place ramekins in a 15x10x1-inch
baking pan; set aside.

2. In a heavy small saucepan, combine
chocolate and the ¾ cup butter. Cook and
stir over low heat until chocolate melts.
Remove pan from heat; set aside.

3. In a large mixing bowl, beat eggs, egg
yolks, granulated sugar and vanilla with an
electric mixer on high speed for 8 to
10 minutes or until thick and lemon colored.
Fold one-third of the chocolate mixture
into egg mixture. Fold remaining chocolate
mixture and the flour into egg mixture.
Spoon about ⅔ cup batter into each
prepared ramekin, dividing evenly.

4. Bake in a 425° oven about 12 minutes
or until cake edges feel firm. Cool in
ramekins on a wire rack for 2 to 3 minutes.
Using a knife, loosen cakes from sides
of ramekins. Invert onto dessert plates.
Sift with powdered sugar and serve with
fresh raspberries and mint leaves. Serve
immediately. **Makes 6 servings.**

Nutrition facts per serving: 544 cal., 45 g fat, 282 mg chol.,
233 mg sodium, 36 g carbo., 4 g fiber, 7 g pro.

Molten Chocolate Lava Cakes

Chai Cupcakes

Prep: 20 minutes Bake: 16 minutes Oven: 350°

1 package 2-layer-size white cake mix
1¼ cups half-and-half or light cream
½ cup cooking oil
2 eggs
1½ teaspoons chai spice blend*
    Butter Frosting (recipe follows) or
    purchased vanilla frosting
    Chai spice blend

1. Line twenty-four 2½-inch muffin cups
with paper bake cups. Set aside.

2. In a large mixing bowl, combine the
cake mix, half-and-half, oil, eggs and
1½ teaspoons spice blend. Beat with an
electric mixer on medium speed for
2 minutes. Spoon into bake cups, filling each
about two-thirds full.

3. Bake in a 350° oven for 16 to 18 minutes
or until a toothpick inserted near the centers
comes out clean. Cool cupcakes in pans on
wire racks for 5 minutes. Remove cupcakes
from pans; cool completely on wire racks.
Frost cooled cupcakes with Butter Frosting
and sprinkle with additional chai spice blend.
Makes 24 cupcakes.

Butter Frosting: In a large mixing bowl, beat
½ cup softened butter with an electric mixer
on medium speed until smooth. Gradually
add 2 cups powdered sugar, beating well.
Beat in 3 tablespoons milk and 1½ teaspoons
vanilla. Gradually beat in 4 cups powdered
sugar. Beat in additional milk to reach
spreading consistency, if necessary.

*Note: If desired, substitute 1 teaspoon
pumpkin pie spice or apple pie spice and
½ teaspoon ground cardamom for the
1½ teaspoons chai spice blend. Sprinkle
frosted cupcakes with additional pumpkin
pie spice or apple pie spice.

Nutrition facts per cupcake: 305 cal., 12 g fat, 33 mg chol.,
184 mg sodium, 48 g carbo., 0 g fiber, 2 g pro.

Chai Cupcakes

combined. Spoon mixture into prepared muffin cups.

3. Bake in a 350° oven for 15 to 20 minutes or until cupcakes spring back when pressed lightly in center. If you like, sprinkle with powdered sugar. Serve warm or cool. **Makes 8 cupcakes.**

Nutrition facts per cupcake: 137 cal., 5g fat, 0 mg chol., 82 mg sodium, 20 g carbo., 1 g fiber, 2 g pro.

Black Tie Cupcakes

Prep: 45 minutes   Bake: 15 minutes
Cool: 10 minutes   Stand: 20 minutes   Oven: 350°

1¼ cups all-purpose flour
¼ cup unsweetened cocoa powder
½ teaspoon baking powder
¼ teaspoon baking soda
¼ teaspoon salt
¼ teaspoon ground cinnamon
⅓ cup butter, softened
1 cup sugar
2 eggs
2 ounces semisweet chocolate, bittersweet chocolate or milk chocolate, melted and cooled
1½ teaspoons vanilla
¾ cup milk
⅓ cup seedless red raspberry or blackberry preserves
Chocolate Ganache (recipe follows)
Decorating Icing (recipe follows)

1. Line twenty 2½-inch muffin cups with foil bake cups; set aside. In a medium bowl, stir together flour, cocoa powder, baking powder, baking soda, salt and cinnamon. Set aside.

2. In a large mixing bowl, beat the butter with an electric mixer on medium to high speed for 30 seconds. Add sugar; beat until combined. Add eggs, one at a time, beating for 30 seconds after each addition. Beat in chocolate and vanilla. Alternately add flour mixture and milk to chocolate mixture, beating on low speed after each addition until well combined.

3. Spoon batter into prepared muffin cups, filling each nearly two-thirds full. Bake in a 350° oven for 15 to 18 minutes or until a toothpick inserted near the centers comes out clean. Cool in muffin cups on wire racks for 10 minutes. Remove from pans and cool completely on wire racks.

4. Place cupcakes 2 inches apart on wire racks set over waxed paper. Spread a scant 1 teaspoon of the preserves over each cupcake.

5. Slowly drizzle a small amount of the Chocolate Ganache over each cupcake, allowing it to spread and cover the preserves and top of the cupcake. If necessary, spread ganache gently so it covers the preserves completely. Let stand for 20 minutes.

6. To decorate, fill a decorating bag fitted with a small round tip with Decorating Icing (or place icing in a resealable plastic bag and snip a small piece off one corner to use as a piping bag). Pipe small dots or swirls of Decorating Icing on top of each cupcake. Use a toothpick to swirl some of the ganache into each dot. **Makes 20 cupcakes.**

Chocolate Ganache: In a small saucepan, bring ½ cup whipping cream just to boiling over medium-high heat. Remove from heat. Chop 7 ounces semisweet chocolate, bittersweet chocolate or milk chocolate. Add to hot cream (do not stir). Let stand for 5 minutes. Stir until smooth. Let stand at room temperature until completely cool but still drizzling consistency before drizzling over the cupcakes. Makes about 1 cup.

Decorating Icing: In a medium bowl, combine 1½ cups powdered sugar and enough milk (4 to 7 teaspoons) to make of piping consistency. If desired, stir in a few drops of food coloring. Makes about ⅓ cup.

Nutrition facts per cupcake: 247 cal., 10 g fat, 38 mg chol., 89 mg sodium, 37 g carbo., 1 g fiber, 3 g pro.

Gingerbread Cupcakes

Gingerbread Cupcakes

Prep: 10 minutes   Bake: 15 minutes   Oven: 350°

1 cup all-purpose flour
½ teaspoon baking powder
½ teaspoon ground ginger
½ teaspoon ground cinnamon
¼ teaspoon baking soda
Dash salt
1 slightly beaten egg white
⅓ cup molasses
⅓ cup water
3 tablespoons cooking oil
Sifted powdered sugar (optional)

1. Line eight 2½-inch muffin cups with paper bake cups; set aside. In a medium mixing bowl, stir together flour, baking powder, ginger, cinnamon, soda and salt; set aside.

2. In a small mixing bowl, stir together the egg white, molasses, the water and oil. Stir molasses mixture into flour mixture just until

Black Tie Cupcakes

White Chocolate Cheesecake
with Triple-Raspberry Sauce

White Chocolate Cheesecake with Triple-Raspberry Sauce

Prep: 30 minutes Bake: 45 minutes Cool: 2 hours Chill: 4 hours Oven: 350°

    1 cup crushed shortbread cookies (about
      4 ounces)
    3 tablespoons finely chopped slivered
      almonds, toasted
  ¼ cup butter, melted
    2 8-ounce packages cream cheese,
      softened
    1 6-ounce package white chocolate
      baking squares with cocoa butter,
      melted and cooled
  ⅔ cup sugar
  ⅔ cup dairy sour cream
    1 teaspoon vanilla
    3 eggs
      Triple-Raspberry Sauce (recipe follows)

1. For crust: In a small bowl, combine crushed cookies and almonds. Stir in melted butter. Press crushed cookie mixture onto the bottom of an 8-inch springform pan. Set aside.

2. For filling: In a large mixing bowl, combine cream cheese and cooled white chocolate; beat with an electric mixer on medium to high speed until combined. Beat in sugar, sour cream and vanilla until mixture is fluffy.

3. Add the eggs; beat on low speed just until combined. Pour into the crust-lined pan. Place in a shallow baking pan.

4. Bake in a 350° oven 45 to 50 minutes or until center is nearly set when you shake the cheesecake gently. Cool on a wire rack for 15 minutes. Loosen from side of pan. Cool for 30 minutes more; remove side of pan. Cool completely.* Cover and chill for at least 4 hours or up to 24 hours.

5. To serve, cut into wedges and drizzle some of the Triple-Raspberry Sauce over each serving. **Makes 12 servings.**

Triple-Raspberry Sauce: In a small saucepan, melt one 10- to 12-ounce jar seedless raspberry preserves over low heat. Add 1 cup fresh red raspberries or frozen red raspberries. Heat gently just until sauce simmers. Cool. If desired, stir in 1 to 2 tablespoons raspberry liqueur. Cover and chill until serving time. Makes 1¾ cups.

*Note: This cheesecake puffs during baking and then settles as it cools.

Nutrition facts per serving: 458 cal., 28 g fat, 116 mg chol., 228 mg sodium, 44 g carbo., 1 g fiber, 7 g pro.

Baby Citrus Cheesecakes

Prep: 25 minutes Bake: 20 minutes Chill: 2 hours Oven: 350°

  12 vanilla or chocolate wafers
    1 8-ounce package cream cheese,
      softened
    1 3-ounce package cream cheese,
      softened
  ½ of an 8-ounce carton mascarpone
      cheese
  ½ cup granulated sugar
    1 tablespoon all-purpose flour
    1 teaspoon vanilla
    2 eggs, lightly beaten
  ½ teaspoon finely shredded lemon peel
  ½ teaspoon finely shredded orange peel
      Whipped cream
      Glazed Kumquats (recipe follows)
      (optional)

1. Line twelve, 2½-inch muffin cups with paper bake cups. Place a wafer on the bottom of each bake cup.

2. For filling: In a large mixing bowl, beat cream cheese, mascarpone cheese, sugar, flour and vanilla with an electric mixer until combined. Stir in eggs, lemon peel and orange peel.

3. Pour filling into muffin cups, filling two-thirds full. Bake in a 350° oven 20 minutes or until edges are set.

4. Cool in pan on wire racks. Remove and chill for at least 2 hours. Top each serving with a dollop of whipped cream and a kumquat half, if you like. **Makes 12 servings.**

Glazed Kumquats: Halve kumquats. In a small saucepan, stir together ½ cup sugar and ½ cup water. Heat to simmering, stirring to dissolve sugar. Add kumquats. Cook about 10 minutes or until syrup thickens and kumquats soften. Remove kumquats from syrup, allowing excess to drip off, and cool on a baking sheet lined with parchment paper.

Nutrition facts per serving: 232 cal., 18 g fat, 86 mg chol., 122 mg sodium, 15 g carbo., 0 g fiber, 5 g pro.

Baby Citrus Cheesecakes

Amaretti

Prep: 15 minutes Stand: 30 minutes
Bake: 10 minutes Oven: 375°

2 egg whites
1 8-ounce can almond paste (1 cup)
1 cup sugar
  Sugar

1. Place egg whites in a small bowl; let stand at room temperature for 30 minutes. Line two cookie sheets with parchment paper, plain brown paper or foil; set aside.

2. In a free-standing electric mixer or food processor, break up and crumble almond paste. Add 1 cup sugar. Beat or process until combined. Add egg whites, one at a time, beating or processing until mixture is stiff (it will not form peaks) and sugar is dissolved.

3. Spoon egg white mixture into a pastry bag fitted with a ½-inch round tip. Pipe into 1-inch rounds (about the size of a quarter coin) 2 inches apart onto the prepared cookie sheets. (Or place the egg white mixture in a resealable plastic bag; seal bag and snip off a corner of bag. Pipe as above.) Sprinkle each cookie with additional sugar.

4. Bake in a 375° oven for 10 to 12 minutes or until set and lightly browned. Remove from oven. Cool completely on cookie sheet. Carefully peel cookies from paper or foil. (To store, layer cookies between waxed paper in an airtight container; cover. Store at room temperature up to 5 days).
Makes about 52 cookies.

Nutrition facts per cookie: 37 cal., 1 g fat, 0 mg chol., 3 mg sodium, 6 g carbo., 0 g fiber, 1 g pro.

Chocolate Waffle Turtle Cookies

Prep: 15 minutes Cook: 2 minutes each batch

  1 cup butter or margarine, melted
1½ cups granulated sugar
  4 eggs, lightly beaten
  ½ cup unsweetened cocoa powder
  2 teaspoons vanilla
  2 cups all-purpose flour
  ¼ cup butter
  3 tablespoons water
  3 tablespoons unsweetened cocoa powder
1½ cups powdered sugar
  1 teaspoon vanilla
  ½ cup caramel ice cream topping
  1 cup chopped toasted pecans (optional)

1. Preheat waffle iron. In a large bowl, stir together melted butter, granulated sugar, eggs, ½ cup cocoa powder and 2 teaspoons vanilla. Add flour; stir just until combined.

2. Drop heaping teaspoonfuls of batter into center of each waffle grid. Cook on medium-high heat about 2 minutes, adjusting heat as necessary. Using a fork, transfer cookies to rack; cool. Repeat with remaining batter. When cool, mound cookies on a platter.

3. For glaze: In a small saucepan, heat ¼ cup butter and the water over low heat until melted. Add the 3 tablespoons cocoa and stir until smooth. Remove from heat. Beat in powdered sugar and the 1 teaspoon vanilla. Stir in additional hot water, if needed, to reach drizzling consistency. Drizzle over cookies along with caramel topping. Sprinkle with pecans, if you like. **Makes about 48 cookies.**

Nutrition facts per cookie: 118 cal., 5 g fat, 30 mg chol., 52 mg sodium, 17 g carbo., 1 g fiber, 1 g pro.

Amaretti

Chocolate Waffle Turtle Cookies

Crisp Pistachio Biscotti

Prep: 35 minutes Cool: 1 hour
Bake: 20 minutes/16 minutes Oven: 375°/325°

  ¾ cup butter, softened
  ½ cup sugar
  1 teaspoon baking powder
  1 egg
  1 teaspoon vanilla
  1 cup cornmeal
  1½ cups all-purpose flour
  1 cup chopped pistachio nuts
  2 teaspoons finely shredded orange peel
  5 ounces white baking chocolate,
    coarsely chopped
  1 tablespoon shortening
  ½ cup chopped pistachio nuts

1. In a large mixing bowl, beat butter with an electric mixer on medium to high speed for 30 seconds. Add sugar and baking powder. Beat until combined, scraping sides of bowl occasionally. Beat in egg and vanilla. Beat in cornmeal. Beat in as much of the flour as you can with the mixer. Using a wooden spoon, stir in any remaining flour, the 1 cup pistachio nuts and orange peel.

2. Divide dough into thirds. Shape each portion into an 8-inch loaf. Place loaves 4 inches apart on an ungreased cookie sheet; flatten until 2 inches wide. Bake in a 375° oven for 20 minutes or until a toothpick inserted near centers comes out clean. Cool on cookie sheet for 1 hour.

3. Reduce oven temperature to 325°. Transfer loaves to a cutting board. Using a serrated knife, cut each loaf diagonally into ½-inch slices. Place slices on ungreased large cookie sheet. Bake for 8 minutes. Turn cookies over; bake for 8 to 10 minutes more or until lightly browned. Transfer to wire racks; cool.

4. In a small saucepan, combine white chocolate and shortening. Cook and stir over low heat until melted. Dip top of each cookie into chocolate. Sprinkle with ½ cup pistachio nuts. Let stand until set. **Makes 42 cookies.**

Nutrition facts per cookie: 115 cal., 7 g fat, 14 mg chol., 37 mg sodium, 13 g carbo., 1 g fiber, 2 g pro.

Lemon Walnut Biscotti

Prep: 40 minutes Chill: 15 minutes
Bake: 25 minutes/12 minutes Cool: 45 minutes
Oven: 325°/300°

  3 cups all-purpose flour
  1 teaspoon baking powder
  ½ teaspoon salt
  ¼ teaspoon baking soda
  10 tablespoons butter, softened
  1⅓ cups granulated sugar
  4½ teaspoons finely shredded lemon peel
  2 eggs
  3 tablespoons lemon juice
  2 cups chopped walnuts
  1 egg white, lightly beaten
  3 tablespoons turbinado sugar

1. Lightly grease two cookie sheets or line with parchment. In a small bowl, mix flour, baking powder, salt and baking soda.

2. In a large mixing bowl, beat butter with an electric mixer for 30 seconds. Add granulated sugar and lemon peel. Beat until combined, scraping sides of bowl. Beat in the two eggs, one at a time, until combined. Beat in lemon juice until combined. Beat in as much of the flour mixture as you can with the mixer. Using a wood spoon, stir in remaining flour mixture. Stir in walnuts.

3. Turn dough out onto a lightly floured surface; divide into three equal parts. Shape each portion into a 10-inch-long loaf about 1½ inches wide. Place loaves 3 inches apart on cookie sheets; flatten loaves until about 2 inches wide. Brush loaves with egg white. Sprinkle with turbinado sugar. Place cookie sheets in refrigerator and chill for 15 minutes.

4. Bake in a 325° oven for 25 to 30 minutes, or until firm and light brown. Cool on cookie sheets for 45 minutes. Reduce oven temperature to 300°.

5. Transfer loaves to a cutting board. Use a serrated knife to cut each loaf diagonally into ½-inch slices. Put slices on cookie sheets, cut sides down. Bake about 7 minutes or until lightly browned. Turn the cookie slices over;

bake for 5 to 6 minutes more or until lightly browned, crisp and dry. Remove and cool on wire racks. Store in an airtight container at room temperature or freeze the biscotti for up to 3 months. **Makes about 50 cookies.**

Nutrition facts per cookie: 105 cal., 6 g fat, 15 mg chol., 56 mg sodium, 13 g carbo., 1 g fiber, 2 g pro.

Vanilla Bean Biscotti

Prep: 25 minutes Bake: 45 minutes
Cool: 15 minutes Oven: 325°

  1 vanilla bean, split lengthwise
  2¾ cups all-purpose flour
  1½ cups sugar
  1½ teaspoons baking powder
  1 teaspoon salt
  2 eggs
  2 egg yolks
  6 tablespoons butter, melted

1. Grease two cookie sheets; set aside. Scrape seeds from bean with tip of a small sharp knife; discard.

2. In a large bowl, stir together flour, sugar, baking powder and salt. Make a well in center of flour mixture. Place eggs and egg yolks in well and stir into flour mixture. Add melted butter and vanilla seeds; stir until dough starts to form a ball.

3. Turn dough out onto a lightly floured surface; divide into thirds. Shape each portion into a 14-inch loaf. Place loaves 3 inches apart on the prepared cookie sheets; flatten slightly until about 1½ inches wide.

4. Bake in a 325° over for 25 minutes or until lightly browned, switching pan positions halfway through baking. Cool on cookie sheets for 15 minutes.

5. Transfer loaves to a cutting board. Using a serrated knife, cut each loaf diagonally into ½-inch slices. Place slices on cookie sheets. Bake for 10 minutes. Turn cookies over; bake for 10 to 15 minutes more or until lightly browned, crisp and dry. Transfer to wire racks; cool. **Makes about 72 cookies.**

Nutrition facts per cookie: 46 cal., 1 g fat, 14 mg chol., 46 mg sodium, 8 g carbo., 0 g fiber, 1 g pro.

Crisp Pistachio Biscotti,
Lemon Walnut Biscotti
and Vanilla Bean Biscotti

Danish Pastry Apple Bars

Prep: 30 minutes Bake: 50 minutes Oven: 375°

2½ cups all-purpose flour
1 teaspoon salt
1 cup shortening
1 egg yolk
  Milk
1 cup cornflakes
8 to 10 tart cooking apples, peeled,
  cored and sliced (8 cups)
¾ to 1 cup granulated sugar
1 teaspoon ground cinnamon
1 egg white, lightly beaten
1 cup powdered sugar
2 to 3 teaspoons milk

1. In a large bowl, combine flour and salt. Using a pastry blender, cut in shortening until the mixture resembles coarse crumbs. In a liquid measuring cup, beat egg yolk lightly.

Add enough milk to make ⅔ cup liquid. Stir well to combine. Stir milk mixture into flour mixture with a fork until combined (dough will be slightly sticky). Divide mixture in half.

2. On a well-floured surface, roll half of the dough to a 17x12-inch rectangle. Fold dough crosswise into thirds. Transfer to a 15x10x1-inch baking pan and unfold dough, pressing to fit into the bottom and sides of the pan. Sprinkle with cornflakes. Top evenly with apples. In a small bowl, combine granulated sugar and cinnamon. Sprinkle mixture over apples. Roll remaining dough to a 15x10-inch rectangle. Fold dough crosswise into thirds. Place atop apples and unfold dough. Crimp edges or use the tines of a fork to seal. Cut slits in the top. Brush top with beaten egg white.

3. Bake in a 375° oven for 50 minutes or until golden and apples are tender, covering with foil after the first 25 minutes of baking time to prevent overbrowning.

4. In a small bowl, combine powdered sugar and 2 to 3 teaspoons milk to make a drizzling consistency. Drizzle over warm bars. Let cool completely on a wire rack. Cut into bars. Makes 32 bars.

Nutrition facts per bar: 147 cal., 7 g fat, 7 mg chol., 83 mg sodium, 21 g carbo., 1 g fiber, 1 g pro.

Sour Cream Pumpkin Bars

Prep: 25 minutes Bake: 25 minutes Oven: 350°

½ cup butter, softened
1⅓ cups sugar
1½ teaspoons baking powder
¼ teaspoon baking soda
¼ teaspoon salt
2 eggs
1 cup canned pumpkin
½ cup dairy sour cream
¼ cup milk
1 teaspoon vanilla

1½ cups all-purpose flour
½ cup whole wheat flour
1 cup chopped pecans or walnuts
  Browned Butter Frosting (recipe
  follows)
  Chopped pecans or walnuts (optional)

1. Grease a 15x10x1-inch baking pan; set aside.

2. In a large mixing bowl, beat the butter with an electric mixer for 30 seconds. Beat in sugar, baking powder, baking soda and salt until combined. Add eggs, pumpkin, sour cream, milk and vanilla; beat until combined. Add all-purpose and whole wheat flours; beat until combined. Stir in 1 cup nuts.

3. Spread mixture evenly into prepared baking pan. Bake in a 350° oven about 25 minutes or until a wooden toothpick inserted near the center comes out clean. Cool in pan on wire rack.

4. Prepare Browned Butter Frosting; spread over cooled bars. If you like, sprinkle with additional nuts. Cut into bars. **Makes 48 bars.**

Browned Butter Frosting: In a small saucepan, heat ½ cup butter over low heat until melted. Continue heating until the butter turns a light brown. Remove from heat and transfer butter to a medium mixing bowl. Add 3 cups powdered sugar, 2 tablespoons milk and 1 teaspoon vanilla. Beat with an electric mixer until combined. Beat in additional milk, 1 teaspoon at a time, to make a spreadable frosting. Use immediately. Makes about 1 cup.

Nutrition facts per bar: 130 cal., 6 g fat, 20 mg chol., 63 mg sodium, 18 g carbo., 1 g fiber, 1 g pro.

Danish Pastry Apple Bars

Sour Cream Pumpkin Bars

Fudge Brownie Hearts

Fudge Brownie Hearts

*Prep: 30 minutes Bake: 35 minutes Chill: 12 hours
Oven: 350°*

　Butter
1 cup butter
8 ounces bittersweet chocolate, coarsely
　chopped
3 ounces semisweet chocolate, coarsely
　chopped
4 eggs, lightly beaten
¾ cup granulated sugar
¾ cup packed brown sugar
2 teaspoons vanilla
1 cup all-purpose flour
1½ teaspoons baking powder
½ teaspoon salt
1 cup coarsely chopped pecans or
　walnuts, toasted
　Vanilla Glaze (recipe follows)

1. Line a 13x9x2-inch baking pan with heavy foil, extending foil over edges of the pan. Butter the foil; set pan aside.

2. In a heavy large saucepan, heat 1 cup butter and the chocolates over low heat, stirring constantly, until chocolate is melted and smooth. Set aside to cool slightly. In a medium bowl, stir together eggs, granulated sugar, brown sugar and vanilla. Stir into warm chocolate mixture; cool to room temperature.

3. In a small bowl, stir together flour, baking powder and salt. Fold flour mixture into chocolate mixture. Stir in pecans. Spread the batter in the prepared pan.

4. Bake in a 350° oven for 35 to 40 minutes or until brownies appear shiny, begin to crack on top and appear set. (Do not overbake.) Cool in pan on a wire rack. Store, covered, in the refrigerator for 12 to 24 hours before serving.

5. To serve, remove pan from refrigerator. Use foil to lift brownies out of pan. Cut brownies with 3-inch heart-shape cookie cutters. Drizzle with Vanilla Glaze. Chill until glaze is set. **Makes 10 to 12 heart shapes or 15 bars.**

Vanilla Glaze: In a small bowl, stir together ⅔ cup powdered sugar, 1 teaspoon milk and ½ teaspoon vanilla. Stir in enough additional milk, ½ teaspoon at a time, to make glaze of drizzling consistency. Makes about ½ cup.

Nutrition facts per bar: 417 cal., 27 g fat, 89 mg chol., 211 mg sodium, 45 g carbo., 3 g fiber, 6 g pro.

Brownie Heartthrob Sundaes: Divide 1 quart tin roof sundae ice cream or vanilla ice cream into six chilled heart-shape serving dishes or shallow bowls. Top each serving with a heart-shape brownie (omit Vanilla Glaze). Drizzle brownie with warm chocolate-fudge ice cream topping. Top each with whipped cream, coarsely chopped nuts and a maraschino cherry. Makes 6 servings.

Spiced Cherry Pie

*Prep: 30 minutes Bake: 1 hour Stand: 2 hours
Cool: 2 hours Oven: 375°*

5 cups frozen unsweetened pitted tart
　red cherries
　Cherry juice or water
1 15-ounce package rolled refrigerated
　unbaked piecrust (2 crusts)
1 cup granulated sugar
¼ cup cornstarch
1 teaspoon ground cinnamon
¼ teaspoon salt
¼ teaspoon ground allspice
2 tablespoons butter
　Coarse sugar (optional)

1. Thaw frozen cherries in a colander over a medium bowl, reserving juice. Measure drained juice; add enough cherry juice to measure ¾ cup.

2. Let piecrust stand at room temperature according to package directions. Unroll piecrusts. Ease one piecrust into a 9-inch pie plate, being careful not to stretch pastry. Do not prick pastry. Cut remaining piecrust in ½-inch-wide strips; set aside.

3. For filling: In a medium saucepan, combine granulated sugar, cornstarch, cinnamon, salt and allspice. Add the ¾ cup reserved juice and the butter. Cook and stir over medium heat until thickened and bubbly. Remove from heat. Stir in thawed cherries.

4. Pour filling into the pastry-lined pie plate. Weave strips over filling in a lattice pattern. Press strip ends into bottom pastry rim. Fold bottom pastry over strip ends; seal and crimp edge. To prevent overbrowning, cover edge of pie with foil.

5. Place pie on an oven rack positioned over a baking sheet on the rack below. Bake in a 375° oven for 30 minutes. Remove foil. Bake for 30 to 35 minutes more or until filling is bubbly in the center and piecrust is golden. Cool on a wire rack for at least 2 hours before serving. To serve, sprinkle with some coarse sugar, if you like. **Makes 8 servings.**

Nutrition facts per serving: 432 cal., 17 g fat, 17 mg chol., 312 mg sodium, 68 g carbo., 2 g fiber, 2 g pro.

Spiced Cherry Pie

Cherry Crisp Pie

Prep: 20 minutes Stand: 45 minutes Bake: 1 hour
Cool: 2 hours Oven: 350°

 1 cup granulated sugar
 3 tablespoons quick-cooking tapioca or
   cornstarch
 2 16-ounce packages frozen
   unsweetened pitted tart red cherries
   Single-Crust Pie Shell (recipe follows)
 ²/₃ cup rolled oats
 ²/₃ cup all-purpose flour
 ¹/₂ cup packed brown sugar
 ¹/₄ teaspoon salt
 ¹/₄ teaspoon ground cinnamon
 6 tablespoons butter

1. In a very large bowl, stir together the granulated sugar and quick-cooking tapioca; add frozen cherries. Gently toss until coated. Let mixture stand about 45 minutes or until fruit is partially thawed but still icy; stirring occasionally.*

2. Transfer cherry mixture to a 4-quart Dutch oven. Add 2 tablespoons water. Cook and stir over medium heat until slightly thickened and bubbly. Let cool to room temperature. Cover and chill in the refrigerator while preparing pastry.

3. Prepare and roll out Single Crust Pie Shell pastry. Line a 9-inch pie plate with pastry. Trim overhang to 1 inch all the way around. Tuck the crust under and flute the edges. Do not prick pastry.

4. For crumb topping: In a medium bowl, stir together the oats, flour, brown sugar, salt and cinnamon. Using a pastry blender, cut in butter until mixture resembles coarse crumbs.

5. Transfer cherry mixture to the pastry-lined pie plate. Sprinkle crumb topping over cherry mixture. To prevent overbrowning, loosely cover pie with foil.

6. Place pie plate on middle shelf in oven; place foil-lined baking sheet on lower rack beneath pie. Bake in a 350° oven for 20 minutes. Remove foil. Bake 40 to 45 minutes more or until filling is bubbly and crumb topping is golden brown. Cool on a wire rack at least 2 hours before serving. **Makes 8 servings.**

*Note: If using cornstarch, it isn't necessary to let mixture stand 45 minutes.

Nutrition facts per serving: 634 cal., 24 g fat, 62 mg chol., 425 mg sodium, 99 g carbo., 4 g fiber, 8 g pro.

Cherry Berry Berry Pie

Prep: 35 minutes Bake: 45 minutes
Cool: 2 hours Oven: 400°

   Single-Crust Pie Shell (recipe follows)
 1 cup granulated sugar
 ¹/₄ cup cornstarch
 4¹/₂ cups frozen unsweetened pitted tart
   red cherries
 ³/₄ cup frozen red raspberries
 ³/₄ cup frozen blueberries
 ¹/₂ teaspoon finely shredded lemon peel
 1 teaspoon lemon juice
 ¹/₂ teaspoon almond extract
 ¹/₂ cup all-purpose flour
 ¹/₂ cup granulated sugar
 ¹/₄ cup packed brown sugar
 ¹/₈ teaspoon salt
 ¹/₄ cup butter, cut into small pieces

1. Prepare and roll out Single Crust Pie Shell pastry. Line a 9-inch pie plate with pastry. Trim overhang to 1 inch all the way around. Tuck the crust under and flute the edges. Do not prick pastry. Put pastry-lined pie plate in freezer while preparing pie filling.

2. In a large saucepan, stir together the 1 cup granulated sugar and the cornstarch; add cherries. Gently toss until coated. Cook and stir over medium heat until bubbly. Add raspberries and blueberries. Cook and stir until thickened and bubbly. Cook and gently stir for 1 minute more. Remove from heat. Stir in lemon peel, lemon juice and almond extract. Set aside.

3. For crumb topping: In a medium bowl, stir together the flour, ¹/₂ cup sugar, the brown sugar and salt. Using a pastry blender, cut in butter until mixture resembles coarse crumbs. Set aside.

4. Transfer cherry mixture to the pastry-lined pie plate. Spread crumb mixture over cherry mixture. To prevent overbrowning, loosely cover pie with foil.

5. Bake in a 400° oven for 25 minutes. Remove foil. Bake for 20 to 25 minutes more or until filling is bubbly and crumb topping is golden brown. Cool on a wire rack at least 2 hours before serving. **Makes 8 servings.**

Single-Crust Pie Shell: In a medium bowl, stir together 1³/₄ cups cake flour or all-purpose flour, ¹/₃ cup all-purpose flour and ³/₄ teaspoon salt. Using a pastry blender, cut in 6 tablespoons butter, cut into pieces, and 3 tablespoons shortening until pieces are pea size. In a small bowl, stir together 4 tablespoons of cold water, 1 lightly beaten egg yolk and 1 teaspoon lemon juice or vinegar. Using a large fork, gently toss the flour mixture and egg mixture together. If there are any dry parts, add 1 tablespoon cold water and gently toss to moisten evenly (should be a mass of very large crumbs). Turn crumb mixture out onto a lightly floured surface. Using your fingers, gently form a ball. Using just a bit of flour, knead four or five times to form a ball. Using your hands, flatten into a disk about 1 inch thick. If necessary, wrap the dough in plastic wrap and chill in the refrigerator for 1 to 2 hours or until easy to handle. On a lightly floured surface, roll dough from center to edges into a 12 inch circle. To transfer pastry, wrap it around the rolling pin. Unroll pastry into a 9-inch pie plate. Ease pastry into pie plate without stretching it, and gently fit pastry into dish. Trim the overhang to 1 inch all the way around. Tuck the crust under and flute the edges. Bake as directed in individual recipes. Makes 1 piecrust.

Nutrition facts per serving: 574 cal., 20 g fat, 54 mg chol., 366 mg sodium, 95 g carbo., 3 g fiber, 5 g pro.

Cherry Crisp Pie

Cherry Berry Berry Pie

Michigan Tart Cherry Pie

Michigan Tart Cherry Pie

Prep: 30 minutes Stand: 45 minutes
Bake: 1 hour 15 minutes Oven: 375° Cool: 2 hours

1¼ cups sugar
  2 tablespoons quick-cooking tapioca
  2 tablespoons cornstarch
5½ cups fresh or frozen unsweetened
    pitted tart red cherries
  1 tablespoon lemon juice
    Two-Crust Pie Shell (recipe follows)
    Water
  1 tablespoon sugar

1. In a large bowl, stir together 1¼ cups granulated sugar, the quick-cooking tapioca and cornstarch; add frozen cherries and lemon juice. Gently toss until coated. Let mixture stand about 45 minutes or until fruit is partially thawed but still icy; stirring occasionally. (If using fresh cherries, let cherry mixture stand about 15 minutes or until a syrup forms; stirring occasionally.)

2. Prepare Two-Crust Pie Shell pastry. Line a 9-inch pie plate with half of the pastry.

3. Transfer cherry mixture to the pastry-lined pie plate. Cut slits in remaining pastry to make a pretty design; place on filling. (Or, cut in strips and create a lattice top.) Trim overhangs to 1 inch all the way around. Tuck crusts under and flute edges. Lightly brush top pastry with a little water. Sprinkle the 1 tablespoon sugar on top pastry. To prevent overbrowning, cover edge of pie with foil.

4. Place pie plate on middle shelf in oven; place foil-lined baking sheet on lower rack beneath pie. Bake in a 375° oven for 25 minutes. Remove foil. Bake about 50 minutes more or until filling is bubbly and crust is golden brown. Cool on a wire rack at least 2 hours before serving. **Makes 8 servings.**

Two-Crust Pie Shell: In a large bowl, stir together 3 cups cake flour, ½ cup all-purpose flour and 1½ teaspoons salt. Using a pastry blender, cut in ¾ cup cold butter (cut into pieces) and ¼ cup shortening until pieces are pea size. In a small bowl, stir together 6 tablespoons cold water; 1 egg, lightly beaten; and 2 teaspoons lemon juice or vinegar. Using a large fork, gently toss the flour mixture and egg mixture together. If there are any dry parts, add 1 tablespoon cold water and gently toss to moisten evenly (should be a mass of very large crumbs). Turn crumb mixture out onto a lightly floured surface. Using your fingers, gently form a ball. Using just a bit of flour, knead four or five times to form a ball. Divide in half. Using your hands, flatten each half into a disk about 1 inch thick. If necessary, wrap the dough in plastic wrap and chill in the refrigerator for 1 to 2 hours or until easy to handle. On a lightly floured surface, roll one disk of dough from center to edges into a 12 inch circle. To transfer pastry, wrap it around the rolling pin. Unroll pastry into a 9-inch pie plate. Ease pastry into pie plate without stretching it, and gently fit pastry into dish. Roll remaining dough disk into a circle 12 inches in diameter.

Nutrition facts per serving: 632 cal., 25 g fat, 72 mg chol., 573 mg sodium, 97 g carbo., 3 g fiber, 7 g pro.

Sugar & Spice Strawberry Pie

Prep: 40 minutes Bake: 13 minutes Cool: 1 hour
Chill: 4 hours Oven: 450°

½ of a 15-ounce package rolled
    refrigerated unbaked piecrust
    (1 crust)
  2 teaspoons cinnamon-sugar
½ to ¾ cup sugar
  2 tablespoons cornstarch
    Dash salt
  1 cup water
½ of a 3-ounce package (about
    3 tablespoons) strawberry-flavor
    gelatin
  6 cups fresh strawberries
    Whipped cream
    Cinnamon-sugar (optional)

1. Let piecrust stand at room temperature as directed on package. Line a 9-inch pie plate with piecrust; fold under edge. Crimp as desired. Prick pastry all over with a fork. Sprinkle 2 teaspoons cinnamon-sugar on the bottom crust. Line pastry with a double thickness of foil. Bake in a 450° oven for 8 minutes. Remove foil. Bake for 5 to 6 minutes more or until golden. Cool on a wire rack. Set aside.

2. In a small saucepan, combine sugar (the amount of sugar depends upon the sweetness of the berries), cornstarch and salt. Stir in the water. Bring to boiling; reduce heat. Stir in strawberry-flavor gelatin. Cook and stir over medium heat until thickened; remove from heat. Transfer gelatin mixture to a large bowl; cover and let cool to room temperature (about 1 hour).

3. Meanwhile, remove stems from strawberries. Cut any large strawberries in half lengthwise. Add berries to cooled gelatin mixture; stir gently to coat. Spoon strawberry mixture into cooled pastry shell. Cover; chill at least 4 hours or until firm. To serve, top with whipped cream. Sprinkle with additional cinnamon-sugar, if you like. **Makes 8 servings.**

Nutrition facts per serving with whipped cream: 282 cal., 13 g fat, 25 mg chol., 155 mg sodium, 41 g carbo., 2 g fiber, 2 g pro.

Sugar & Spice Strawberry Pie

Apple-Pear Praline Pie

Prep: 50 minutes Bake: 1 hour 2 minutes
Cool: 4 hours Oven: 375°

Nut Pastry (recipe follows)
¾ cup granulated sugar
¼ cup all-purpose flour
½ teaspoon ground nutmeg
½ teaspoon ground cinnamon
Dash salt
3 cups thinly sliced peeled pears
3 cups thinly sliced peeled tart apples
2 tablespoons butter, cut up
Milk (optional)
Granulated sugar (optional)
¼ cup butter
½ cup packed brown sugar
2 tablespoons milk, half-and-half or
 light cream
½ cup chopped hickory nuts or pecans

1. Prepare and roll out Nut Pastry. Line a 9-inch pie plate with a pastry circle.

2. In a large mixing bowl, combine ¾ cup granulated sugar, the flour, nutmeg, cinnamon and salt. Add pears and apples; toss to coat. Transfer mixture to the pastry-lined pie plate. Dot with 2 tablespoons butter. Trim bottom pastry to edge of pie plate. Cut slits in remaining pastry circle; place on filling and seal. Crimp edge as desired.

3. If you like, brush top with milk and sprinkle with a little granulated sugar. To prevent overbrowning, cover edge of pie with foil. Place pie in a 375° oven. Place a foil-lined baking sheet on the rack below pie in oven. Bake for 40 minutes. Remove foil from pie. Bake 20 minutes more until filling is bubbly.

4. After baking pie for 50 minutes, in a small saucepan, melt ¼ cup butter; gradually stir in brown sugar and 2 tablespoons milk. Cook and stir until mixture comes to a boil. Carefully spoon atop baked pie; sprinkle with nuts. Return to oven and bake 2 to 3 minutes or until topping starts to bubble. Cool on wire rack. **Makes 8 servings.**

Nut Pastry: In a medium bowl, combine 2¼ cups all-purpose flour, ¼ cup ground toasted hickory nuts or pecans, and ¾ teaspoon salt. Cut in ⅔ cup shortening until pieces are pea size. Sprinkle 1 tablespoon water over part of the flour mixture; toss with a fork. Push moistened pastry to side of bowl. Repeat moistening flour mixture using 1 tablespoon water at a time (5 to 6 tablespoons total) until flour mixture is moistened. Divide pastry in half; form halves into balls. On a lightly floured surface, use your hands to slightly flatten one pastry ball. Roll it from center to edge into a 12 inch circle. Repeat with remaining pastry.

Nutrition facts per serving: 629 cal., 34 g fat, 23 mg chol., 307 mg sodium, 80 g carbo., 5 g fiber, 4 g pro.

Shaker Sugar Pie

Prep: 15 minutes Bake: 45 minutes Oven: 350°

½ of a 15-ounce package rolled
 refrigerated unbaked piecrust
 (1 piecrust)
1 cup packed brown sugar
⅓ cup all-purpose flour
2 cups (1 pint) half-and-half or light
 cream
1 teaspoon vanilla
2 tablespoons butter, cut into small
 pieces
Ground nutmeg

1. Let piecrust stand at room temperature according to package directions. Unroll piecrust. Ease piecrust into a 9-inch pie plate without stretching it. Crimp edges as desired. Set aside.

2. In a small bowl, combine brown sugar and flour. In another small bowl, combine half-and-half and vanilla. Evenly spread brown sugar mixture in the bottom of the unbaked piecrust. Pour half-and-half mixture over brown sugar mixture. Evenly distribute butter pieces over filling. Lightly sprinkle with nutmeg. To prevent overbrowning, cover edge of the pie with foil.

3. Bake in a 350° oven for 25 minutes. Remove foil. Bake about 20 minutes more or until bubbly and lightly browned on top (pie will not appear set but will set when cool). Cool on a wire rack. Cover and chill within 2 hours. **Makes 10 servings.**

Nutrition facts per serving: 278 cal., 13 g fat, 26 mg chol., 129 mg sodium, 37 g carbo., 0 g fiber, 2 g pro.

Shaker Sugar Pie

Apple-Pear Praline Pie

Fantasy Chocolate Pie

Prep: 30 minutes Bake: 50 minutes Oven: 350°

Pastry for Single-Crust Pie (recipe
   follows)
3 eggs
1 cup light-color corn syrup
½ cup granulated sugar
⅓ cup butter, melted
1 teaspoon vanilla
¼ teaspoon salt
½ cup milk chocolate pieces
½ cup semisweet chocolate pieces
½ cup semisweet and white chocolate
   swirled pieces
1 cup flaked coconut
½ cup pecan pieces
½ cup slivered almonds
   Whipped cream (optional)
   Toasted coconut and/or semisweet
   chocolate curls (optional)

1. Prepare Pastry for Single-Crust Pie. To transfer pastry, wrap it around the rolling pin. Unroll pastry into a 9-inch pie plate. Ease pastry into pie plate without stretching. Trim pastry to ½ inch beyond edge of pie plate. Fold under extra pastry. Crimp edge. (Do not prick.) Set aside.

2. For filling: In a medium bowl, combine eggs, corn syrup, granulated sugar, butter, vanilla and salt.

3. In pastry shell, layer milk chocolate pieces, semisweet chocolate pieces, semisweet and white chocolate pieces, 1 cup coconut, the pecans and almonds. Slowly pour egg mixture over all, allowing egg mixture to sink down into filling. To prevent overbrowning, cover edge of pastry shell with foil.

4. Bake the pie in a 350° oven for 30 minutes. Remove the foil; bake for 20 to 25 minutes more or until the center of pie appears set when gently shaken. Cool completely on a wire rack. Cover and store in refrigerator within 2 hours. If you like, serve with whipped cream and sprinkle with toasted coconut and/or chocolate curls. **Makes 8 to 10 servings.**

Pastry for Single-Crust Pie: In a large bowl, stir together 1¼ cups all-purpose flour, ½ teaspoon ground cinnamon and ¼ teaspoon salt. Using a pastry blender, cut in ⅓ cup shortening until pieces are pea size. Sprinkle 1 tablespoon of cold water over part of the mixture; gently toss with a fork. Push moistened dough to the side of the bowl. Repeat moistening dough, using 1 tablespoon cold water at a time, until all the dough is moistened (4 to 5 tablespoons cold water total). Form dough into a ball. On a lightly floured surface, use your hands to slightly flatten dough. Roll dough from center to edges into a 12-inch circle. Continue as directed in Step 1.

Nutrition facts per serving: 766 cal., 43 g fat, 102 mg chol., 317 mg sodium, 92 g carbo., 4 g fiber, 9 g pro.

Fantasy Chocolate Pie

Raspberry Cream Tart

Prep: 20 minutes Bake: 35 minutes
Cool: 30 minutes Oven: 350°

1 16.5-ounce roll refrigerated sugar
   cookie dough, cut into ½-inch-thick
   slices
2 3-ounce packages cream cheese,
   softened
¼ cup granulated sugar
1 egg
1 teaspoon finely shredded lemon peel
1 tablespoon lemon juice
½ teaspoon vanilla
2 cups fresh red raspberries, blueberries
   and/or blackberries
2 teaspoons granulated sugar
   Powdered sugar
   Fresh red raspberries, blueberries and/
   or blackberries (optional)

1. Press cookie dough slices into bottom and fluted sides of a greased 11-inch tart pan with removable bottom. Do not prick. (Or press onto bottom of greased 12-inch pizza pan.) Bake in a 350° oven 20 minutes or until light brown. Remove from oven; set aside.

2. In a small bowl, beat cream cheese with an electric mixer on medium to high speed for 30 seconds. Add ¼ cup sugar, the egg, lemon peel, lemon juice and vanilla. Beat until combined. Pour cheese mixture over warm crust and spread evenly.

3. Place the 2 cups raspberries in a single layer on top of cheese mixture. Sprinkle raspberries with 2 teaspoons sugar. Bake for 15 to 17 minutes more or until cheese mixture is set. Transfer to a wire rack; let cool for 30 minutes before serving.

4. Just before serving, sprinkle with powdered sugar. Garnish with additional fresh berries, if you like. **Makes 8 servings.**

Nutrition facts per serving: 388 cal., 20 g fat, 67 mg chol., 319 mg sodium, 47 g carbo., 2 g fiber, 5 g pro.

Raspberry Cream Tart

Cherry-Pecan Cobbler

Prep: 25 minutes Bake: 20 minutes Cool: 1 hour
Oven: 400°

- 1 cup all-purpose flour
- 2 tablespoons granulated sugar
- 1½ teaspoons baking powder
- 1 teaspoon finely shredded lemon peel
- ¼ teaspoon salt
- ¼ cup butter
- ½ cup toasted chopped pecans
- 6 cups fresh or frozen unsweetened pitted tart red cherries
- 1 cup granulated sugar
- 3 tablespoons cornstarch
- 1 egg
- ¼ cup milk
- 2 tablespoons coarse sugar or granulated sugar
  Ice cream (optional)

1. For topping: In a medium bowl, stir together flour, 2 tablespoons granulated sugar, the baking powder, lemon peel and salt. Cut in butter until mixture resembles coarse crumbs. Stir in pecans; set aside.

2. For filling: In a large saucepan, combine the cherries, the 1 cup granulated sugar and the cornstarch. Cook over medium heat until cherries release juices, stirring occasionally. Continue to cook, stirring constantly, over medium heat until thickened and bubbly. Keep filling hot.

3. In a small bowl, stir together the egg and milk. Add to flour mixture, stirring just until moistened. Transfer hot filling to a 2-quart square (8x8-inch) baking dish. Using a spoon, immediately drop topping into six mounds on top of filling. Sprinkle mounds with coarse sugar.

4. Bake in a 400° oven for 20 to 25 minutes or until topping is golden brown. Let cool in dish on wire rack about 1 hour. Serve warm with ice cream, if you like. **Makes 6 servings.**

Nutrition facts per serving: 479 cal., 16 g fat, 56 mg chol., 263 mg sodium, 83 g carbo., 4 g fiber, 6 g pro.

Ginger-Cinnamon Apple Crisp

Prep: 35 minutes Bake: 55 minutes
Cool: 20 minutes Oven: 375°

- Nonstick cooking spray
- ¾ cup packed dark brown sugar
- ½ cup all-purpose flour
- 1½ teaspoons ground ginger
- 1 teaspoon ground cinnamon
  Dash salt
- 6 tablespoons unsalted butter, cut into pieces
- ½ cup chopped walnuts
- ½ cup chopped pecans
- ½ cup packed dark brown sugar
- ¼ cup cornstarch
- ¾ teaspoon ground ginger
- ½ teaspoon ground cinnamon
- 3 pounds Granny Smith apples, peeled, cored and thinly sliced (about 8 cups)
  Vanilla ice cream or whipped cream (optional)

1. Lightly coat a 2½- to 3-quart (13x9-inch) baking dish with cooking spray; set aside.

2. For topping: In a large bowl, whisk together the ¾ cup brown sugar, the flour, the 1½ teaspoons ginger, the 1 teaspoon cinnamon and the salt. Using a pastry blender, cut in butter until the mixture resembles coarse crumbs. Stir in walnuts and pecans; set aside.

3. In a very large mixing bowl, whisk together the ½ cup brown sugar, cornstarch, the ¾ teaspoon ginger and the ½ teaspoon cinnamon. Add apples slices. Gently toss until coated.

4. Transfer apple mixture to prepared dish. Sprinkle topping over the apples. Cover the dish with foil.

5. Bake in a 375° oven for 30 minutes. Remove the foil and bake for 25 to 30 minutes more or until top is browned and apples are tender. Let cool for 20 to 30 minutes before serving. If you like, serve with ice cream. **Makes 8 servings.**

Nutrition facts per serving: 402 cal., 19 g fat, 23 mg chol., 29 mg sodium, 60 g carbo., 3 g fiber, 3 g pro.

Cherry-Pecan Cobbler

Ginger-Cinnamon Apple Crisp

Whole-Apple Crisp

Whole Apple Crisp

Prep: 30 minutes Bake: 1 hour Cool: 30 minutes
Oven: 350°

8 medium baking apples, such as
   McIntosh or Rome
1 cup orange juice
1 cup rolled oats
½ cup packed brown sugar
⅓ cup slivered almonds, toasted
1 tablespoon all-purpose flour
¾ teaspoon ground cinnamon
¼ teaspoon ground nutmeg
⅓ cup butter, melted
⅓ cup honey
1 6- to 7-ounce carton Greek-style
   yogurt or other creamy-style yogurt
   Cinnamon sticks

1. Remove a ½-inch slice from tops of the
apples. With a melon baller remove core,
stopping about ½ inch from the bottom
of the apple. Arrange the prepared apples
in a 13x9x2-inch baking dish (3-quart
rectangular) and brush with 1 tablespoon of
the orange juice. (If necessary, remove a thin
slice from the bottoms of the apples so they
sit flat in the baking dish.)

2. In a medium bowl, combine oats,
brown sugar, almonds, flour, cinnamon and
nutmeg. Stir in butter until combined. Fill and
top apples with oat mixture.

3. When ready to bake, pour remaining
orange juice around the apples and cover
with foil. Bake in a 350° oven for 50 minutes.
Remove foil; bake for 10 to 15 minutes more
or until tender. Cool about 30 minutes.
Transfer to a platter or plates and drizzle
with honey. Serve with yogurt. Garnish with
cinnamon sticks. **Makes 8 servings.**

Make-Ahead Tip: After Step 2, apples can
be covered and refrigerated up to 24 hours
before baking.

Nutrition facts per serving: 383 cal., 14 g fat, 24 mg chol.,
67 mg sodium, 63 g carbo., 6 g fiber, 6 g pro.

Rhubarb Crunch

Prep: 30 minutes Stand: 15 minutes
Bake: 35 minutes Cool: 30 minutes Oven: 375°

1 cup granulated sugar
1½ teaspoons finely shredded orange peel
2 tablespoons orange juice
6 cups sliced fresh rhubarb (about
   2 pounds) or frozen unsweetened
   sliced rhubarb, thawed but not
   drained (about 1½ pounds)
1 tablespoon butter, softened
2 slices firm-texture white or whole
   wheat sandwich bread, cut into
   quarters
¾ cup finely chopped pecans, macadamia
   nuts or almonds
½ cup finely crushed graham crackers
½ cup packed brown sugar
1 teaspoon ground cinnamon or apple
   pie spice
¼ teaspoon ground ginger or ground
   nutmeg
⅛ teaspoon salt
¼ cup butter, melted
   Vanilla ice cream or whipped cream

1. For filling: In a large bowl, stir together
granulated sugar, orange peel and orange
juice. Add rhubarb; gently toss until coated.
Let mixture stand about 15 minutes or until a
syrup forms, stirring occasionally.

2. Using the 1 tablespoon butter, generously
coat bottom and sides of a 2-quart square or
rectangular baking dish. Set aside.

3. Place steel blade in a food processor. Add
bread quarters. Cover and pulse with on/
off turns until bread forms fluffy, soft bread
crumbs. Transfer bread crumbs to a large
bowl. Add pecans, crushed graham crackers,
brown sugar, cinnamon, ginger and salt;
gently toss until combined.

4. Evenly scatter one-third of the crumb
mixture onto the bottom of the prepared
baking dish. Top with the rhubarb mixture.
Sprinkle the remaining crumb mixture over
the rhubarb. Drizzle melted butter over all.

5. Bake in a 375° oven for 35 to 40 minutes
or until the filling is bubbly and tender and
the crumbs are nicely browned. Cool for
30 minutes on a wire rack. Serve warm with
ice cream. **Makes 6 servings.**

Nutrition facts per serving: 597 cal., 29 g fat, 75 mg chol.,
243 mg sodium, 82 g carbo., 4 g fiber, 6 g pro.

Rhubarb-Berry Crunch: Prepare as directed,
except substitute 1½ cups blueberries,
blackberries, raspberries or coarsely chopped
strawberries for 1½ cups of the sliced
rhubarb. Continue as directed.

Rhubarb Crunch

**Single-Serving
Caramel Apples**

Make-Ahead Tip: To make ahead, prepare as directed through Step 4. Cover each dish with plastic wrap. Chill up to 6 hours. To serve, uncover; bake as directed above.

Nutrition facts per serving: 573 cal., 37 g fat, 66 mg chol., 284 mg sodium, 58 g carbo., 3 g fiber, 7 g pro.

Maple-Baked Stuffed Pears

Prep: 20 minutes Bake: 40 minutes Oven: 350°

  4 medium firm pears with stems
  ¼ cup dried cranberries or dried tart red
      cherries
  3 tablespoons toasted chopped walnuts
  1 tablespoon lemon juice
2½ teaspoons sugar
  ¼ cup water
  ¼ cup pure maple syrup
      Sweetened whipped cream
      Fresh mint leaves (optional)

1. Peel whole pears, leaving the stems intact. Cut a thin slice from the bottom of each pear so the pears stand up. Working through the bottom of each pear, use a melon baller to remove the core.

2. In a small mixing bowl, combine cranberries, walnuts, lemon juice and sugar. Spoon mixture into bottom of each pear. Stand pears in a 2-quart square baking dish. Add the water to baking dish. Pour maple syrup over and around pears. Sprinkle any remaining filling into bottom of dish.

3. Bake, covered, in 350° oven for 20 minutes. Uncover; bake for 20 to 25 minutes more or until pears are tender, basting occasionally with cooking liquid.

4. To serve, spoon whipped cream in the center of four dessert plates. Place pears in cream. Spoon any remaining cooking liquid over pears. If you like, garnish with mint leaves. Serve warm. **Makes 4 servings.**

Nutrition facts per serving: 330 cal., 15 g fat, 41 mg chol., 16 mg sodium, 52 g carbo., 6 g fiber, 2 g pro.

Single-Serving Caramel Apples

*Prep: 30 minutes Bake: 20 minutes
Cool: 10 minutes Oven: 400°*

  1 17.3-ounce package frozen puff pastry
      sheets (2 sheets), thawed
      Butter
  4 medium Granny Smith, Jonagold
      and/or Fuji apples, peeled, cored
      and thinly sliced
  2 tablespoons packed brown sugar
  3 tablespoons butter, cut up
  ½ cup caramel-flavor ice cream topping
  1 egg yolk, lightly beaten
  2 tablespoons granulated sugar
      Whipped cream

1. Unfold pastry sheets onto a lightly floured surface. Arrange eight* 4- to 5-inch individual quiche dishes, pie plates or individual shallow casserole dishes atop pastry sheets, top sides down. (If the pastry sheets are not large enough for all the dishes to fit, roll out the pastry sheets until they are large enough.)

2. Using a small knife, cut out pastry around the dishes. Discard excess pastry. Set pastry aside. Butter insides of dishes; set aside.

3. In a large bowl, toss together apple slices and brown sugar. Arrange apple slices in buttered dishes. Dot with the 3 tablespoons butter. Drizzle apples with ice cream topping.

4. Place a cut-out pastry piece atop each dish. Press pastry against the top insides of the dishes. Brush pastry with egg yolk; sprinkle with granulated sugar. Place dishes on a very large baking sheet.

5. Bake in a 400° oven about 20 minutes or until pastry is golden brown and apples are just tender. Cool slightly. Serve warm with whipped cream. **Makes 8 servings.**

*Tip: If you do not have eight of the same kind of dish, use a combination of dishes.

Maple-Baked Stuffed Pears

Peach Pinwheel Dumplings

Peach Pinwheel Dumplings

Prep: 45 minutes Bake: 45 minutes
Cool: 30 minutes Oven: 350°

- ½ cup butter or margarine
- 2 cups sugar
- 2 cups water
- 1 teaspoon vanilla
- 2 cups self-rising flour
- ½ cup shortening
- ½ cup milk
- 5 cups chopped, pitted and peeled peaches or frozen unsweetened peach slices, thawed and chopped
- ½ teaspoon ground cinnamon
- ¼ to ½ teaspoon ground nutmeg
  Vanilla ice cream

1. Place butter in a 3-quart rectangular baking dish and set dish in a 350° oven to melt butter, allowing 5 to 8 minutes. (Be sure to watch carefully to avoid overbrowning the butter.) Remove dish from oven; set aside.

2. For syrup: In a medium saucepan, combine sugar and the water. Cook and stir over medium heat until sugar is dissolved; bring to boiling and boil, uncovered, for 5 minutes. Remove saucepan from heat; stir in vanilla. Cover and keep warm.

3. For dough: Place 2 cups flour in a large mixing bowl. Use a pastry blender to cut shortening into flour until pieces are pea size. Make a well in center. Add milk all at once. Stir just until moistened. Knead dough on a lightly floured 14x12-inch piece of waxed paper 10 to 12 strokes or until nearly smooth. Lightly sprinkle dough with flour. Cover with another 14x12-inch piece of waxed paper. Roll out dough to a 12x10-inch rectangle (about ¼ inch thick).

4. For filling: In another large bowl, combine peaches, cinnamon and nutmeg. Spoon 3 cups of the peaches on top of the melted butter in the baking dish, spreading evenly to form a single layer. Spoon the remaining 2 cups peaches evenly over the dough rectangle. Roll dough into a spiral, starting from a long side. Pinch seam to seal. Cut into

twelve 1-inch-thick pieces. Arrange rolls, cut sides down, over the peaches in the dish. Pour syrup carefully around rolls. (This will look like too much syrup, but the rolls will absorb the liquid during baking.)

5. Bake in the 350° oven for 45 to 50 minutes or until golden. Cool on a wire rack 30 minutes. Serve warm in dishes with a scoop of vanilla ice cream. **Makes 12 servings.**

Nutrition facts per serving: 378 cal., 17 g fat, 21 mg chol., 324 mg sodium, 56 g carbo., 2 g fiber, 3 g pro.

Chocolate Crepes with Nutmeg Vanilla Sauce

Prep: 30 minutes Stand: 20 minutes .
Cook: 18 minutes

- 1 cup all-purpose flour
- ⅓ cup sugar
- ⅓ cup unsweetened cocoa powder
- 2 eggs, lightly beaten
- 1 cup milk
- 2 tablespoons butter, melted
- 1 teaspoon vanilla
- ½ cup whipping cream
- 2 tablespoons sugar
  Nutmeg Vanilla Sauce (recipe follows)
  Chocolate curls

1. In a small mixing bowl, stir together flour, ⅓ cup sugar and the cocoa powder; set aside. In a medium bowl, whisk together eggs, milk, butter and vanilla; add flour mixture and whisk until combined. Let batter stand at room temperature for 20 minutes.

2. Heat a lightly greased 8-inch skillet over medium-high heat; remove from heat. Pour 3 tablespoons of batter into center of skillet. Lift and tilt skillet to spread batter and coat bottom of pan. Return skillet to heat; cook one side only about 1½ minutes or until the top is no longer shiny. Invert pan over paper towels to remove finished crepes. Repeat with remaining batter, making 12 crepes total. (Adjust heat as necessary during cooking, greasing skillet and stirring batter if needed.)

3. In a chilled medium bowl, combine whipping cream and 2 tablespoons sugar.

Beat with an electric mixer on medium speed until soft peaks form.

4. To serve, fold each crepe in half. Fold in half again, forming a triangle. Place two crepes on each of six shallow dessert plates. Drizzle with Nutmeg Vanilla Sauce; top with whipped cream and chocolate curls. **Makes 6 servings.**

Nutmeg Vanilla Sauce: In a small saucepan, stir together three egg yolks, ¾ cup milk and 2 tablespoons sugar. Cook and stir continuously with a wooden spoon or heatproof rubber spatula over medium heat until mixture thickens and just coats the back of a clean metal spoon. Remove pan from heat. Stir in 1 teaspoon vanilla and ¼ teaspoon freshly grated nutmeg or ⅛ teaspoon ground nutmeg. Quickly cool the custard sauce by placing the saucepan in a large bowl of ice water for 1 to 2 minutes, stirring constantly. Pour custard sauce into a bowl. Cover the surface with plastic wrap to prevent a skin from forming. Chill for at least 1 hour, without stirring, before serving. Makes about 1 cup.

Nutrition facts per serving: 371 cal., 18 g fat, 219 mg chol., 92 mg sodium, 43 g carbo., 1 g fiber, 10 g pro.

**Chocolate Crepes with
Nutmeg Vanilla Sauce**

Cherry-Berry Rich Shortcakes

Prep: 30 minutes Bake: 10 minutes
Cool: 5 minutes Oven: 425°

- 2 cups fresh or frozen unsweetened blueberries, thawed
- 1 cup fresh or frozen unsweetened raspberries, thawed, or sliced strawberries
- 1 cup fresh or frozen unsweetened pitted sweet cherries, thawed
- 1/4 cup sugar
- 3 cups packaged biscuit mix
- 1/4 teaspoon ground nutmeg or ground cinnamon
- 1/4 cup cold butter
- 2/3 cup half-and-half, light cream or whole milk
  Sugar
- 1 cup whipping cream
- 2 tablespoons sugar
- 1/2 teaspoon vanilla

1. In a large bowl, combine blueberries, raspberries, cherries and 1/4 cup sugar; set aside.

2. For shortcake: In a large bowl, stir together biscuit mix and nutmeg. Use a pastry blender to cut butter into flour mixture until mixture resembles coarse crumbs. Make a well in the center of the mixture. Add half-and-half all at once. Using a fork, stir just until moistened. Drop dough into six mounds on an ungreased baking sheet; flatten each mound with the back of a spoon until about 3/4 inch thick. Lightly sprinkle each mound with additional sugar.

3. Bake in a 425° oven for 10 to 12 minutes or until golden. Cool on a wire rack for 5 minutes.

4. In a chilled medium bowl, beat whipping cream, 2 tablespoons sugar and the vanilla with an electric mixer with chilled beaters on medium speed until soft peaks form.

5. To serve, split warm shortcakes in half horizontally. Using a wide spatula, carefully lift off the top layer. Place bottom layers in six shallow dessert dishes. Spoon whipped cream over the bottom layer. Spoon fruit mixture over whipped cream. Carefully replace the top layers. Serve immediately.
Makes 6 servings.

Nutrition facts per serving: 604 cal., 35 g fat, 86 mg chol., 855 mg sodium, 67 g carbo., 4 g fiber, 7 g pro.

Gingered Cantaloupe & Blackberry Shortcakes

Prep: 30 minutes Bake: 12 minutes Oven: 400°

- Honey-Ginger Fruit (recipe follows)
- 2 cups all-purpose flour
- 1/4 cup sugar
- 1 tablespoon baking powder
- 1/4 teaspoon salt
- 1/3 cup cold butter, cut into small pieces
- 1 egg, lightly beaten
- 1/2 cup cold milk
- 1 1/2 teaspoons finely snipped crystallized ginger or 1/2 teaspoon ground ginger
- 1 1/2 teaspoons vanilla
- 2 cups whipping cream, whipped with 2 tablespoons sugar

1. Prepare Honey-Ginger Fruit. Cover and store in refrigerator while preparing the shortcake.

2. Lightly grease a baking sheet; set aside. In a medium bowl, combine flour, sugar, baking powder and salt. Using a pastry blender, cut in butter until mixture resembles coarse crumbs. Make a well in the center of flour mixture.

3. In a small bowl, combine egg, milk, 1 1/2 teaspoons finely snipped crystallized ginger and the vanilla. Add egg mixture all at once to flour mixture. Using a fork, stir just until moistened.

4. Drop dough into eight mounds on the prepared baking sheet. Bake in a 400° oven for 12 to 15 minutes or until golden and a toothpick inserted into centers comes out clean. Remove from baking sheet; cool on wire rack.

5. To serve, split shortcakes in half horizontally; place bottoms in dessert dishes. Spoon half of the Honey-Ginger Fruit and syrup on shortcake bottoms; top with half of the whipped cream. Add shortcake tops. Spoon remaining fruit and syrup on shortcake tops. Dollop with remaining whipped cream. Garnish with additional snipped crystallized ginger, if you like.
Makes 8 servings.

Honey-Ginger Fruit: In a small saucepan, combine 1/3 cup honey; 1/3 cup white grape juice, apple juice or unsweetened pineapple juice; and 1 1/2 teaspoons finely snipped crystallized ginger. Cook and stir over medium heat just until boiling. Remove from heat and stir in 1/4 teaspoon vanilla; transfer hot mixture to a heatproof medium bowl and cool for 15 minutes. Add 2 cups coarsely chopped cantaloupe and/or honeydew melon and 1 1/2 cups fresh blackberries or blueberries to honey mixture; gently stir to coat. Cover and chill in the refrigerator. Makes about 3 cups fruit and syrup.

Nutrition facts per serving: 418 cal., 89 mg chol., 299 mg sodium, 55 g carbo., 3 g fiber, 6 g pro.

Cherry-Berry Rich Shortcakes

Gingered Cantaloupe &
Blackberry Shortcakes

Vanilla Bean Soufflé with
Quick Vanilla Custard Sauce

Vanilla Bean Soufflé with Quick Vanilla Custard Sauce

Prep: 30 minutes Bake: 40 minutes Oven: 350°

Butter, softened
Sugar
1¼ cups half-and-half, light cream or
    whole milk
1 4- to 6-inch vanilla bean or
    1 tablespoon vanilla
¼ cup butter
⅓ cup all-purpose flour
6 egg yolks, lightly beaten
6 egg whites
1 teaspoon vanilla
½ cup sugar
    Quick Vanilla Custard Sauce (recipe
    follows)
    Fresh mint sprigs (optional)

1. Butter the sides of a 2-quart soufflé dish and sprinkle with sugar. To make a collar for the soufflé dish, measure enough foil to wrap around the top of the soufflé dish and add 3 inches. Fold the foil in thirds lengthwise. Lightly butter one side of the foil and sprinkle with sugar. Attach the foil, sugar side in, around the outside of the dish so the foil extends 2 inches above the dish. Tape or pin the ends of the foil together; set aside. Adjust the oven rack to the lowest position.

2. In a small saucepan, heat half-and-half and vanilla bean (if using) until bubbles form at the edge of the saucepan. Remove from heat. Remove vanilla bean; let cool for 5 minutes. Using a paring knife, slit vanilla bean lengthwise. Scrape out seeds. Stir seeds (or the 1 tablespoon vanilla, if using) into half-and-half.

3. In another small saucepan, melt the ¼ cup butter. Stir in the flour. Add half-and-half mixture. Whisk over medium heat until thickened and bubbly. Remove from heat (mixture will be thick). Gradually whisk the mixture into the beaten yolks; set aside.

4. In a large mixing bowl, beat egg whites and the 1 teaspoon vanilla with an electric mixer on medium speed until soft peaks form (tips curl). Gradually add the ½ cup sugar, about 1 tablespoon at a time, beating on medium-high speed until stiff peaks form (tips stand straight).

5. Gently fold the egg yolk mixture into the egg white mixture. Spoon mixture into the prepared soufflé dish. Place soufflé dish in a 15x10x1-inch baking pan. Bake in a 350° oven 40 to 45 minutes or until a knife inserted near the center comes out clean. Serve at once with Quick Vanilla Custard Sauce. If you like, garnish each serving with a fresh mint sprig. **Makes 6 servings.**

Quick Vanilla Custard Sauce: Allow 1½ cups good-quality vanilla bean ice cream to soften, covered, in the refrigerator about 3 hours to become pourable consistency. When ready to serve over hot soufflés, stir in ¼ teaspoon vanilla. Makes about 1 cup.

Nutrition facts per serving: 448 cal., 27 g fat, 300 mg chol., 176 mg sodium, 39 g carbo., 0 g fiber, 10 g pro.

Wisconsin Honey Bee & Vanilla Bean Pudding

Prep: 35 minutes Cool: 15 minutes Chill: 3 hours

2 cups whole milk
1 to 2 4- to 6-inch vanilla beans
1 cup whipping cream or heavy cream
3 egg yolks
½ cup sugar
¼ cup mild-flavor Wisconsin honey or
    other honey
3 tablespoons cornstarch
⅛ teaspoon salt
1 tablespoon butter or unsalted butter
    Candied orange peel (optional)

1. In a heavy medium saucepan, bring milk to boiling over medium heat, stirring occasionally. Remove from heat. Using the tip of a paring knife, slit the vanilla beans down the center. Scrape the seeds into the hot milk and add the pods. Cool 15 minutes. Cover and chill 2 to 24 hours. Remove the vanilla pods; using two fingers, press the milk out of the pods into the milk mixture to extract all the seeds; discard pods.

2. In the same saucepan, heat the milk and 1 cup whipping cream over medium heat until boiling, stirring occasionally. Remove from heat.

3. Meanwhile, in a medium bowl, beat egg yolks with an electric mixer for 1 minute on medium speed. Beat in sugar, honey, cornstarch and salt until well combined. Gradually beat in about 1 cup of the hot milk mixture until well combined.

4. Add the egg yolk mixture to the remaining milk mixture in the saucepan. Bring to a gentle boil over medium heat, stirring constantly; reduce heat. Cook and stir for 2 minutes more. Remove from heat. Stir in butter until melted. If necessary, strain mixture to remove any lumps.

5. Pour pudding into four or five 6- to 8-ounce individual dessert dishes or a 3½- to 4-cup serving bowl. Cover surface of pudding with plastic wrap. Chill at least 1 hour for individual dishes or at least 3 hours for the large serving bowl or until pudding is completely chilled. (Do not stir during chilling.) Top pudding with candied orange peel, if you like. **Makes 4 or 5 servings.**

Nutrition facts per serving: 600 cal., 38 g fat, 280 mg chol., 178 mg sodium, 59 g carbo., 1 g fiber, 8 g pro.

Wisconsin Honey Bee & Vanilla Bean Pudding

Vanilla Cake Batter Ice Cream

Vanilla Cake Batter Ice Cream

Prep: 30 minutes Cool: 1 hour Chill: 2 hours

2 cups half-and-half, light cream or
   whole milk
1 package 1-layer-size white cake mix
½ cup sugar
2 cups whipping cream or heavy cream
1 tablespoon vanilla

1. In a medium saucepan, stir together half-and-half, cake mix and sugar. Gently heat and stir until mixture just bubbles. Pour mixture into a large heatproof mixing bowl and whisk briskly. Cover and cool for 1 hour. Stir in whipping cream and vanilla. Cover the bowl with plastic wrap, then chill in the refrigerator for at least 2 hours or until the mixture is well chilled.

2. Pour into a 1½-quart ice cream freezer and freeze according to the manufacturer's instructions. Transfer to a freezer container and freeze overnight to ripen. **Makes 5 cups.**

Nutrition facts per ½-cup serving: 370 cal., 26 g fat, 84 mg chol., 198 mg sodium, 34 g carbo., 0 g fiber, 3 g pro.

Birthday Cake Batter Ice Cream: Prepare as directed above; pour the mixture into an ice cream freezer. Freeze according to the manufacturer's instructions. Stir in 2 tablespoons colored sprinkles and, if you like, stir ½ cup miniature chocolate pieces, chopped nuts and/or coarsely chopped maraschino cherries into the ice cream mixture before freezing overnight to ripen.

Chocolate Cake Batter Ice Cream: Prepare as directed above, except substitute one package one-layer chocolate cake mix for white cake mix. Pour the mixture into an ice cream freezer. Freeze according to the manufacturer's instructions. Stir ⅔ cup miniature chocolate pieces into the ice cream mixture before freezing overnight to ripen.

Cappuccino Mousse

Prep: 35 minutes Chill: 4 hours

2 tablespoons instant espresso coffee
   powder or regular instant coffee
   crystals
¼ cup water
1 teaspoon unflavored gelatin
6 egg yolks
½ cup sugar
2 cups whipping cream or heavy cream
   Bittersweet chocolate shavings or curls

1. In a small bowl, dissolve coffee powder in the water. Sprinkle gelatin over coffee; let stand for 10 minutes.

2. In a large metal bowl or the top of a double boiler, beat egg yolks and sugar with a wire whisk until combined. Place over gently boiling water (metal bowl or upper pan should not touch water). Cook, stirring rapidly with a whisk, about 10 minutes or until egg mixture begins to thicken and coats a metal spoon (160°). Remove from heat.

3. Add coffee-gelatin mixture to warm egg mixture; whisk until combined. Beat egg-gelatin mixture with an electric mixer on medium speed about 5 minutes or until mixture is cool; set aside.

4. Thoroughly wash beaters. In a chilled mixing bowl, beat whipping cream with an electric mixer on medium speed until stiff peaks form. Gently fold whipped cream, one-third at a time, into egg-gelatin mixture.

5. Divide mixture evenly among eight chilled wine or parfait glasses (or place in a large glass bowl). Cover and chill at least 4 hours. To serve, garnish with chocolate shavings or curls. **Makes 8 servings.**

Nutrition facts per serving: 319 cal., 27 g fat, 240 mg chol., 31 mg sodium, 18 g carbo., 0 g fiber, 4 g pro.

Honey-Tangerine Mousse

Prep: 20 minutes Chill: 6 hours

1½ teaspoons finely shredded tangerine peel
½ cup tangerine juice
1 teaspoon unflavored gelatin
½ cup refrigerated or frozen egg
   product, thawed
¼ cup honey
1 cup whipping cream

1. In a small saucepan, combine tangerine peel, juice and gelatin. Stir over low heat until gelatin is dissolved; cool.

2. In a mixing bowl, beat egg product with electric mixer until soft peaks form. Gradually beat in the honey on medium-high speed until combined. Continue beating about 3 minutes more or until mixture is very thick with soft peaks

3. In another medium mixing bowl, beat whipping cream with electric mixer on high speed until soft peaks form. Fold in the tangerine mixture and beaten honey mixture.

4. Spoon into eight sherbet glasses. Cover and chill for at least 6 hours or overnight until set. **Makes 8 servings.**

Nutrition facts per serving: 151 cal., 11 g fat, 41 mg chol., 41 mg sodium, 11 g carbo., 0 g fiber, 2 g pro.

Cappuccino Mousse

**Honeyed Frozen
Yogurt Sundaes**

Ice Cream Sandwich Sundaes

*Prep: 20 minutes Freeze: 1 hour to 1 week
Cook: 5 minutes Stand: 5 minutes*

1½ to 2 cups vanilla or desired-flavor ice
    cream
32 1½-inch shortbread cookies (such as
    Lorna Doone)
  2 small ripe pears or apples, peeled,
    cored and finely chopped
  1 cup caramel ice cream topping
⅓ cup chopped pecans or walnuts,
    toasted
    Whipped cream or frozen whipped
    dessert topping, thawed (optional)

1. Place a small scoop of ice cream on the
bottom side of half of the cookies. Top with
remaining cookies, bottom sides down,
pressing together lightly. Place in an airtight
container and freeze until ready to serve, up
to 1 week.

2. To serve, combine pears and caramel
topping in a small saucepan. Heat over
medium-low heat until pears start to
soften, 5 to 8 minutes. Remove ice cream
sandwiches from the freezer. Let stand about
5 minutes. Place two sandwiches in each of
eight serving bowls. Top with caramel
mixture, nuts and if you like, whipped cream.
Makes 8 servings.

Nutrition facts per serving: 425 cal., 17 g fat, 37 mg chol.,
255 mg sodium, 63 g carbo., 2 g fiber, 5 g pro.

Honeyed Frozen Yogurt Sundaes

Start To Finish: 15 minutes

1 quart low-fat or fat-free vanilla frozen
    yogurt or vanilla ice cream
    Toasted almonds and/or toasted
    coconut*
    Honey, such as wildflower, orange
    blossom or clover
    Waffle cone or bowl, broken into small
    pieces
    Edible flowers

1. Divide yogurt or ice cream among
six serving dishes. Top each serving with
toasted almonds and/or toasted coconut.
Drizzle with honey. Sprinkle with pieces of
waffle cone and edible flowers. **Makes
6 servings.**

***Note:** To toast almonds and/or coconut,
spread in a single layer in a shallow baking
pan. Bake in a 350° oven for 5 to 10 minutes
or until nuts and/or coconut are lightly
golden, stirring once or twice. Cool nuts
completely.

Nutrition facts per serving: 231 cal., 6 g fat, 13 mg chol.,
101 mg sodium, 40 g carbo., 3 g fiber, 7 g pro.

Ice Cream Sandwich Sundaes

Ice Cream-Cookie Cake

Ice Cream-Cookie Cake

Prep: 30 minutes Freeze: 7 hours

    1 to 2 pints cherry vanilla, real strawberry
      or black cherry ice cream
    2 cups coarsely crushed shortbread
      cookies, cinnamon shortbread cookies
      or fudge-striped shortbread cookies
      (about thirty 1½-inch square cookies
      or 6 to 7 ounces)
    ⅓ cup butter or margarine, melted and
      cooled slightly
    ½ cup toffee pieces, shredded coconut,
      miniature semisweet chocolate pieces
      or toasted slivered almonds
    1 pint pistachio, peanut butter cup or
      French vanilla ice cream, softened*
    1 pint chocolate or chocolate chip ice
      cream, softened*

1. Working quickly, scoop cherry vanilla ice cream into 1½- to 2-inch balls. Place balls on a chilled, waxed paper-lined baking sheet; freeze. In a medium bowl, combine crushed cookies and butter. Stir in toffee pieces.

2. Press half of the cookie mixture on the bottom of a 9-inch springform pan. Freeze for 10 minutes or until firm. Carefully spread softened pistachio ice cream evenly over cookie mixture. Freeze for 1 hour to set. Carefully spread softened chocolate ice cream evenly over pistachio ice cream.

3. Place ice cream balls over ice cream layer, leaving ½ to 1 inch at edges. Sprinkle with remaining cookie mixture. Cover and freeze at least 6 hours or overnight.

4. To serve, remove the sides of the pan. Cut into wedges. Serve immediately with whipped cream. Cover and store any remaining ice cream cake in the freezer. **Makes 12 to 16 servings.**

*To soften ice cream: Place ice cream in a chilled bowl. Use a wooden spoon to stir ice cream and press against sides of bowl until evenly softened and ice cream will spread easily.

Nutrition facts per serving: 411 cal., 29 g fat, 110 mg chol., 197 mg sodium, 35 g carbo., 1 g fiber, 5 g pro.

Ice Cream Waffle Sundaes

Start to finish: 20 minutes

    ½ cup hot fudge-flavor ice cream topping
    1 to 2 tablespoons crème de cacao or
      1 tablespoon coffee liqueur or peanut
      butter
    2 giant waffle ice cream cones or bowls
      or 4 regular waffle cones
    2 cups tin roof sundae ice cream, coffee
      ice cream, dulce de leche caramel
      ice cream, caramel swirl ice cream or
      favorite flavor ice cream
    ½ cup sliced banana or quartered
      strawberries
    2 tablespoons chopped chocolate-
      covered peanut butter cups

1. In a heavy small saucepan, stir ice cream topping and crème de cacao over medium-low heat until smooth. Remove saucepan from heat. Place each waffle cone in a tall cup or bowl. Scoop ice cream into cones. Top with banana slices. Drizzle with sauce. Top with chopped peanut butter cups. **Makes 2 large or 4 small servings.**

Nutrition facts per large serving: 842 cal., 35 g fat, 66 mg chol., 257 mg sodium, 124 g carbo., 4 g fiber, 17 g pro.

**Ice Cream
Waffle Sundaes**

Lemon Drop Bark

Prep: 20 minutes Chill: 30 minutes

    1 pound vanilla-flavor candy coating,
        cut up
    6 ounces white baking chocolate,
        coarsely chopped
    ¾ cup finely crushed lemon drops,
        peppermint candy canes or fruit-
        flavor hard candy (about 6 ounces)
    ¼ cup finely chopped macadamia nuts or
        slivered almonds (optional)

1. Line a large baking sheet with foil; set aside. In a heavy medium saucepan, heat candy coating and white baking chocolate over low heat, stirring frequently until melted and smooth. Remove from heat.

2. Stir in ½ cup of the crushed candy. Pour mixture onto the prepared baking sheet; spread to about ⅜ inch thick. Sprinkle with

Lemon Drop Bark

remaining crushed candy and, if you like, macadamia nuts; press slightly.

3. Chill candy about 30 minutes or until firm. (Or let candy stand at room temperature for several hours until firm.) Use foil to lift candy from the baking sheet; carefully peel off foil and break candy into pieces.

4. To store, layer candy pieces between waxed paper in airtight container; cover. Store in refrigerator up to 2 weeks or freeze up to 3 months. Serve at room temperature. **Makes about 1¾ pounds (about thirty-six 2-inch pieces).**

Nutrition facts per piece: 118 cal., 6 g fat, 1 mg chol., 6 mg sodium, 16 g carbo., 0 g fiber, 0 g pro.

Old-Fashioned Ice Cream Sundae Cake

Prep: 45 minutes Bake: 25 minutes
Cool: 10 minutes Freeze: 13 hours
Stand: 20 minutes Oven: 350°

      2 cups all-purpose flour
      2 teaspoons baking powder
      ¾ teaspoon salt
      ¾ cup shortening
    1½ cups sugar
      1 tablespoon vanilla
      1 cup whole milk
      5 egg whites
      1 pint chocolate ice cream, softened*
      ⅔ cup finely chopped firm banana
          (1 small)
      1 pint vanilla ice cream, softened*
      1 8-ounce can crushed pineapple, well
          drained
      1 pint strawberry ice cream, softened*
      ⅔ cup finely chopped strawberries
      1 12-ounce carton frozen whipped
          dessert topping, thawed
      ½ cup shredded coconut, toasted
          Maraschino cherries with stems

1. Grease and lightly flour two 9x1½-inch round baking pans. In a small bowl, combine flour, baking powder and salt; set aside.

2. In a large mixing bowl, beat shortening with an electric mixer on medium to high

speed for 30 seconds. Add sugar and vanilla; beat until combined. Alternately add flour mixture and milk, beating on low to medium speed after each addition just until combined. Thoroughly wash beaters.

3. In another large mixing bowl, beat egg whites on medium to high speed until stiff peaks form (tips stand straight). Gently fold egg whites into flour mixture. Pour batter into prepared pans.

4. Bake in a 350° oven for 25 to 30 minutes or until a wooden toothpick inserted in centers comes out clean. Cool in pans on wire racks for 10 minutes. Remove from pans; cool completely on wire racks. Slice each cake layer in half horizontally with a long-bladed serrated knife.

5. Place a 9-inch springform pan in a 15x10x1-inch baking pan. Place one layer of cake in the springform pan. Gently stir together chocolate ice cream and banana; spread over cake in pan. (It is ok if some ice cream runs down sides of cake.) Cover and freeze 30 minutes. Top with a second cake layer. Gently stir together vanilla ice cream and pineapple; spread atop second cake layer. Cover and freeze 30 minutes. Top with a third cake layer. Gently stir together strawberry ice cream and strawberries; spread atop third cake layer. Top with remaining cake layer. (Cake layer will rise above the top of springform pan.) Cover and freeze for 12 to 24 hours.

6. To serve, remove cake from freezer. Remove from springform pan and place on a serving platter. Frost top and sides with dessert topping. Sprinkle with coconut and top with maraschino cherries. Let stand 20 minutes before serving. Cut into wedges. Store any remaining cake covered in the freezer. **Makes 16 servings.**

*To soften ice cream: Place ice cream in a large bowl. Let stand 5 minutes; stir with a wooden spoon until just softened and spreadable but not melted.

Nutrition facts per serving: 431 cal., 21 g fat, 29 mg chol., 203 mg sodium, 55 g carbo., 1 g fiber, 5 g pro.

Old-Fashioned Ice Cream
Sundae Cake

Sticky Toffee Pudding,
page 209

HOLIDAY BAKING

Cranberry-Sour Cream Pound Cake

Prep: 30 minutes Stand: 40 minutes
Bake: 1 hour 10 minutes Oven: 325°

¾ cup butter
3 eggs
⅔ cup dried cranberries, snipped dried cherries and/or dried blueberries
2½ cups all-purpose flour
1 teaspoon baking powder
½ teaspoon salt
½ teaspoon baking soda
1¼ cups granulated sugar
1 tablespoon finely shredded orange or lemon peel
1½ teaspoons vanilla
1 8-ounce carton dairy sour cream
Powdered sugar (optional)

1. Allow butter and eggs to stand at room temperature for 30 minutes. Meanwhile,

Cranberry-Sour Cream Pound Cake

grease and lightly flour a 9x5x3-inch loaf pan; set aside. In a small bowl, pour boiling water over dried cranberries; let stand for 10 minutes. Drain well; set aside. In a medium bowl, combine flour, baking powder, salt and baking soda; set aside.

2. In a large mixing bowl, beat butter with an electric mixer on medium to high speed for 30 seconds. Gradually add sugar, 3 tablespoons at a time, beating on medium speed about 6 minutes or until very light and fluffy. Add orange peel and vanilla. Add eggs, one at a time, beating on low to medium speed after each addition, scraping sides of bowl frequently. Alternately add flour mixture and sour cream to butter mixture, beating on low after each addition just until combined. Stir in cranberries. Pour batter into prepared pan.

3. Bake in a 325° oven about 1 hour 10 minutes or until a wooden toothpick inserted near center comes out clean. (Cake will be high in pan.) Cool for 10 minutes in pan on a wire rack. Remove from pan and completely cool on wire rack. If you like, sift powdered sugar over cake just before serving. **Makes 10 to 12 servings.**

Nutrition facts per serving: 417 cal., 20 g fat, 110 mg chol., 336 mg sodium, 54 g carbo., 1 g fiber, 6 g pro.

Coconut-Tangerine Snowball Cupcakes

Prep: 40 minutes Stand: 30 minutes
Bake: 18 minutes Cool: 1 hour Oven: 350°

3 eggs
1⅓ cups buttermilk or sour milk*
2⅔ cups all-purpose flour
1 teaspoon baking powder
½ teaspoon baking soda
½ teaspoon salt
½ cup butter, softened
1⅔ cups sugar
2 teaspoons finely shredded tangerine, orange or lemon peel

1 teaspoon vanilla
⅔ cup flaked coconut, toasted
Tangerine Creamy Frosting (recipe follows)
Flaked coconut (optional)

1. Allow eggs and buttermilk to stand at room temperature for 30 minutes. Line twenty-four 2½-inch muffin cups with paper bake cups; set aside. In a medium bowl, stir together flour, baking powder, baking soda and salt; set aside.

2. In a large mixing bowl, beat butter with an electric mixer on medium to high speed for 30 seconds. Add sugar, tangerine peel and vanilla; beat until well combined. Add eggs, one at a time, beating well after each addition. Alternately add flour mixture and buttermilk to butter mixture, beating on low speed after each addition just until combined. Stir in toasted coconut.

3. Fill prepared muffin cups two-thirds full. Bake in a 350° oven for 18 to 20 minutes or until cupcakes are golden brown and spring back when lightly pressed. Cool on a wire rack for 5 minutes. Remove cupcakes from pan and cool completely before frosting.

4. Frost cupcakes with Tangerine Creamy Frosting and, if you like, sprinkle with additional flaked coconut. **Makes 24 cupcakes.**

Tangerine Creamy Frosting: In a large mixing bowl, beat one 3-ounce package cream cheese, softened; 3 tablespoons butter, softened; ¾ teaspoon vanilla; and ½ to ¾ teaspoon finely shredded tangerine, orange or lemon peel with an electric mixer on medium speed until combined. Gradually add 1¾ cups powdered sugar, beating until smooth. Makes about 1⅓ cups frosting.

*To make sour milk: In a 2-cup glass measure place 4 teaspoons lemon juice or vinegar. Add enough milk to make 1⅓ cups; stir. Let stand for 5 minutes before using.

Nutrition facts per cupcake: 229 cal., 9 g fat, 45 mg chol., 170 mg sodium, 36 g carbo., 1 g fiber, 3 g pro.

Coconut-Tangerine
Snowball Cupcakes

Red Velvet Cheesecake

Sticky Toffee Pudding

Prep: 30 minutes Bake: 20 minutes
Cool: 13 minutes Oven: 350°

  1 cup pitted whole dates, chopped
¾ cup water
  1 tablespoon mild-flavor molasses
  1 cup all-purpose flour
  1 teaspoon baking powder
¼ teaspoon baking soda
¼ teaspoon salt
¼ teaspoon ground cinnamon
¼ teaspoon ground nutmeg
½ cup butter, softened (1 stick)
½ cup packed dark brown sugar
  1 egg
½ teaspoon vanilla
    Honey Toffee Sauce (recipe follows)
    Chocolate-covered toffee pieces

1. In a medium saucepan, combine dates and the water. Bring to boiling; reduce heat. Cook, covered, for 15 minutes or until most of the liquid is absorbed, stirring occasionally. Remove from heat; stir in molasses. Set aside.

2. Grease eight 6-ounce ramekins, soufflé dishes or custard cups. Place in a 15x10x1-inch baking pan. In a medium bowl, stir together flour, baking powder, baking soda, salt, cinnamon and nutmeg; set aside.

3. In a large mixing bowl, beat butter with an electric mixer on medium for 30 seconds. Add brown sugar; beat until well combined. Add egg and vanilla; beat for 1 minute more. Add date mixture to butter mixture, beating on low speed just until combined. With a wooden spoon, stir in flour mixture until combined. Spoon about ⅓ cup batter into each prepared ramekin.

4. Bake in a 350° oven for 20 to 25 minutes or until top springs back when lightly touched. Cool in ramekins on a wire rack for 3 minutes. Using a knife, loosen pudding from sides of ramekins. Invert onto dessert plates. Spoon 3 tablespoons of Honey Toffee Sauce over each pudding, allowing it to drip down the sides and cover the top. Top with toffee pieces. **Makes 8 servings.**

Honey Toffee Sauce: Slit half of a vanilla bean lengthwise. Scrape out seeds. In a small saucepan, bring 1 cup whipping cream and vanilla seeds just to boiling, stirring frequently. Remove from heat. In a heavy medium saucepan, combine ⅓ cup butter, ⅓ cup packed dark brown sugar and ⅛ teaspoon salt. Cook and stir over medium heat for 3 to 5 minutes or until mixture just comes to a full boil. Slowly whisk the hot whipping cream mixture into butter mixture. Simmer, stirring constantly, over medium to medium-low heat for 6 minutes more. Remove from heat; stir in 2 tablespoons honey. Serve warm. Makes about 1½ cups.

Nutrition facts per serving: 549 cal., 37 g fat, 139 mg chol., 351 mg sodium, 54 g carbo., 2 g fiber, 4 g pro.

Red Velvet Cheesecake

Prep: 45 minutes Bake: 1 hour
Cool: 1 hour 45 minutes Chill: 4 hours Oven: 350°

  1 pound milk chocolate, chopped
½ cup butter
  1 9-ounce package chocolate wafer
    cookies (40 to 45 cookies)
  1 cup semisweet chocolate pieces
  1 cup slivered almonds
½ cup packed brown sugar
½ cup butter, melted
  4 8-ounce packages cream cheese,
    softened
  1 8-ounce carton dairy sour cream
⅓ cup granulated sugar
⅓ cup buttermilk
  1 1-ounce bottle red food coloring
  4 eggs
  2 egg yolks
    Powdered sugar

1. In a medium saucepan, melt chocolate and ½ cup butter over low heat; transfer to a bowl and cool completely.

2. For crust: Place wafer cookies, chocolate pieces, almonds and brown sugar in a large food processor. Cover and process until finely ground. Add the ½ cup melted butter; cover and process until well combined. Transfer crumbs to a 10x3-inch springform pan with a

removable bottom. Press crumbs onto bottom and up the sides of the pan, leaving a ½-inch space at the top of the pan. Set aside.

3. In a very large mixing bowl, beat chocolate mixture, cream cheese, sour cream, sugar, buttermilk and food coloring with an electric mixer on medium to high speed until combined. Add four eggs and two egg yolks. Beat on low until combined.

4. Pour filling into crumb crust-lined springform pan. Place springform pan in a shallow baking pan on the oven rack. Bake in a 350° oven about 1 hour or until 2 inches of outside edge appear set when shaken gently.

5. Remove springform pan from baking pan. Cool cheesecake in pan on a wire rack for 15 minutes. Use a small metal spatula to loosen cheesecake from sides of pan. Cool 30 minutes more. Remove sides of pan. Cool for 1 hour; cover and chill at least 4 hours.

6. Use a doily to create design with powdered sugar on top. **Makes 20 servings.**

Nutrition facts per serving: 546 cal., 42 g fat, 148 mg chol., 319 mg sodium, 40 g carbo., 2 g fiber, 9 g pro.

Sticky Toffee Pudding

Key Lime Spritz Cookies

Key Lime Spritz Cookies

Prep: 30 minutes   Bake: 6 minutes per batch
Stand: 20 minutes   Oven: 400°

1 cup unsalted butter, softened
¾ cup granulated sugar
¼ teaspoon salt
¼ teaspoon baking powder
1 egg
1 teaspoon finely shredded Key lime or lime peel (set aside)
2½ cups all-purpose flour
2 teaspoons Key lime or lime juice
   Coarse sugar (optional)
   Lime Icing (optional) (recipe follows)
   Green colored sugar (optional)

1. In a large mixing bowl, beat butter with an electric mixer on medium to high speed for 30 seconds. Add granulated sugar, salt and baking powder. Beat until combined, scraping sides of bowl. Beat in egg and juice until combined. Beat in as much of the flour as you can with the mixer. Using a wooden spoon, stir in any remaining flour and the lime peel.

2. Place unchilled dough into cookie press fitted with template. Force dough through cookie press, forming desired shapes 1 inch apart on ungreased cookie sheets. If you like, sprinkle cookies with coarse sugar.

3. Bake in a 400° oven for 6 to 8 minutes or until edges are firm but not brown. Transfer cookies to wire racks and let cool. If you like, drizzle with Lime Icing; let stand 20 minutes or until set. Or dip tops of cookies in Lime Icing, if you like, and sprinkle with green sugar. Let stand until set.

4. Store uniced cookies in tightly covered container at room temperature for up to 3 days or in the freezer for up to 6 months. **Makes about 84 cookies.**

Lime Icing: In a bowl, stir together ¾ cup powdered sugar, 1½ teaspoons lime juice and enough milk (2 to 3 teaspoons) to make drizzling consistency. If desired, tint pale green with food coloring. Makes about ⅓ cup icing.

Nutrition facts per cookie: 41 cal., 2 g fat, 8 mg chol., 9 mg sodium, 5 g carbo., 0 g fiber, 0 g pro.

Hazelnut-Chocolate Chunk Cookies

Prep: 25 minutes   Bake: 12 minutes per batch
Oven: 325°

3 cups all-purpose flour
¾ teaspoon baking powder
½ teaspoon baking soda
½ teaspoon salt
1 cup butter, softened
½ cup shortening
1 cup granulated sugar
1 cup packed brown sugar
2 eggs
2 teaspoons vanilla or hazelnut liqueur
1 12-ounce package miniature semisweet chocolate pieces
6 ounces premium white baking chocolate, cut into ½-inch chunks
1 cup hazelnuts, toasted, skins removed and chopped, or 1 cup chopped pecans

1. In a medium bowl, combine flour, baking powder, baking soda and salt; set aside.

2. In a very large mixing bowl, beat butter and shortening with an electric mixer on medium to high speed for 30 seconds. Add granulated sugar and brown sugar. Beat until combined, scraping sides of bowl occasionally. Add eggs and vanilla. Beat until combined. Gradually add flour mixture, beating on low speed just until combined (dough will be stiff). Using a wooden spoon, stir in semisweet chocolate pieces, white baking chocolate chunks and hazelnuts.

3. Drop dough from a rounded measuring tablespoon 2 inches apart onto ungreased cookie sheets.

4. Bake in a 325° oven for 12 to 14 minutes or until edges are light brown (do not overbake). Cool on cookie sheets for 1 minute. Transfer to wire racks and let cool. **Makes about 60 cookies.**

Nutrition facts per cookie: 154 cal., 9 g fat, 16 mg chol., 63 mg sodium, 18 g carbo., 1 g fiber, 2 g pro.

Hazelnut-Chocolate Chunk Cookies

Quadruple Ginger Cookies

Prep: 45 minutes Chill: 1 hour
Bake: 10 minutes per batch
Stand: 1 minute per batch Oven: 350°

2 cups all-purpose flour
1½ to 2½ teaspoons ground ginger
1 teaspoon baking soda
1 teaspoon ground cinnamon
¾ teaspoon salt
½ to 1 teaspoon ground cloves
½ to ¾ cup finely snipped crystallized
   ginger
½ cup shortening
¼ cup butter, softened
1 cup packed light brown sugar
¼ cup dark molasses

Quadruple Ginger Cookies

1 egg
1 teaspoon fresh ginger juice* (optional)
¾ cup Ginger Sugar (recipe follows) or
   granulated sugar

1. In a medium bowl, stir together flour, ground ginger, baking soda, cinnamon, salt and cloves. Stir in snipped ginger; set aside.

2. In a large mixing bowl, beat shortening and butter with an electric mixer on medium to high speed for 30 seconds. Add brown sugar. Beat until combined, scraping sides of bowl occasionally. Beat in molasses and egg until combined. Beat in as much of the flour mixture as you can with the mixer. Using a wooden spoon, stir in any remaining flour mixture. If you like, stir in fresh ginger juice. Cover and chill dough for 1 hour or until dough is easy to handle.

3. Place Ginger Sugar in a small bowl. Using the palms of your hands, shape dough into 1-inch balls. Roll balls in the Ginger Sugar. Place 1½ inches apart on lightly greased cookie sheets. Bake in a 350° oven for 10 to 12 minutes or until edges are set. Cool on cookie sheets 1 minute. Transfer to wire racks and let cool. **Makes about 48 cookies.**

Ginger Sugar: Coarsely chop enough fresh ginger to equal ¼ cup; combine in a small bowl with ¾ cup granulated sugar. Let stand 1 hour (sugar will clump slightly from moisture in ginger). Place mixture in a fine-mesh sieve set over a bowl; stir gently so sugar separates from ginger. Discard ginger.

*Note: A garlic press works well to juice fresh ginger. Cut the pieces to fit the press and juice them over a small bowl. Be careful to clean it well to make sure there isn't any garlic flavor mixing in with the ginger juice.

Nutrition facts per cookie: 86 cal., 3 g fat, 7 mg chol., 74 mg sodium, 14 g carbo., 0 g fiber, 1 g pro.

Fat Molasses Cookies

Prep: 40 minutes Chill: 1 hour
Bake: 10 minutes per batch Oven: 375°

5 cups all-purpose flour
2 teaspoons baking soda
1 teaspoon ground ginger
1 teaspoon ground cinnamon
¼ teaspoon salt
1 cup shortening
1 cup packed brown sugar
2 eggs
2 tablespoons water
2 tablespoons vinegar
1 cup molasses
   Coarse sugar

1. In a large bowl, combine the flour, baking soda, ground ginger, cinnamon and salt. Set aside.

2. In a very large bowl, beat shortening for 30 seconds. Add brown sugar and beat until fluffy. Add eggs, the water, vinegar and molasses; beat until combined. Add flour mixture and beat until combined. Divide dough in half. Cover and chill for 1 hour or until easy to handle.

3. On a floured surface, roll out half of the dough to ½-inch thickness. Cut dough using a 3-inch scalloped or round cutter. Place cookies 2½ inches apart on ungreased cookie sheets. Sprinkle with coarse sugar.

4. Bake in a 375° oven about 10 minutes or until edges are firm. Remove and cool on wire racks. Store cookies at room temperature for up to 3 days. **Makes 26 cookies.**

Nutrition facts per cookie: 239 cal., 8 g fat, 16 mg chol., 134 mg sodium, 38 g carbo., 1 g fiber, 1 g pro.

Fat Molasses Cookies

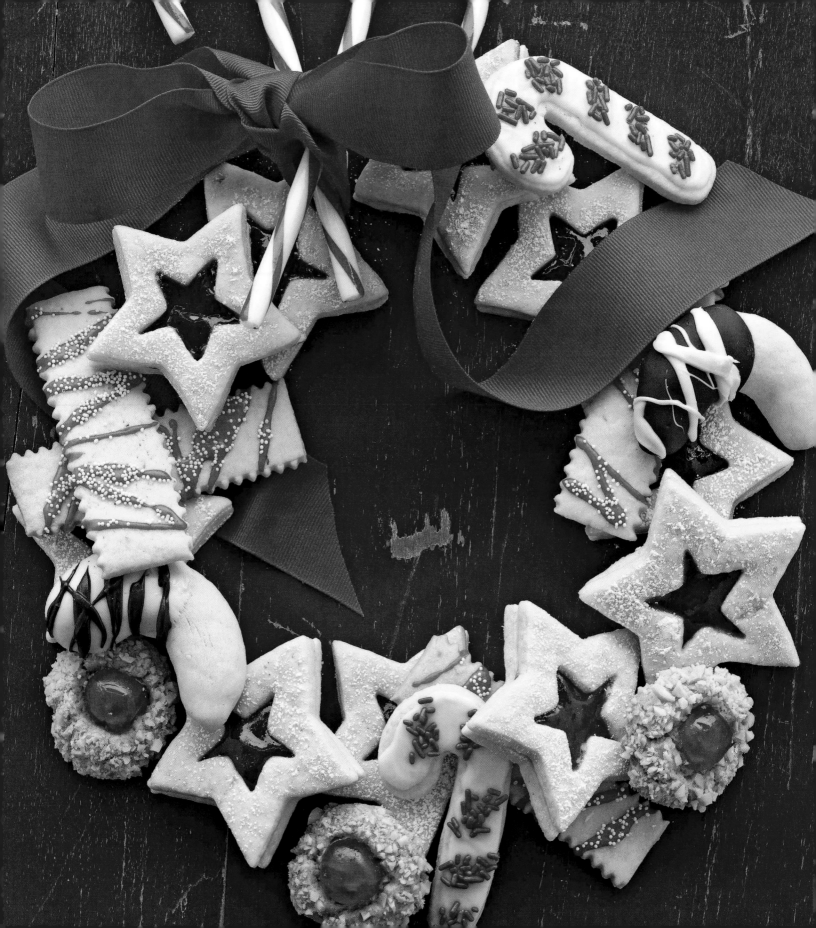

Basic Sugar Cookie Dough

Use this basic dough as the base for the nine cookies that follow. Read the basic recipe and the variation before making your cookie choice. In some cases, you'll substitute ingredients.

Prep: 20 minutes

    3 cups all-purpose flour
 1/3 cup cornstarch
    1 cup butter, softened
    1 3-ounce package cream cheese,
        softened
 3/4 cup sugar
    1 teaspoon baking powder
 1/2 teaspoon salt
    1 egg
    1 tablespoon vanilla

1. In a medium bowl, combine flour and cornstarch; set aside.

2. In a large mixing bowl, beat butter and cream cheese with an electric mixer on medium to high speed for 30 seconds. Add sugar, baking powder and salt. Beat until combined, scraping sides of bowl occasionally. Beat in egg and vanilla. Beat in as much of the flour mixture as you can with the mixer. Stir in any remaining flour mixture with a wooden spoon. Continue as directed in the following recipes.

Tip: To store the cookie dough, pack it into an airtight container and refrigerate for up to 3 days or freeze for up to 1 month. Take frozen cookie dough from the freezer a day before using and thaw in the refrigerator.

Rosemary & Lemon Ribbons

Prep: 30 minutes Bake: 6 minutes per batch Cool: 1 hour Oven: 375°

    Basic Sugar Cookie Dough (recipe
        above)
    2 teaspoons finely snipped fresh
        rosemary or 3/4 teaspoon dried
        rosemary, finely crushed
    2 teaspoons finely shredded lemon peel
 2 1/2 cups powdered sugar
    2 tablespoons milk
    1 teaspoon lemon juice

1. Prepare Basic Sugar Cookie Dough as directed, except add rosemary and lemon peel with the sugar.

2. For piped ribbons: Pack cookie dough (do not chill dough) into a cookie press fitted with the ribbon plate. Force dough through press onto ungreased cookie sheets. Cut into 2- to 3-inch lengths. Place 1 inch apart on ungreased cookie sheets. Continue as directed in Step 6.

3. For rolled-out ribbons and/or cutout diamonds: Divide dough in half and tightly wrap each piece with plastic wrap and chill for 1 hour or until dough is easy to handle.

4. For ribbons: On a lightly floured surface, roll half the dough (keep remaining dough in refrigerator) into a 16x10-inch rectangle. Using a fluted pastry wheel, cut each rectangle lengthwise into eight 1 1/4-inch strips. Cut strips crosswise into 4-inch pieces. Place about 1 inch apart on ungreased cookie sheets. If you like, curve pieces slightly. Continue as directed in Step 6.

5. For diamonds: On a lightly floured surface, roll half the dough (keep remaining dough in refrigerator) until 1/4 inch thick. Using a 2 1/2x1 3/4-inch diamond-shape cutter with fluted sides, cut out dough. Place about 1 inch apart on ungreased cookie sheets.

6. Bake in 375° oven for 6 to 8 minutes or until edges are firm when lightly touched and bottoms are very lightly browned. Cool on cookie sheet for 1 minute. Transfer cookies to wire racks; cool.

7. To decorate, in a small bowl, combine powdered sugar, milk and lemon juice. Stir in additional milk, 1 teaspoon at a time, until drizzling consistency. Drizzle a very thin line of glaze in a zigzag pattern over tops of cookies. Let set before serving.
Makes about 64 cookies.

Nutrition facts per cookie: 83 cal., 3 g fat, 12 mg chol., 50 mg sodium, 12 g carbo., 0 g fiber, 1 g pro.

Lemon Curd Sugar Tartlets

Prep: 50 minutes Chill: 1 hour Bake: 15 minutes Cool: 2 hours Oven: 350°

    Basic Sugar Cookie Dough (recipe
        at left)
    1 10-ounce jar lemon or lime curd
 1/4 cup dairy sour cream
 1/2 teaspoon finely shredded lemon or
        lime peel
    1 tablespoon lemon or lime juice
        Sweetened whipped cream
    2 kiwifruits, peeled, sliced and quartered
        (optional)
   40 red raspberries (optional)
        Finely snipped crystallized ginger
        (optional)

1. Prepare Basic Sugar Cookie Dough. If necessary, wrap and chill dough 1 hour or until easy to handle.

2. Press about 1 tablespoon of dough into the bottoms and up the sides of ungreased 1 3/4-inch muffin cups. Bake in a 350° oven for 10 minutes until dough is firm but not set. Remove muffin cups from oven.

3. Use the back of a round 1/2-teaspoon measuring spoon to gently press a shallow indentation into each shell. Bake about 5 minutes more or until the edges of tart shells are firm and lightly browned. Cool tart shells in muffin cups on a wire rack for 2 minutes. Transfer shells to wire racks; cool.

4. For filling: In a small bowl, combine lemon curd, sour cream, lemon peel and juice. Spoon a slightly rounded teaspoon of filling into each cooled shell. Cover and chill for 1 to 24 hours.

5. To serve, top each tartlet with whipped cream. If you like, top with a quartered kiwi slice and a raspberry or snipped crystallized ginger. **Makes 48 tartlets.**

Nutrition facts per tartlet: 114 cal., 6 g fat, 24 mg chol., 72 mg sodium, 15 g carbo., 1 g fiber, 1 g pro.

Brown Sugar Thumbprints

Prep: 30 minutes Chill: 1 hour
Bake: 15 minutes per batch Cool: 1 hour
Oven: 325°

Basic Sugar Cookie Dough (recipe page 215)
¾ cup packed brown sugar
1 teaspoon ground cinnamon
1 teaspoon ground allspice
1 teaspoon ground ginger
1 egg white
1 tablespoon water
1 cup very finely chopped almonds
Candied red and/or green cherries, halved

1. Prepare Basic Sugar Cookie Dough as directed, except substitute brown sugar for granulated sugar and add cinnamon, allspice and ginger. Continue as directed. Tightly wrap dough with plastic wrap and chill for 1 hour or until dough is easy to handle.

2. Lightly grease cookie sheets or line with foil and lightly coat foil with nonstick cooking spray; set aside. In a shallow dish, use a fork to lightly beat egg white with the water.

3. Shape dough into 1-inch balls. Roll balls in egg white mixture then in almonds. Place balls about 2 inches apart on prepared cookie sheets. Press a cherry half in center of each cookie.

4. Bake in a 325° oven for 15 to 17 minutes or until edges are firm and bottoms are very lightly browned. Cool on cookie sheets for 1 minute. Transfer cookies to wire racks and let cool. **Makes 55 cookies.**

To store: Place cookies between sheets of waxed paper in an airtight container; cover. Store at room temperature for up to 3 days or freeze up to 3 months.

Nutrition facts per cookie: 101 cal., 5 g fat, 14 mg chol., 60 mg sodium, 13 g carbo., 0 g fiber, 1 g pro.

Layered Coconut Dream Bars

Prep: 30 minutes Bake: 30 minutes Oven: 350°

Basic Sugar Cookie Dough (recipe page 215)
1½ cups shredded coconut
1 cup snipped dried apricots, dried cherries and/or dried cranberries
1 cup chopped pecans
½ cup semisweet chocolate pieces
½ cup white baking pieces
1 14-ounce can sweetened condensed milk

1. Prepare Basic Sugar Cookie Dough. Press and flatten dough with your hands to evenly cover the bottom of an ungreased 15x10x1-inch baking pan. Bake in a 350° oven for 10 minutes.

2. Sprinkle coconut, apricots, pecans, semisweet chocolate pieces and white baking pieces evenly over the cookie dough. Drizzle sweetened condensed milk evenly over all.

3. Return to oven and bake about 20 minutes more or until top is golden brown. Cool completely in pan on a wire rack. Cut into bars. **Makes 36 bars.**

Nutrition facts per bar: 221 cal., 12 g fat, 26 mg chol., 108 mg sodium, 26 g carbo., 1 g fiber, 3 g pro.

Frosty Chocolate Snowballs

Prep: 30 minutes Bake: 14 minutes per batch
Cool: 1 hour Oven: 325°

Basic Sugar Cookie Dough (recipe page 215)
3 ounces bittersweet or semisweet chocolate, melted and cooled
1 cup miniature semisweet chocolate pieces
½ cup very finely chopped pistachios, macadamia nuts or almonds
¾ cup powdered sugar

1. Prepare Basic Sugar Cookie Dough as directed, except beat in cooled chocolate after beating in the sugar. Continue as directed. Stir in chocolate pieces and nuts.

2. Shape dough into 1-inch balls. Place about 2 inches apart on ungreased cookie sheets.

3. Bake in a 325° oven for 14 to 15 minutes or until edges are set when touched lightly and bottoms are very lightly browned. Cool on cookie sheet for 1 minute. Transfer cookies to wire racks and let cool.

4. Place the powdered sugar in a plastic bag; gently shake cooled cookies, a few at a time, in bag to coat. **Makes about 80 cookies.**

Nutrition facts per cookie: 82 cal., 4 g fat, 10 mg chol., 43 mg sodium, 10 g carbo., 0 g fiber, 1 g pro.

Layered Coconut Dream Bars

Christmas Spirals & Bull's-Eyes

Prep: 35 minutes Chill: 2 hours
Bake: 8 to 10 minutes Cool: 1 hour Oven: 350°

    Basic Sugar Cookie Dough (recipe page 215)
1/2 teaspoon peppermint or almond extract (optional)
    Red paste food coloring or 10 drops red food coloring
    Green paste food coloring or 10 drops green food coloring
    Sugar

1. For spirals: Prepare Sugar Cookie Dough, adding peppermint or almond extract, if you like, when you add the vanilla. Divide dough into three equal portions. Tint one portion of the dough with red food coloring; tint another portion with green food coloring. Leave remaining dough portion plain. Tightly wrap each piece with plastic wrap and chill for 1 hour or until dough is easy to handle.

2. Divide each piece of dough into four equal portions. On a lightly floured surface, roll each portion into a 1/2-inch-diameter rope. Place one red, one green and one plain rope side by side. Twist together. Repeat with remaining ropes. Wrap with plastic wrap and chill rolls of dough about 30 minutes or until firm.

3. To slice, take one roll at a time out of the refrigerator; remove the wrap. If the rolls have flattened, reshape by gently rolling on the countertop. Using a sharp thin-bladed knife, cut each roll crosswise into 1/2-inch-thick slices. To avoid flattening the roll, rotate the roll a quarter turn after each slice. Place about 2 inches apart on ungreased cookie sheets. Using the bottom of a glass dipped in sugar, flatten each ball to 1/4-inch thickness.

4. Bake in a 350° oven for 10 to 12 minutes or edges are firm and bottoms are very lightly browned. Cool on cookie sheet for 1 minute. Transfer cookies to wire racks; cool.

5. For bull's-eyes: Prepare Sugar Cookie Dough. Divide dough into four equal portions. Tint one portion of the dough with red food coloring; tint another dough portion with green food coloring. Leave the remaining two dough portions plain. Tightly wrap each piece with plastic wrap and chill for 1 hour before rolling out.

6. Divide red and green dough portions in half. On a lightly floured surface, roll each red and green dough portion into a 3/4-inch-diameter rope, each measuring 11 inches long. Transfer the red and green ropes to a baking sheet and chill about 20 minutes or until firm.

7. Divide plain dough portions in half, making a total of four portions. On a lightly floured surface, roll each of the plain dough portions into an 11x4-inch rectangle. Transfer the pieces to a large baking sheet and chill about 20 minutes or until firm.

8. Place a red rope along a long edge of one plain dough rectangle. Roll plain dough with your hands to enclose the red rope. Trim excess. Gently pinch dough to seal. Transfer roll to a baking sheet and chill 20 minutes or until firm. Repeat with remaining plain dough rectangles and red and green ropes.

9. To slice, take one roll at a time out of the refrigerator. Using a sharp thin-bladed knife, cut each roll crosswise into 1/4-inch-thick slices. To avoid flattening the roll, rotate the roll a quarter turn after each slice. Place slices about 2 inches apart on ungreased cookie sheets.

10. Bake in a 350° oven for 8 to 10 minutes or until edges are firm and bottoms are very lightly browned. Cool on cookie sheet for 1 minute. Transfer cookies to wire racks; cool.
Makes about 48 (2 1/2-inch) spiral cookies.
Makes about 64 bull's-eye cookies.

Nutrition Facts per cookie (Christmas Spirals): 87 cal., 5 g fat, 17 mg chol., 66 mg sodium, 10 g carbo., 0 g fiber, 1 g pro.

Shining Star Sandwich Cookies

Prep: 30 minutes Chill: 1 hour Bake: 6 minutes
Stand: 1 minute per batch Oven: 375°

    Basic Sugar Cookie Dough (recipe page 215)
2 cups powdered sugar
1/3 cup cherry or currant jelly or apricot jam
1/2 teaspoon almond extract

Shining Star Sandwich Cookies

1/4 teaspoon ground nutmeg or ground cinnamon
    Powdered sugar
    Cherry or currant jelly or apricot jam, melted and cooled

1. Prepare Basic Sugar Cookie Dough. Divide dough in half and tightly wrap each piece with plastic wrap. Cover and chill for 1 hour or until easy to handle.

2. On a lightly floured surface, roll half the dough (keep remaining dough in refrigerator) until 1/8 to 1/4 inch thick. Using a 2 1/2- to 3-inch star-shape cookie cutter, cut dough. Using a 1- to 1 1/2-inch star-shape cookie cutter, cut holes in the centers of half of the cookies. Place about 1 1/2 inches apart on ungreased cookie sheets. Reroll and cut centers, if you like.

3. Bake in a 375° oven for 6 to 7 minutes or until edges are firm and bottoms are lightly brown. Cool on cookie sheet for 1 minute. Transfer cookies to wire racks and let cool.

4. For filling: In a medium bowl, stir together the 2 cups powdered sugar, 1/3 cup jelly, the almond extract and nutmeg.

5. To assemble, sift additional powdered sugar over tops of cookies with holes in centers. Spread filling on the bottoms of the cookies without holes. Top each of these cookies with the remaining cookies, powdered sugar side up. Fill the hole of each cookie with a small spoonful of additional jelly. **Makes 40 cookies.**

Nutrition facts per cookie: 147 cal., 6 g fat, 20 mg chol., 81 mg sodium, 23 g carbo., 0 g fiber, 1 g pro.

Holiday Sugar Cookie Cutouts

Prep: 45 minutes Chill: 1 hour
Bake: 6 minutes per batch Cool: 1 hour Oven: 375°

  Basic Sugar Cookie Dough (recipe
    page 215)
 3 cups powdered sugar
 3 tablespoons milk
 ½ teaspoon vanilla or ½ teaspoon
    peppermint, rum or almond extract
    Assorted colors of paste food coloring
    Clear or white edible glitter, pearl
    sugar, fine sanding sugar, colored
    sprinkles and/or coarse sugar

1. Prepare Basic Sugar Cookie Dough. Divide dough in half and tightly wrap each half with plastic wrap and chill for 1 hour or until dough is easy to handle.

2. On a lightly floured surface, roll half the dough (keep remaining dough in refrigerator) until ⅛ to ¼ inch thick. Using assorted 2½- to 3-inch cookie cutters, cut dough into desired shapes. Place about 1½ inches apart on ungreased cookie sheets.

3. Bake in a 375° oven for 6 to 7 minutes or until edges are firm and bottoms are lightly brown. Cool on cookie sheet for 1 minute. Transfer cookies to a wire rack and let cool.

4. To decorate, in a medium bowl, combine powdered sugar, milk and vanilla. Stir in additional milk, 1 teaspoon at a time, until glazing consistency. If you like, tint with paste food coloring. Glaze cookies with white or tinted icing. Sprinkle with glitter or sugar. Let set before serving.
Makes about 48 cookies.

To store: Place plain cookies between sheets of waxed paper in an airtight container; cover. Store at room temperature for up to 3 days or freeze up to 3 months.

Nutrition facts per cookie: 118 cal., 5 g fat, 17 mg chol., 66 mg sodium, 18 g carbo., 0 g fiber, 1 g pro.

Chocolate Drizzled Crescents

Prep: 30 minutes Bake: 15 minutes per batch
Cool: 1 hour Chill: 1 hour Oven: 325°

  Basic Sugar Cookie Dough (recipe
    page 215)
 2 tablespoons whiskey, rum or brandy
 3 ounces bittersweet or semisweet
    chocolate, chopped
 2 teaspoons shortening
 3 ounces white baking chocolate, chopped

1. Prepare Basic Sugar Cookie Dough as directed, except substitute 2 tablespoons whiskey for 1 tablespoon vanilla. Continue as directed. Tightly wrap dough with plastic wrap and chill for 1 hour or until dough is easy to handle.

2. Pinch off pieces of dough the size of a walnut (about 1½-inch balls). Roll each piece into a 3-inch log; shape logs into crescents, tapering ends slightly. Place crescents about 2 inches apart on ungreased cookie sheets.

3. Bake in a 325° oven for 15 to 20 minutes or until edges are firm when touched lightly and bottoms are very lightly browned. Cool on cookie sheet for 1 minute. Transfer cookies to wire racks and let cool.

4. To decorate, in a heavy small saucepan, heat and stir bittersweet chocolate and 1 teaspoon of the shortening over low heat until melted and smooth. In another heavy small saucepan, heat and stir white baking chocolate and remaining 1 teaspoon shortening over low heat until melted and smooth. Drizzle each crescent with some of the bittersweet chocolate and then drizzle with some of the white chocolate. Place crescents on waxed paper and let stand until set. **Makes 36 crescents.**

To store: Place plain cookies between sheets of waxed paper in an airtight container; cover. Store at room temperature for up to 3 days or freeze up to 3 months.

Nutrition facts per crescent: 145 cal., 8 g fat, 23 mg chol., 91 mg sodium, 16 g carbo., 0 g fiber, 2 g pro.

Snowcapped Crescents: Prepare as above except omit drizzling with chocolates. Cool cookies slightly on a wire rack. In a plastic bag, gently shake warm crescents, a few at a time, with 1 cup powdered sugar. Cool completely on the wire racks. Sift additional powdered sugar over tops of the cooled crescents.

Chocolate Drizzled Crescents

Snowmen Shortbread Cookies

Gumdrop Hats and Scarves: Sprinkle a cutting board with granulated sugar. Place a gumdrop on the board; sprinkle with more sugar. With a rolling pin, roll gumdrop to about ⅛- to ¼-inch thickness. Cut into desired hat and scarf shapes.

Oh So Lemony Glazed Spritz Cookies

Prep: 50 minutes Bake: 8 minutes per batch
Stand: 30 minutes Oven: 375°

1½ cups butter, softened
1 cup granulated sugar
1 teaspoon baking powder
1 egg
1 teaspoon vanilla
½ teaspoon lemon extract
3½ cups all-purpose flour
   Lemon Glaze (recipe follows)
   Colored sugar (optional)

1. In a large mixing bowl, beat butter with an electric mixer on medium speed for 30 seconds. Add granulated sugar and baking powder. Beat until combined, scraping sides of bowl occasionally. Beat in egg, vanilla and lemon extract until combined. Beat in as much flour as you can. Stir in any remaining flour with a wooden spoon. Do not chill dough.

2. Pack unchilled dough into a cookie press. Force dough through press onto ungreased cookie sheets.

3. Bake in a 375° oven for 8 to 10 minutes or until edges of cookies are firm but not brown. Transfer to a wire rack and let cool. Drizzle or brush with Lemon Glaze; sprinkle with sugar, if you like. Dry for 30 minutes on waxed paper. **Makes about 70 cookies.**

Lemon Glaze: In a small bowl, stir together 1½ cups powdered sugar, 2 teaspoons finely shredded lemon peel and 1½ teaspoons lemon juice. Stir in milk, 1 teaspoon at a time, until icing is drizzling consistency.

Nutrition facts per serving: 80 cal., 4 g fat, 13 mg chol., 34 mg sodium, 10 g carbo., 0 g fiber, 5 g sugar, 1 g pro.

Snowmen Shortbread Cookies

Prep: 45 minutes Bake: 12 minutes per batch
Oven: 350°

2 cups unsalted butter, softened
1½ cups sifted powdered sugar
1 tablespoon vanilla
1 teaspoon baking powder
½ teaspoon salt
4 cups all-purpose flour
1 tablespoon finely shredded tangerine
   or orange peel
   Powdered Sugar Icing (recipe follows)
   Small candies (optional)
   Gumdrop Hats and Scarves (optional)

1. In a large mixing bowl, beat butter with an electric mixer on medium to high speed for 30 seconds. Add powdered sugar, vanilla, baking powder and salt. Beat until combined, scraping sides of bowl occasionally. Beat in as much of the flour as you can with the mixer. Using a wooden spoon, stir in tangerine peel and any remaining flour. Divide dough in half. If necessary, cover and chill dough 30 minutes or until easy to handle.

2. On a lightly floured surface, roll half the dough at a time until about ¼ inch thick. Cut dough into shapes using a 3- to 4-inch snowman-shape cookie cutter. Place 1 inch apart on ungreased cookie sheets.

3. Bake in a 350° oven about 12 minutes or until edges are firm and bottoms are very lightly browned. Transfer to a wire rack and let cool. Frost with Powdered Sugar Icing. If you like, while icing is still wet, decorate with small candies for nose and buttons and add Gumdrop Hats and Scarves.
Makes about 50 cookies.

Powdered Sugar Icing: In a small bowl, combine 2 cups sifted powdered sugar, ½ teaspoon vanilla and 2 tablespoons milk. Stir in additional milk, 1 teaspoon at a time, until icing reaches desired consistency.

Nutrition facts per serving: 123 cal., 8 g total fat (5 g sat. fat), 22 mg chol., 34 mg sodium, 11 g carb., 0 g dietary fiber, 1 g protein.

Pumpkin Chess Pie

Pumpkin Chess Pie

Prep: 30 minutes Bake: 1 hour Oven: 400°/350°

    Single-Crust Pie Shell (recipe page 176)
6 tablespoons butter, softened
1⅓ cups sugar
4 teaspoons cornmeal
1 cup canned pumpkin
⅓ cup half-and-half or light cream
2 egg, lightly beaten
1 teaspoon vanilla
½ teaspoon salt
½ teaspoon ground cinnamon
¼ teaspoon ground nutmeg
¼ teaspoon ground ginger
¼ teaspoon ground cloves

1. Prepare and roll out Single Crust Pie Shell pastry. Line a 9-inch pie plate with pastry. Trim overhang to 1 inch all the way around. Tuck the crust under and flute the edges. Do not prick pastry. Line pastry with a double thickness of foil; add pie weights, if you like. Bake in a 400° oven for 15 minutes to partially bake pastry shell. Remove foil and pie weights. Reduce oven temperature to 350°.

2. In a medium mixing bowl, beat butter with an electric mixer on medium to high speed for 30 seconds. Add sugar and cornmeal. Beat until combined, scraping the sides of the bowl occasionally. Add pumpkin, half-and-half, eggs, vanilla, salt, cinnamon, nutmeg, ginger and cloves. Beat just until combined.

3. Place the pastry-lined pie plate on the oven rack. Carefully pour the pumpkin mixture into the pastry shell. To prevent overbrowning, cover the edge of the pie with foil.

4. Bake in a 350° oven for 25 minutes. Remove foil. Bake for 20 to 25 minutes more or until a knife inserted near the center comes out clean. Cool on a wire rack. Cover and store in the refrigerator within 2 hours. Makes 8 servings.

Nutrition facts per serving: 507 cal., 25 g fat, 118 mg chol., 516 mg sodium, 65 g carbo., 2 g fiber, 6 g pro.

Mommy's Pumpkin Pie

Prep: 30 minutes Bake: 1 hour Oven: 400°

    Single-Crust Pie Shell (recipe page 176)
1 15-ounce can pumpkin
¾ cup packed brown sugar
1¼ teaspoons ground cinnamon
1 teaspoon ground ginger
½ teaspoon salt
¼ teaspoon ground cloves
¼ teaspoon finely shredded orange peel
4 eggs, lightly beaten
1½ cups half-and-half or light cream
    Whipped cream
    Granulated sugar
    Ground cinnamon

1. Prepare and roll out Single-Crust Pie Shell pastry. Line a 9-inch pie plate with pastry. Trim overhang to 1 inch all the way around. Tuck the crust under and flute the edges high. Do not prick pastry. Line pastry with a double thickness of foil; add pie weights, if you like. Bake in a 400° oven for 15 minutes to partially bake pastry shell. Remove foil and pie weights.

2. In a large bowl, combine pumpkin, brown sugar, 1¼ teaspoons cinnamon, the ginger, salt, cloves and orange peel. Add eggs; beat lightly with a fork just until combined. Gradually add half-and-half; stir until combined.

3. Place the partially baked piecrust on the oven rack. Carefully pour pumpkin mixture into the pastry shell. To prevent overbrowning, cover edge of the pie with foil.

4. Bake in 400° oven for 20 minutes. Remove foil. Bake 25 to 30 minutes more or until a knife inserted near the center comes out clean. Cool on a wire rack. Cover and store in the refrigerator within 2 hours. Serve with whipped cream sprinkled with granulated sugar and additional cinnamon. Makes 8 servings.

Nutrition facts per serving: 509 cal., 28 g fat, 182 mg chol., 499 mg sodium, 58 g carbo., 3 g fiber, 9 g pro.

Pumpkin Cream Cheese Pie

Prep: 20 minutes Bake: 55 minutes Oven: 425°/350°

    Single-Crust Pie Shell (recipe page 176)
1 15-ounce can pumpkin
¾ cup sugar
1 teaspoon ground cinnamon
¼ teaspoon salt
2 eggs, lightly beaten
1 5-ounce can (⅔ cup) evaporated milk
1 8-ounce package cream cheese, softened
⅓ cup sugar
1 egg, lightly beaten
½ teaspoon vanilla

1. Prepare and roll out Single Crust Pie Shell pastry. Line a 9-inch pie plate with pastry. Trim overhang to 1 inch all the way around. Tuck the crust under and flute the edges high. Do not prick pastry.

2. In a medium bowl, combine pumpkin, ¾ cup sugar, the cinnamon and salt. Add two eggs; beat lightly with a fork just until combined. Gradually beat in evaporated milk.

3. In a large mixing bowl, beat cream cheese and ⅓ cup sugar with an electric mixer on medium speed until smooth. Add one egg and the vanilla. Beat until combined.

4. Transfer cream cheese mixture to the pastry-lined pie plate. Place the pie plate on the oven rack. Carefully pour pumpkin mixture over cream cheese mixture. To prevent overbrowning, cover the edge of the pie with foil.

5. Bake in a 425° oven for 15 minutes. Remove foil; reduce oven temperature to 350°. Bake for 40 to 50 minutes more or until a knife inserted near the center comes out clean. Cool on a wire rack. Cover and store in the refrigerator within 2 hours. Makes 8 servings.

Nutrition facts per serving: 527 cal., 27 g fat, 155 mg chol., 490 mg sodium, 62 g carbo., 2 g fiber, 10 g pro.

Peppermint Brownie Pie

Peppermint Brownie Pie

Prep: 20 minutes   Cool: 20 minutes
Bake: 55 minutes   Oven: 350°

  ½ cup butter or margarine
  3 ounces unsweetened chocolate,
    chopped
    Single-Crust Pie Shell (recipe page 176)
  3 eggs, lightly beaten
1½ cups granulated sugar
  ½ cup all-purpose flour
  1 teaspoon vanilla
  1 cup mint-flavor semisweet chocolate
    pieces
    Whipped cream

1. For filling: In a heavy small saucepan, melt butter and chocolate over low heat, stirring frequently. Cool 20 minutes.

2. Meanwhile, prepare and roll out pastry. Line a 9-inch pie plate with pastry; trim and crimp edge.

3. In a mixing bowl, combine eggs, sugar, flour and vanilla. Stir in the chocolate mixture and chocolate pieces. Pour into pastry-lined pie plate.

4. Bake pie in a 350° oven about 55 minutes or until filling is evenly puffed and edges of filling are slightly cracked. Cool on wire rack (center will sink slightly as pie cools). Serve with whipped cream. **Makes 10 servings.**

Nutrition facts per serving: 542 cal., 31 g fat, 98 mg chol., 150 mg sodium, 64 g carbo., 3 g fiber, 6 g pro.

Pumpkin Trifle

Prep: 30 minutes   Chill: 2 hours

  1 10¾-ounce frozen pound cake,
    thawed and cut into ½-inch cubes
  ⅓ cup apricot brandy, apricot liqueur,
    apricot nectar or orange juice
  1 16-ounce can whole cranberry sauce
  ⅓ cup apricot jam
  1 15-ounce can pumpkin
  1 4-serving-size package instant vanilla
    pudding mix

Pumpkin Trifle

  1 cup milk
  1 teaspoon ground cinnamon
  ½ teaspoon ground nutmeg
  1 cup whipping cream
  2 tablespoons sugar
  1 teaspoon apricot brandy, apricot
    liqueur or vanilla
  2 1.4-ounce bars chocolate-covered
    toffee bars, coarsely chopped, or
    ½ cup chopped toasted pecans

1. Divide cake cubes evenly among eight 10- to 12-ounce 4-inch-tall glasses. Or layer all cake cubes in a 2½-quart clear serving bowl or soufflé dish. Sprinkle with ⅓ cup brandy.

2. In a medium bowl, stir together the cranberry sauce and apricot jam. Spoon mixture over cake cubes. In a large bowl, whisk together pumpkin, pudding mix, milk, cinnamon and nutmeg until well combined. Spoon the mixture over cranberry layer.

3. In a chilled large mixing bowl, combine whipping cream, sugar and 1 teaspoon apricot brandy. Beat with chilled beaters of an electric mixer on medium speed until soft peaks form. Gently spread over pumpkin layer. Cover; chill for 2 to 5 hours. Sprinkle with chopped toffee bars before serving. **Makes 8 servings.**

Nutrition facts per serving: 558 cal., 23 g fat, 131 mg chol., 411 mg sodium, 80 g carbo., 3 g fiber, 4 g pro.

Eggnog Muffins

Prep: 25 minutes Bake: 18 minutes
Cool: 5 minutes Oven: 375°

2¼ cups all-purpose flour
  1 cup sugar
  2 teaspoons baking powder
  ½ teaspoon ground nutmeg
  2 eggs, lightly beaten
  1 cup dairy eggnog
  ½ cup butter, melted and cooled
  1 teaspoon vanilla
  ½ teaspoon rum extract
    Nutmeg-Streusel Topping (recipe
    follows)

1. Grease twelve 2½-inch muffin cups or line with paper bake cups; set aside. In a medium bowl, combine flour, sugar, baking powder and nutmeg. Make a well in center of flour mixture; set aside.

2. In a small bowl, combine eggs, eggnog, melted butter, vanilla and rum extract. Add egg mixture all at once to the flour mixture. Stir just until moistened (batter should be lumpy). Spoon batter into muffin cups, filling each two-thirds full. Sprinkle Nutmeg Streusel Topping over muffin batter in cups.

3. Bake in a 375° oven for 18 to 20 minutes or until golden and a wooden toothpick inserted in centers comes out clean. Cool in muffin cups on a wire rack for 5 minutes. Remove from muffin cups; serve warm. **Makes 12 muffins.**

Nutmeg-Streusel Topping: In a small bowl, mix ⅓ cup all-purpose flour, ⅓ cup sugar and ½ teaspoon ground nutmeg using pastry blender. Cut in 2 tablespoons butter until the mixture resembles coarse crumbs.

Nutrition facts per muffin: 312 cal., 12 g fat, 73 mg chol., 132 mg sodium, 46 g carbo., 1 g fiber, 5 g pro.

Chocolate-Pistachio Wreath Bread

Prep: 30 minutes Stand: 30 minutes
Rise: 1 hour 45 minutes Bake: 25 minutes
Oven: 375°

3½ to 4½ cups all-purpose flour
  1 cup warm milk (105° to 115°)
  2 teaspoons sugar
  1 package active dry yeast
  2 eggs
  ½ cup sugar
  ⅓ cup unsweetened cocoa powder
  ⅓ cup finely chopped pistachio nuts or
    almonds
  2 teaspoons finely shredded orange peel
  ¾ teaspoon salt
  ⅓ cup butter, cut into small pieces and
    softened
  1 egg, lightly beaten
  1 tablespoon milk
    Chocolate Icing (recipe follows)
    Chopped pistachio nuts

1. In a large mixing bowl, combine 1 cup of the flour, 1 cup warm milk, 2 teaspoons sugar and the yeast. Beat with an electric mixer on medium speed about 2 minutes or until smooth. Cover; let stand at room temperature for 30 minutes or until bubbly.

2. Add the two eggs, ½ cup sugar, cocoa powder, finely chopped pistachio nuts, orange peel and salt to flour mixture; stir in another ½ cup of the flour. Beat with an electric mixer on medium speed about 2 minutes or until smooth. Add butter, a few pieces at a time, and beat until well combined. Using a wooden spoon, stir in as much of the remaining flour as you can.

3. Turn out onto a lightly floured surface. Knead in enough remaining flour to make a moderately stiff dough that is smooth and elastic. Shape dough into a ball. Place dough in a lightly greased bowl, turning dough to coat all surfaces. Cover; let rise in a warm place until double in size (about 1 hour).

4. Punch down dough. Turn out onto lightly floured surface. Divide dough into three equal portions. Cover; let rest for 10 minutes.

5. Roll each portion of dough into a thick rope that is 20 inches long. Line up the ropes, 1 inch apart on the lightly floured surface. Starting in the middle, braid by bringing left rope underneath center rope; lay it down. Then bring right rope under new center rope; lay it down. Repeat to end. On the other end, braid by bringing outside ropes alternately over center rope to center. (Braid ropes loosely so bread has room to expand.) Join ends of braid to form a wreath. Transfer to a greased baking sheet, placing a greased ball of foil in center to help hold shape. Cover; let rise until almost double in size (45 to 60 minutes).

6. Stir together the one egg and 1 tablespoon milk. Brush over top of wreath. Bake in a 375° oven 25 minutes or until bread sounds hollow when tapped. Cover with foil the last 10 minutes, if necessary, to prevent overbrowning. Remove from baking sheet; cool slightly. Remove foil from center.

7. Spread bread with Chocolate Icing. Top with additional pistachio nuts. **Makes 16 to 20 servings.**

Chocolate Icing: In a small saucepan, melt ½ cup milk chocolate pieces and 2 tablespoons butter over low heat, stirring frequently. Remove from heat. Stir in 1 cup powdered sugar and 2 tablespoons hot water. If needed, stir in additional hot water to make a smooth and creamy icing of spreading consistency. Makes ¾ cup icing.

Nutrition facts per serving: 282 cal., 10 g total fat, 56 mg chol., 178 mg sodium, 42 g carbo., 1 g fiber, 6 g pro.

Eggnog Muffins

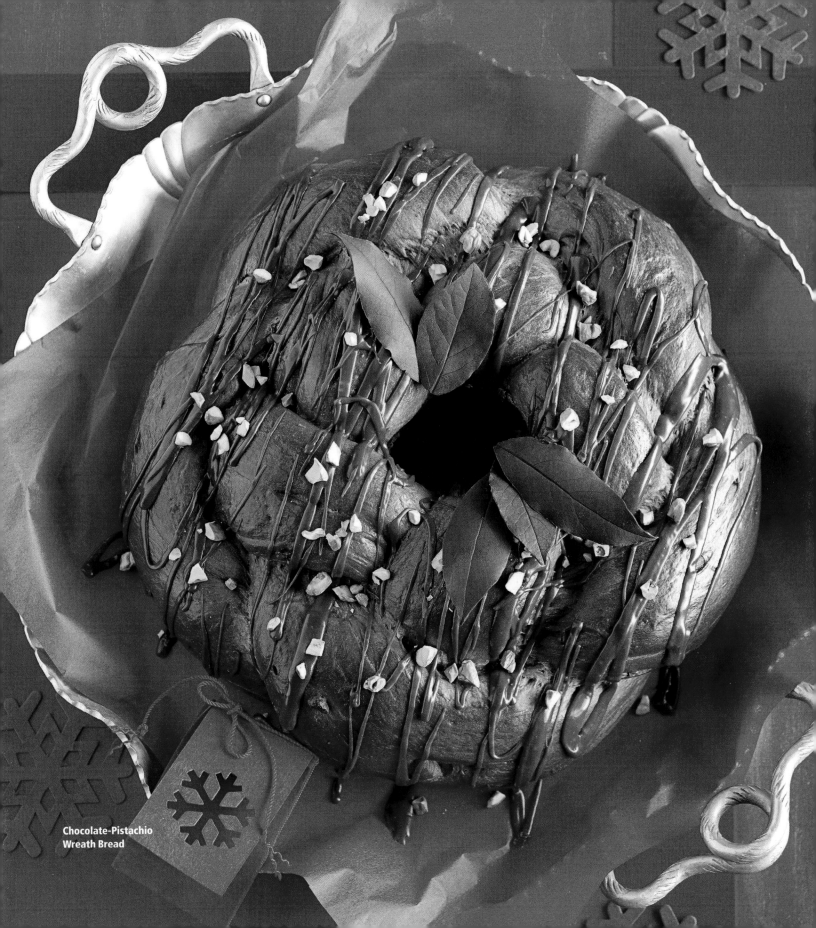

Chocolate-Pistachio
Wreath Bread

METRIC INFORMATION

The charts on this page provide a guide for converting measurements from the U.S. customary system, which is used throughout this book, to the metric system.

PRODUCT DIFFERENCES

Most of the ingredients called for in the recipes in this book are available in most countries. However, some are known by different names. Here are some common American ingredients and their possible counterparts:

- ◻ Sugar (white) is granulated, fine granulated, or castor sugar.
- ◻ Confectioners' sugar is icing sugar.
- ◻ All-purpose flour is enriched, bleached, or unbleached white household flour. When self-rising flour is used in place of all-purpose flour in a recipe that calls for leavening, omit the leavening agent (baking soda or baking powder) and salt.
- ◻ Light-colored corn syrup is golden syrup.
- ◻ Cornstarch is cornflour.
- ◻ Baking soda is bicarbonate of soda.
- ◻ Vanilla or vanilla extract is vanilla essence.
- ◻ Green, red, or yellow sweet peppers are capsicums or bell peppers.
- ◻ Golden raisins are sultanas.

VOLUME AND WEIGHT

The United States traditionally uses cup measures for liquid and solid ingredients. The chart, top right, shows the approximate imperial and metric equivalents. If you are accustomed to weighing solid ingredients, the following approximate equivalents will be helpful.

- ◻ 1 cup butter, castor sugar, or rice = 8 ounces = $1/2$ pound = 250 grams
- ◻ 1 cup flour = 4 ounces = $1/4$ pound = 125 grams
- ◻ 1 cup icing sugar = 5 ounces = 150 grams

Canadian and U.S. volume for a cup measure is 8 fluid ounces (237 ml), but the standard metric equivalent is 250 ml. 1 British imperial cup is 10 fluid ounces.

In Australia, 1 tablespoon equals 20 ml, and there are 4 teaspoons in the Australian tablespoon.

Spoon measures are used for smaller amounts of ingredients. Although the size of the tablespoon varies slightly in different countries, for practical purposes and for recipes in this book, a straight substitution is all that's necessary. Measurements made using cups or spoons always should be level unless stated otherwise.

COMMON WEIGHT RANGE REPLACEMENTS

Imperial / U.S.	Metric
½ ounce	15 g
1 ounce	25 g or 30 g
4 ounces (¼ pound)	115 g or 125 g
8 ounces (½ pound)	225 g or 250 g
16 ounces (1 pound)	450 g or 500 g
1¼ pounds	625 g
1½ pounds	750 g
2 pounds or 2¼ pounds	1,000 g or 1 Kg

OVEN TEMPERATURE EQUIVALENTS

Fahrenheit Setting	Celsius Setting*	Gas Setting
300°F	150°C	Gas Mark 2 (very low)
325°F	160°C	Gas Mark 3 (low)
350°F	180°C	Gas Mark 4 (moderate)
375°F	190°C	Gas Mark 5 (moderate)
400°F	200°C	Gas Mark 6 (hot)
425°F	220°C	Gas Mark 7 (hot)
450°F	230°C	Gas Mark 8 (very hot)
475°F	240°C	Gas Mark 9 (very hot)
500°F	260°C	Gas Mark 10 (extremely hot)
Broil	Broil	Grill

*Electric and gas ovens may be calibrated using celsius. However, for an electric oven, increase celsius setting 10 to 20 degrees when cooking above 160°C. For convection or forced air ovens (gas or electric) lower the temperature setting 25°F/10°C when cooking at all heat levels.

BAKING PAN SIZES

Imperial / U.S.	Metric
9×1½-inch round cake pan	22- or 23×4-cm (1.5 L)
9×1½-inch pie plate	22- or 23×4-cm (1 L)
8×8×2-inch square cake pan	20×5-cm (2 L)
9×9×2-inch square cake pan	22- or 23×4.5-cm (2.5 L)
11×7×1½-inch baking pan	28×17×4-cm (2 L)
2-quart rectangular baking pan	30×19×4.5-cm (3 L)
13×9×2-inch baking pan	34×22×4.5-cm (3.5 L)
15×10×1-inch jelly roll pan	40×25×2-cm
9×5×3-inch loaf pan	23×13×8-cm (2 L)
2-quart casserole	2 L

U.S. / STANDARD METRIC EQUIVALENTS

⅛ teaspoon = 0.5 ml	⅓ cup = 3 fluid ounces = 75 ml
¼ teaspoon = 1 ml	½ cup = 4 fluid ounces = 125 ml
½ teaspoon = 2 ml	⅔ cup = 5 fluid ounces = 150 ml
1 teaspoon = 5 ml	¾ cup = 6 fluid ounces = 175 ml
1 tablespoon = 15 ml	1 cup = 8 fluid ounces = 250 ml
2 tablespoons = 25 ml	2 cups = 1 pint = 500 ml
¼ cup = 2 fluid ounces = 50 ml	1 quart = 1 litre